Richard Parker

Kensington

4th February 2005

LAKELAND **FELLRANGER**

THE **CENTRAL** FELLS

by
Mark Richards

Originally published under the same title by HarperCollins*Publishers* 2003
ISBN: 0 00 711365 X

Printed by KHL Printing, Singapore.
A catalogue record for this book is available from the British Library.
Artwork and photographs by the author.

Maps are reproduced with permission from HARVEY Maps,
www.harveymaps.co.uk.

HARVEY

Dedicated to Andrew Carter – a man with a passion for Cumbria

ACKNOWLEDGEMENTS

For the publication of this guide by Cicerone I have re-walked many of the routes, and renewing my acquaintance with the range has been a great pleasure. Frequently it brought back memories of fine days of the recent past. However, I must mention the support I have received from two dedicated local fellwalkers, David Hall and Andrew Leaney. In checking a random selection of routes from the original guide they have been able to clarify and update some important detail. This process has also been a valuable means of finding out how effective the guide is in practice. Between them they have amassed amazing photographic galleries from their regular weekend walks, and if you'd like to watch the changing seasons on the fells from the comfort of your home then check out their dynamic websites, www.davidhalllakedistrictwalks.co.uk and www.leaney.org.uk.

ADVICE TO READERS

While every effort is made by our authors to ensure the accuracy of guidebooks as they go to print, changes can occur during the lifetime of an edition. If we know of any, there will be an Updates tab on this book's page on the Cicerone website (www.cicerone.co.uk), so please check before planning your trip. We also advise that you check information about such things as transport, accommodation and shops locally. Even rights of way can be altered over time. We are always grateful for information about any discrepancies between a guidebook and the facts on the ground, sent by email to info@cicerone.co.uk or by post to Cicerone, 2 Police Square, Milnthorpe LA7 7PY, United Kingdom.

Front cover: Helm Crag from the ridge to Gibson Knott
Previous page: Silver How from Stone Arthur (Chapter 23)

CONTENTS

ABOUT THE AUTHOR

The Cumbrian fells have held a lifetime's attraction for me, as they have for many others. Brought up in the far-flung west Oxfordshire countryside, the romance of the high fells tugged at my emotions from my youth. In 2001 my wife and I were able to up sticks and make a permanent home within sight of Lakeland. The move was triggered by a sought-after commission to write and produce the Lakeland Fellranger series, an eight-part guide for HarperCollins. The series was also soon to find its natural Cumbrian home, with Cicerone Press, thus assuring completion of my task and a long-term future for the series.

My early experience of walking in fell country came in two guises. My mother's cousin was a farm manager on a fell estate near Kirkby Lonsdale. Hence summer holidays were spent gathering sheep and tending cattle. Though busman's holidays from my stockman's life in Oxfordshire, these were great experiences, developing my awareness of the magic of fell country.

By my late teens the lure of mountains for recreation had taken a real hold, and shortly after joining a mountaineering club I met, and became a regular house-guest of, Alfred Wainwright. Just being with such a gifted artist and writer was very special. We shared a delight in drawing and in poring over maps and walking guide ideas. He quickly saw my own appetite for pen and ink and my passion for the countryside, the fells in particular, and he encouraged me to consider creating my own illustrated guides.

My earliest guides were the *Cotswold Way* (1973), *Cornwall North Coast Path* (1974) and *Offa's Dyke Path* (1975). Cicerone commissioned a trio of hand-drawn walking guides to the Peak District that were published in the early 1980s (and subsequently revised). Other books followed, including – thanks to my fascination with historic landscapes – a guide to *Hadrian's Wall Path*.

After 14 years' dedicated research, the magnum opus Lakeland Fellranger series was officially completed in 2013, with all eight individual volumes now also available in a box set! So my attention turns southward to renew acquaintance with the spacious gritstone moors and edges of the Peak District, in order to produce a new volume of *Dark Peak Walks*, replacing my *High Peak Walks*, first published in 1982.

Mark Richards, 2013

FROM FIRESIDE TO FELLSIDE

This land of living dreams we call the Lake District is a cherished blessing to know, love and share. As we lead our normal lives far removed from there, we may take a fleeting moment to reflect that someone, somewhere, will be tramping up a lonely gill or along an airy ridge, peering from a lofty summit or gazing across a wind-blown tarn and taking lingering inspiration from its timeless beauty. The trappings of modern life thrust carpet and concrete under our feet, and it is always wonderful to walk the region's sheep trods and rough trails, and to imprint our soles upon the fells. This guide sets out to give you the impetus and resolve to make time in your life to reclaim the fells.

I love to wander the fells alone, but I know too that they are for sharing, and the majority of fellwalkers choose a friend or two and turn a walk into a party. Yet among such a majestic mountain environment I feel a certain sorrow when I see trains of walkers traipsing up and down Stickle Ghyll and elsewhere, heads down, lost in conversations about everything under the sun, but oblivious to their surroundings.

The regular paths of long tradition deserve consideration. Progressively many of the main paths are being re-set with cobbles and pitching, all highly meritorious. But it has to be said that, in many instances, the best consideration we can give these pathways is rest. They came into being as lines of desire, yet perhaps the modern trail-blazer should show a new 'green' awareness by choosing to tread lightly on the

Harrison Stickle and Millbeck Farm (Chapter 10)

land and to find new ways around the hills. Hence the underlying impulse of this guide is to increase sustainability by presenting a diversity of route options for each and every fell.

THIS GUIDE

While the Central Fells are very familiar, few people think of it as a single area. Everyone knows of the Langdale Pikes, which in the mind's eye belong to Great Langdale; of Loughrigg Fell, Silver How and Helm Crag around Grasmere; the escarpment of Walla Crag above Derwentwater; the exquisite setting of Watendlath and, threading through the Jaws of Borrowdale, Eagle Crag above Stonethwaite. Yet somehow the relationship of these separate parts – all wonderful subjects for a day's walk – fails to register as a coherent whole. Perhaps it is because the range is generally of a lower elevation, with few narrow ridges, and has no incisive roads that marvelling eyes are averted. But the range does harbour heather-clad fells, quiet dales such as Wythburn, Greenburn and Shoulthwaite, and, to cap it all, superlative viewpoints at many levels from Loughrigg Terrace to High Raise.

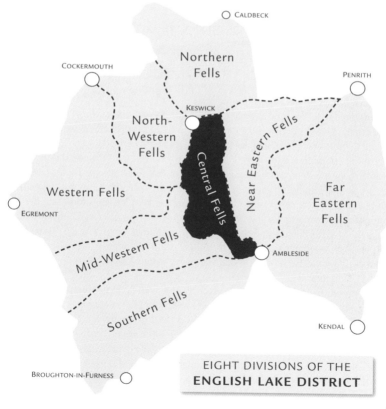

EIGHT DIVISIONS OF THE
ENGLISH LAKE DISTRICT

The Central Fells offer the chance to leave the car some distance from your walk by using either the 555 'Lakeslink' service from Windermere to Keswick via Ambleside and Grasmere, or the 79, the 'Borrowdale Rambler', from Keswick to Seatoller. Both of these Stagecoach bus services are as regular as clockwork, run all year round and give genuine flexibility to your walk plans.

The 555 service with top-deck viewing is enhanced by the booklet 'From A to B to SEE, a guide to your ride', which was prepared for the service whilst researching this guide to give all visitors a sense of the wonderful backdrop of fells seen during the journey. The Derwentwater launch might even be used for walks beginning from either the Ashness Gate or Lodore landing stages. These jetties are convenient for the escarpment from Walla Crag to Grange Fell.

The purpose of this guide is to show the fullest complement of walking routes on each fell. The pressure of boots down the years has taken its toll. Costly capital projects, along with pre-emptive works, have been and continue to be undertaken by the Fix the Fells project, a working partnership between the Lake District National Park Authority, the National Trust and Natural England. Yet 'official' advice on your choice of routes has always been strict, limiting route information to the modern variations of traditional paths and thus concentrating walkers on limited routes. In contrast, Lakeland Fellranger provides a solid reference to the fullest range of reliable contemporary options, a valuable by-product of this being to spread the load more widely over the path network.

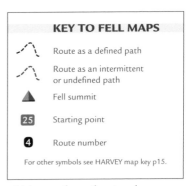

KEY TO FELL MAPS

Route as a defined path

Route as an intermittent or undefined path

Fell summit

25   Starting point

4   Route number

For other symbols see HARVEY map key p15.

For ease of reference the 28 fell chapters are arranged in alphabetical order. Each chapter begins with a customised HARVEY map that illustrates the routes of ascent described in the guide, and shows ridge connections to neighbouring fells to assist in the planning of extended walks. The corresponding text describes routes up the fell from given valley starting points, identified on the map by a number (shown in a blue box). The starting points are listed in the 'Starting Points' table on page 18, and are also given in blue (in brackets) after the ascent route headings in the walks. In many instances there is also a diagram that shows the routes from a given perspective to assist visualisation.

The primary routes to the summit are described, with optional variations given, up to their natural point of connection with the more common route. Where a route follows a defined path this is shown in red dashes, and where the recommended route follows an intermittent path (or there is no path on the ground at all) this is shown in green dashes. Where a route follows a road it is not picked out by dashed lines. Being aware of the safest lines of descent is important and advice is given on these except on the most straightforward of fells. There are far more paths on the fells than are

Pavey Ark and Stickle Tarn (Chapter 18)

Eagle Crag from Stonethwaite Bridge (Chapter 6)

Blencathra from Bell Crags (Chapter 2)

shown on a conventional HARVEY map, and for clarity this guide only shows the paths and routes that are described here.

As a good guide should also be a revelation, a full panorama is provided for each fell summit or better nearby viewpoint. This names the principal fells and picks out key features in their midst, with some more distant features beyond the national park to intrigue. When undertaking the walks in the guide, you are advised to take a map and compass with you (and know how to use them). The map can enhance your day by showing additional landscape features and setting your walk in its wider context, as well as being useful for your own safety. And remember that representation of a route in this guide, in whatever form, does not infer safe passage for all, at any time. The onus is on each individual to weigh up their own capabilities and the prevailing conditions. In fellwalking, as in any mountain travel, knowing when to retreat is often the greater part of valour. The author has taken care to follow time-honoured routes, and kept within bounds of access, yet cannot guarantee rights of way in all cases.

FIX THE FELLS

This series highlights the work of the Fix the Fells project in pitching the most seriously damaged fell paths. The process has been a great learning curve and the more recent pitching is superb, ensuring a flat foot-fall where possible, and being easy to use in ascent and descent. However, invariably these trails are not rights of way, and are therefore beyond the statutory responsibility of the highway authority. Hence this partnership of the National Park Authority, National Trust and Natural England, with additional financial support from the Friends of the

Thirlmere from Raven Crag (Chapter 20)

Lake District, has worked to make good the hill paths. The whole effort has been made possible by third-party match-funding from the Heritage Lottery Fund.

Much work remains to be done, most especially pre-emptive repair to stop paths from washing out in the first place. Nurture Lakeland (www.nurturelakeland.org) also contributes significantly to this work, but with a metre of path costing up to £100 there is every good reason to cultivate the involvement of fellwalkers in a cause that must be dear to their hearts... and soles! Make a beeline for www.fixthefells.co.uk to mark your commitment to the well-being of the fells by giving a modest donation. Clearly the occasional donation is welcome, but as yet this is still only a tiny injection. If it were the culture for regular fellwalkers to make small regular donations, so much the better.

ACCESS
May 2005 saw the implementation of the Countryside and Rights of Way (CROW) Act in Cumbria, from which time most rough open country became conditionally accessible to walkers. The so-called 'right to roam' legislation is in truth something of a sledge hammer to crack a nut. Quite the majority of fellwalkers only feel at ease when striding upon a clear path, especially one that has a time-honoured sense of purpose. The roving instinct, a broad-brush freedom to randomly explore trackless country, appeals to a narrow band of walkers. I love the liberty of exploring open country with a map, but being wedded to the preparation of practical guides, my liberty always has an eye on sensible routes that give the security that guidebook users expect. This guide shows only a few such 'roaming' routes.

The mantra of Open Access should be stressed – Respect, Protect and Enjoy – for liberty to roam brings responsibilities. As wanderers we acknowledge that land has value, not confined to its ownership, and we above all should play our bit-part in its sustaining care. This new liberty has a further purpose, and is seen by Natural England as a flagship for a walking revolution. The notion of biophilia (a love of living things), and an inclusive joining up of natural heritage and people, has broadened the message, for alongside the well-being benefits of stepping out – see Walking the Way to Health (www.whi.org.uk) – Open Access brings new impetus for encouraging a wider range of people to experience the outdoors.

SAFETY

Being constantly alive to, and aware of, the potential dangers of walking in high fell country is essential for everyone, and most especially those who come new to this activity. The National Park Authority provides practical, up-to-date advice from daily weather checks (Weatherline 017687 75757, 24-hour fell forecast) to guided walks aimed at absolute beginners. As a first recourse obtain a copy of their leaflet 'Safety on the Fells' and consult their website: www.lake-district.gov.uk.

ADVISORY NOTE

The National Park have prepared a short advisory note for conscientious walkers:

- Place your feet thoughtfully; every single footstep causes wear and tear on the environment. The slow-growing plants that can survive on mountains are particularly vulnerable.
- Keep to the path surface; do not walk along the vegetation at the edge of the path.
- Do not build or add to cairns – paths need stones more than cairns.
- Do not take shortcuts – water will soon follow your tracks and an erosion scar will develop. Remember, there may be only one of you, but there are another 12 million pairs of feet treading Lake District paths every year.

Let us long love Lakeland and care for its future. May its magic remain an inspiration for each new generation.

THE **CENTRAL** FELLS – four graphic projections of the range

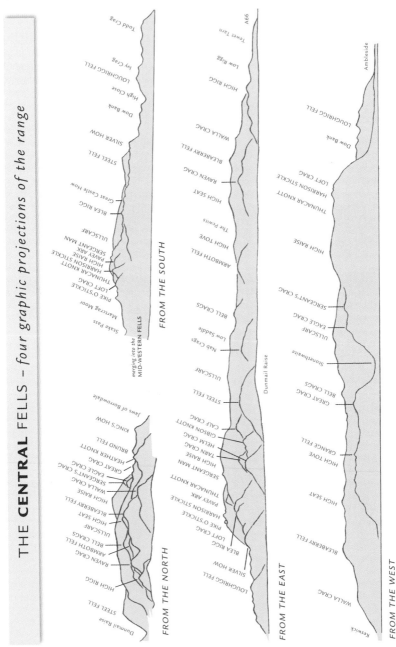

FROM THE SOUTH

FROM THE NORTH

FROM THE EAST

FROM THE WEST

HARVEY MAP KEY

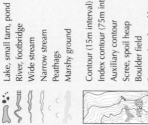

- Lake, small tarn, pond
- River, footbridge
- Wide stream
- Narrow stream
- Peathags
- Marshy ground

- Contour (15m interval)
- Index contour (75m interval)
- Auxiliary contour
- Scree, spoil heap
- Boulder field
- Scattered rock and boulders
- Predominantly rocky ground
- Major crag, large boulder
- O.S. trig pillar, large cairn
- Spot height (from air survey)

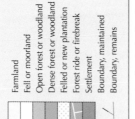

Contours change from brown to grey where the ground is predominantly rocky outcrops, small crags and other bare rock.

- Farmland
- Fell or moorland
- Open forest or woodland
- Dense forest or woodland
- Felled or new plantation
- Forest ride or firebreak
- Settlement
- Boundary, maintained
- Boundary, remains

On moorland, walls, ruined walls and fences are shown. For farmland, only the outer boundary wall or fence is shown.

SCALE 1 : 40,000

- Dual carriageway
- Main road (fenced)
- Minor road (unfenced)
- Track or forest road
- Footpath or old track
- Intermittent path
- Powerline, pipeline
- Building, ruin or sheepfold, shaft

Pike — Fell summits that feature as chapters in this guidebook.

The representation of a road, track or footpath is no evidence of the existence of a right of way.

0 Kilometres

0 Miles

THE CENTRAL FELLS

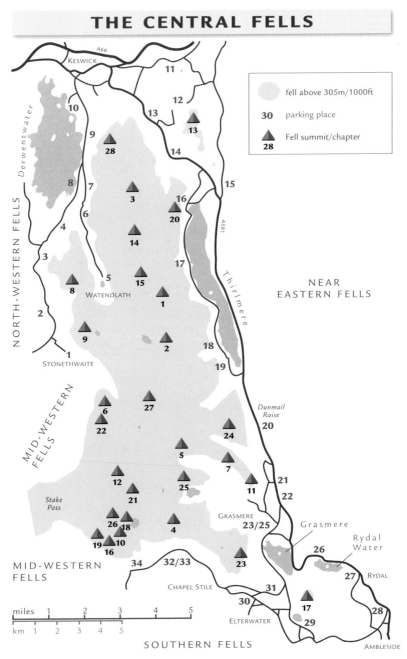

KESWICK

A66

11

12

10

13

13

9

28

fell above 305m/1000ft

30 parking place

28 Fell summit/chapter

Derwentwater

8

7

3

14

16

20

6

14

4

15

A591

3

5

15

8

WATENDLATH

1

Thirlmere

NEAR
EASTERN FELLS

2

9

2

1

STONETHWAITE

18

19

NORTH-WESTERN FELLS

27

Dunmail
Raise

6

22

24

20

MID-WESTERN
FELLS

5

7

12

25

11

21

21

22

Stake
Pass

26

18

4

GRASMERE

23/25

Grasmere

19

10

16

Rydal
Water

26

23

27

RYDAL

MID-WESTERN
FELLS

34

32/33

31

CHAPEL STILE

30

17

28

ELTERWATER

29

miles 1   2   3   4   5

km 1   2   3   4   5

SOUTHERN FELLS

AMBLESIDE

16

FELL MOSAIC

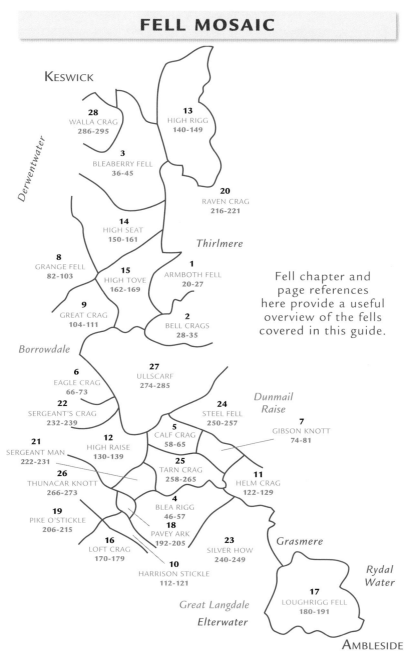

KESWICK

28
WALLA CRAG
286-295

13
HIGH RIGG
140-149

3
BLEABERRY FELL
36-45

Derwentwater

20
RAVEN CRAG
216-221

14
HIGH SEAT
150-161

Thirlmere

8
GRANGE FELL
82-103

15
HIGH TOVE
162-169

1
ARMBOTH FELL
20-27

Fell chapter and
page references
here provide a useful
overview of the fells
covered in this guide.

9
GREAT CRAG
104-111

2
BELL CRAGS
28-35

Borrowdale

6
EAGLE CRAG
66-73

27
ULLSCARF
274-285

*Dunmail
Raise*

22
SERGEANT'S CRAG
232-239

24
STEEL FELL
250-257

7
GIBSON KNOTT
74-81

21
SERGEANT MAN
222-231

12
HIGH RAISE
130-139

5
CALF CRAG
58-65

26
THUNACAR KNOTT
266-273

25
TARN CRAG
258-265

11
HELM CRAG
122-129

19
PIKE O'STICKLE
206-215

4
BLEA RIGG
46-57

18
PAVEY ARK
192-205

23
SILVER HOW
240-249

Grasmere

16
LOFT CRAG
170-179

10
HARRISON STICKLE
112-121

*Rydal
Water*

17
LOUGHRIGG FELL
180-191

Great Langdale

Elterwater

AMBLESIDE

17

STARTING POINTS

	LOCATION	GRID REFERENCE	PARKING	BUS STOP
1	Stonethwaite verge	261 139		B
2	Rosthwaite (NT)	257 149	P	B
3	Quayfoot (NT)	254 168	P	B
4	Leathes lay-by	256 177		B
5	Watendlath (NT)	276 163	P	B
6	Surprise View	268 189	P	
7	Ashness Bridge	269 196	P	
8	Kettlewell (NT)	267 194	P	B
9	Great Wood (NT)	272 214	P	B
10	Keswick, Lake Road	265 229	P	B
11	Tewet Tarn verge	306 238		
12	St John's in the Vale Church	306 225	P	
13	Causeway Foot	293 219	P	B
14	Rough How Bridge	300 205	P	B
15	Legburthwaite	318 195	P	B
16	Thirlmere Dam	306 189	P	
17	Armboth	305 172	P	
18	Dob Gill	316 142	P	
19	Steel End	321 130	P	
20	Dunmail Raise lay-by	329 111		B
21	Mill Bridge	396 092	P	B
22	A591 lay-by	337 086	P	
23	Redbank Road	335 073	P	B
24	Broadgate	338 078	P	B
25	Stock Lane	339 073	P	B
26	White Moss	350 065	P	B
27	Pelter Bridge, Rydal	336 059	P	B
28	Rydal Road, Ambleside	375 047	P	B
29	Tarn Foot	345 039	P	
30	Elterwater (NT)	329 052	P	B
31	High Close	337 053	P	
32	Langdale	295 063	P	B
33	Stickle Ghyll (NT)	294 063	P	B
34	Old Dungeon Ghyll (NT)	286 062	P	B

P – formal car parking facilities (some with coin meters) otherwise informal, limited lay-by parking
B – serviced bus stop close by

In the guide, the starting point for each ascent route is shown in a blue box on the map and given in blue (in brackets) after the route title.

Public transport may be a problem elsewhere, but here in the heart of Lakeland one may confidently plan a day around a reliable rural service, given a proper study of timetables. The Mountain Goat service is supplemented by regular Stagecoach services throughout the district. Pertinent to this guide is the Lakeslink 555 service that runs along the A591, from Windermere via Ambleside and Grasmere crossing Dunmail Raise

bound for Keswick. Two bus services for Borrowdale leave the Keswick bus terminus (situated beside the Lakes Foodstore). You can hop aboard the Honister Rambler 77/77A, a circular service which heads down the shore of Derwentwater bound for Rosthwaite and Seatoller, then crosss the Honister Pass to Buttermere and Lorton, before switching back over the Whinlatter Pass. Alternatively, take the more direct Borrowdale Rambler 79, a shuttle service to Seatoller. The National Trust operate the Watendlath Wanderer from Keswick on summer Sundays only. From Ambleside use the Langdale Rambler 526 for Elterwater, Chapel Stile and the Old Dungeon Ghyll Hotel. For current advice contact: TRAVELINE public transport info 0871 200 22 33, www.traveline.org.uk

Langstrath Beck (Chapter 22)

1 ARMBOTH FELL *(479m, 1572ft)*

Fells do not get more pudding-like than this. Indeed, to add to the analogy, and indignity, Armboth is a squidgy, squadgy fell that looks as if some local monster has set his considerable posterior down precisely on top – by neat coincidence Thirlmere actually translates as 'lake of the giant'. Thankfully there are a few outcrops to distract from its otherwise nondescript demeanour. Summit-baggers are the more likely visitors to this outpost, and its only claim may be that it is the most centrally placed fell in the district. Evidence of Celtic rock art has been spotted on rocks west of the summit, but my own searches have been in vain.

You are never far from water when strolling about this moor. The ageing heather has a hard time keeping its feet dry, and the same may be said of any fellwalker who ventures near the peaty, sphagnum-encroached hollow where Launchy and Fisher Gills have a common sluggish birth. The stretch of plateau to the south has a small erratic that may be inspected while surveying the shapely profile of Bell Crags to the south. You may be lucky enough to spot the small herd of shy red deer that roam this quiet area. Fisher Crag, the best viewpoint and most characterful feature on the fell, is not strictly accessible. Overlooking Thirlmere, Fisher Crag rivals Raven Crag as a brink from which to survey the great fell wall of the Helvellyn range and the more distant Blencathra. As a picturesque subject it must have featured in many a photograph taken from Station Coppice car park, across the dark waters of the reservoir.

ASCENT FROM ARMBOTH (17)

Direct 287m/940ft 3.2km/2 miles

Start from the United Utilities car park (toilets), situated 1 mile south of the dam on the road running down the western shore of Thirlmere. **1** Facing out from the point of entry, go right and first left at the kissing-gate, to the start of the fell path destined for Watendlath, which traverses the intervening ridge via High Tove. A clear path crosses a stout little bridge spanning Middlesteads Gill. Pass through a wall gap, and the hurdles in a wooden sheep pen, to ascend by a group of large rocks on a partly repaired and stepped path rising beside the forestry fence shielding Fisher Gill. The path switches right and enjoys a fine view across the reservoir to the Helvellyn range. Passing under a sycamore and skirting juniper, climb to a wall-gap beside the plantation fence. Keep to the footpath for a matter of 200m, then fork half-left just after entering bracken, on a strong sheep trod, to ford a feeder-gill. Accompany the right-hand rim of the shallow upper ravine of Fisher Gill, shaded by birch and rowan. As the gill winds on with ever decreasing gradient, aim half-left through sickly-looking heather towards

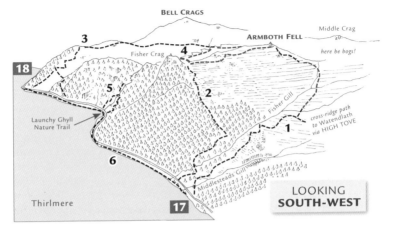

the prominent outcrop, and if you are lucky you might find the one path which leads to that very evident summit outcrop. Only the latter stages of the route can be said to be free of excitement, that is unless you set yourself the challenge of finding the rock art!

Via Fisher Crag   287m/940ft   3.5km/2¼ miles

2 Go left along the reservoir's west shore road to the forestry parking area and gate/stile entry on the right, just before the road crossing of Fisher Gill. A forest track winds uphill crossing Fisher Gill. Note, to the left, the old Armboth Hall summer-house perched among the trees on a knoll – finding contemporary use as a lunch

Fisher Crag from Middlesteads Gill

shelter for forest workers. The track continues more steeply, and drifts away from the gill at a left-hand bend with young plantation fencing on the right. Climb to a ladder-stile with a stone sheepfold and bothy ruin close at hand. The path wends up beside the old wall and fence to crest the moor. Carefully climb over the locked gate in the fence and climb (no path) onto the immediate top

Raptor trap near Fisher Crag

of Fisher Crag, where a cairn nestles among the heather. Is this view an improvement on Raven Crag? Well perhaps not, though its mildly 'illicit' nature does add something! Return to the gate and head basically south-westward, initially over marshy ground, to work a way up the rocky fell to the summit.

ASCENT FROM DOB GILL (18)

Via Stone Hause   287m/940ft   4.2km/2¾ miles

3 Start at the United Utilities Dob Gill car park (toilets) situated 3 miles south of the dam. Exit and follow the road left (north) to where a path commences at a stile on the left and leads through a wall gateway and up the northern edge of the plantation, passing a curious empty metal tree cage, to reach the open track as it exits the forestry. Go right, then quickly left, to a hand-gate in the wall corner. An old shepherds' path winds steeply up the bracken-dogged fellside. As the ground eventually eases on Brown Rigg, pass a couple of old sheepfolds tucked into outcrop nooks. Deer management quad vehicles exit at the top forest gate and have provided a line to follow by Stone Hause, out across the bowl-shaped gathering grounds of Launchy Gill to a ford above Launchy Tarn – actually rather a shallow, lazy meander. Beyond, the tracks are lost en route. Cross the wire fence and climb the rough, though gently angled slope to the summit.

Via Launchy Gill   4.7km/3 miles

4 Fellwalkers with a wanderlust may make a swiping route that ignores the summit altogether. Having forded the upper course of Launchy Gill, amble downstream by Launchy Tarn and the old wall beside the cascaded section, and find a fence-stile at the resumption of the wall approaching the forest edge. From here follow the forest top-wall and gradually rise to Fisher Crag. Turn this excursion into a round-trip using the lakeside road and include the Launchy Ghyll Nature Trail. Should you begin this circuit from the Armboth car park, then the forest track below Brown Rigg will be found useful in reducing the extent of road walking.

Launchy Ghyll Trail ¼ mile

Launchy Ghyll Nature Trail The best series of cataracts falling east into Thirlmere tumbles through the forestry issuing from the lonely wastes between Bell Crags and Armboth Fell – this is Launchy Ghyll. The gill-name contains the Old Norse word *laun* which means 'secret', while the use of the 'ghyll' spelling is a persistence of Victorian affectation, exclusive to the lower tourist-accessible section.

Launchy Ghyll, the upper falls

5 Situated midway between the Armboth and Dob Gill car parks the waymarked forest trail gives a relaxing stroll for casual visitors as it climbs from lay-bys either side of the road bridge situated midway between the Armboth and Dob Gill car parks. At half-height a footbridge crosses the ravine. Above this point the gorge narrows and steepens; not surprisingly the secure trail smartly turns tail, switching back down to the road. As you may suspect the best of the falls lie out of sight higher up. From the top of the steps on the southern side, half-a-dozen steps intimate the beginning of an old unsecured path up through the conifers to two impromptu viewing points. The top fall is supremely elegant and luxuriant. There is no access to the open fell above, as the forest-bounding fence is walker-tight!

THE SUMMIT

A slender rib of ice-worn rock, like the inverted hull of a boat, forms the summit, which has a small cairn precariously perched on the very top. The only evidence of visitation is a narrow trod approaching from the direction of Fisher Gill. Perhaps this lack of obvious human 'damage' is one of the fell's understated virtues. A damp plateau extends south, and a solitary erratic acts as a target for otherwise aimless

Summit cairn, Armboth Fell

Summit outcrop, Armboth Fell

strolls. The southern slopes of the fell, approaching the wide hollow of Launchy Gill, are defined by a tight, fortunately barbless fence, erected to restrict red deer.

SAFE DESCENT

The simplest course is north across a largely pathless moor. Ford Fisher Gill and join the footpath coming down from High Tove, which leads by the forest fence to the security of the Thirlmere shore road at Armboth. The nearest habitation is on the left, beyond the dam at Bridgend Farm (camp site), 1½ miles, and the nearest phone kiosk is at Legburthwaite a further half-mile away.

RIDGE ROUTES

HIGH TOVE	↓45m/150ft	↑75m/250ft	1.3km/¾ mile

Beelines are fine for bees, who enhance their honey with nectar from the heather; they don't have to set foot in the bogs and twist their delicate ankles in the rough moor grass. To minimise time entangled in the marsh, follow the safe descent. Head north, descending to ford Fisher Gill and join the old footpath linking Armboth with Watendlath. The westward-trending path is never very convincing, and even has the temerity to almost 'dissolve' on the wet rise to the summit cairn on the skyline. However, this is far better than following the habits of crows or bees!

BELL CRAGS	↓75m/250ft	↑165m/540ft	1.6km/1 mile

There is no path from start to finish, but it is far sweeter than the spinal ridge track beside the fence from High Tove to Bell Crags! Walk south to the lone erratic boulder, then descend, with the shapely peak of Bell Crags ahead. Carefully cross the plain wire fence and ford Launchy Gill, passing another solitary erratic boulder before mounting above the actual Bell Crags outcrop and climbing past the large sheepfold to the peaked summit.

PANORAMA

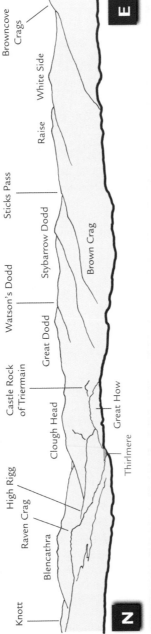

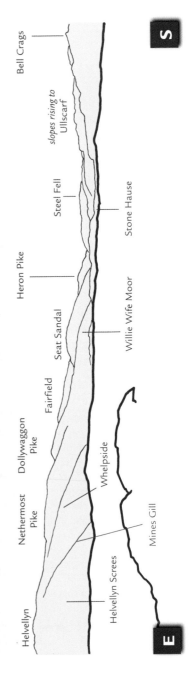

Top panorama (E):
Browncove Crags — White Side — Raise — Sticks Pass — Stybarrow Dodd — Brown Crag — Watson's Dodd — Great Dodd — Castle Rock of Triermain — Great How — Clough Head — Thirlmere — High Rigg — Raven Crag — Blencathra — Knott

Bottom panorama (S / E):
Bell Crags — slopes rising to Ullscarf — Steel Fell — Stone Hause — Heron Pike — Willie Wife Moor — Seat Sandal — Fairfield — Dollywaggon Pike — Whelpside — Nethermost Pike — Mines Gill — Helvellyn — Helvellyn Screes

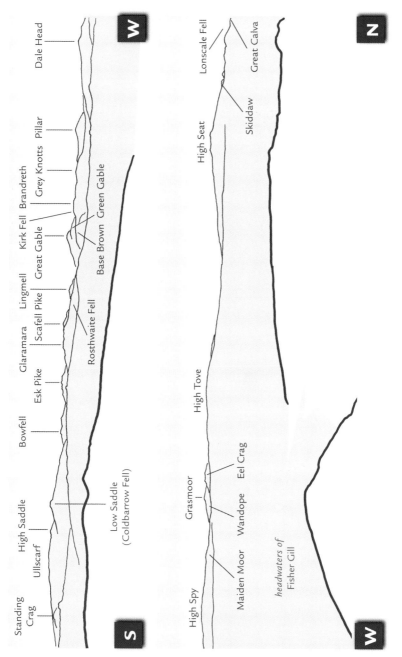

2 BELL CRAGS *(558m, 1831ft)*

By curious convention Bell Crags is not recognised as a separate fell. Sandwiched between Launchy and Dob Gills, the wedge of rough country rising west from the shores of Thirlmere – initially as craggy afforestation but later as a wonderfully wild fell – has been cold-shouldered by those who claim to know a fell when they see one.

There is no doubting the merits of Bleaberry Fell and High Seat, each swelling as distinguished components of the range further north, but as the ridge trends south towards Ullscarf over High Tove, the grounds for separate fell status weaken. This low-slung ridge has two recognised intermediate tops, High Tove and Armboth Fell. Both are beset with soggy peat and grouse, which make their distinctive 'go back, go back' call as they frantically beat their wings in low flight across the rank, sickly looking heather.

Such fells are poor fish beside the far more striking height of Bell Crags. The fell stands smartly to attention above Launchy Gill, master of all it surveys – hardly a quality one can bestow upon its northern neighbours. The old bridle path from Wythburn to Watendlath, via Harrop and Blea Tarns, might be said to prove the point, effectively annexing the fell from the greater mass of Ullscarf. The fell-top can be reached via the long, tendril-like path acutely south-eastward from Watendlath, but more efficiently and scenically from the south-western shores of Thirlmere at Dob Gill.

ASCENT FROM DOB GILL (18)

Via Harrop Tarn   597m/1960ft   3.2km/2 miles

Three paths climb from the vicinity of the United Utilities Dob Gill car park. **1** An engineered path climbs directly from the signboard and winds up the mature forestry to the outflow of Harrop Tarn. **2** Alternatively, the old bridle route begins from the road (modified start) on the south side of the beck, a signpost and hand-gate giving access. Note the Binka Stone, a distinctive ice-smoothed outcrop to the left – a 'bink' being a doorstep, alluding to its stepped appearance. Rise via a second hand-gate after 40m, and the stony stair climbs through dense juniper to a ladder-stile crossing the tall deer fence. The path leads through the forest over a section of

duckboards to the footbridge and ford at the outflow of Harrop Tarn. The tarn forms an attractive scene, and is surrounded by conifers and backed by craggy fellside, the north-eastern slopes of Ullscarf. It can shine like a jewel, though it is much diminished by encroaching marsh. **3** A somewhat circuitous route can be followed that climbs the eastern slope through further juniper beyond the Binka Stone to the cairn on top of Birk Crag, before descending north-west to this point via a deer gate. **4** The old bridle route follows the clear forest track by a small grove of beech. After crossing a footbridge at a shallow feeder-gill, the track swings right but the path heads straight on to quickly link up with a further forest track. As this track bears right again, a signpost indicates the bridle path leading straight on up to a double deer-door gate by an old fold. Exiting the forestry, the bridle path winds purposefully on up the open slope to the broad, damp depression. Standing Crag is the noble feature to the south, and Blea Tarn is in view westward. Do not go through the hand-gate at the ridge-top fence. Instead tip-toe, as best you can, across an uncomfortable marsh to the right (north) to firm ground on course for the summit.

5 Alternatively, follow the forest fence immediately right, branching off at will to climb the fell and finding your own way, there being no hindrance but small outcrops, to an easy pathless ascent. The summit lies at the northern tip of the slightly undulating ridge.

Via Mosshause and Stone Hause   3km/1¾ miles

6 Leave the road a few metres north of the car park at a stile, and a path leads up through a wall gateway and the northern edge of the forest to a track. **7** Pass through the hand-gate into the plantation, and at the first fork in the forest track either go straight ahead or bear up right. Both tracks achieve union with the bridle path, and waymarking guides to the right up to a double deer-door gate by an old fold to leave the forestry as per Route 4. **8** Go right, then quickly left, to a hand-gate in the wall corner. An old shepherds' path winds steeply up the grooved fellside, and fine views back over the head of Thirlmere give scope for a breather or two. As the ground eases, pass a couple of old folds tucked into outcrop nooks. Bell Crags comes into view once the forestry corner is passed. Evade bracken patches while crossing Stone Hause, and mount the ramped slope of the upper fell to the prominent summit.

ASCENT FROM WATENDLATH (5)

The 5 miles from the shores of Derwentwater to Bell Crags, via Watendlath, is split equally between single-track road and fell path (rising via Ashness Bridge, the path section described in Routes 9–10). Also arriving at Watendlath is the popular bridle path from Rosthwaite via the Puddingstone Bank bridle path (see GRANGE FELL Route 8, page 90), and this makes a four-mile off-road fell walk to the summit. However, an excellent idea is to contemplate a range-crossing traverse, linking bus stops at Rosthwaite and Wythburn road-end at the southern end of Thirlmere – thus connecting the Borrowdale Rambler route and the half-hourly 555 Lakeslink bus services (both out of Keswick).

Via Blea Tarn 290m/950ft 4km/2½ miles

9 Most walkers will start from the National Trust car park (pay and display). Exit either over the ladder-stile or go right from the point of entry to a gate. The way-marked footpath fords Raise Beck and soon commences the zig-zag ascent of the steep bank, following centuries-old sled trails used for conveying peat from High Tove for domestic heating. The point of departure from the Armboth path is marked on a slate 'to Wythburn' at the wall corner. The green path contours the hillside, initially with an intake wall for company, though the wall is replaced by strategic cairns as guides on the long gradual south-eastward rise. The path clips the brow, missing the fence corner, and dips to the outflow of Blea Tarn, a wind-whipped sheet of water; the term *blea* means 'coarse or rough ground', explanatory of the immediate environs. The damp path proceeds up the tough tussocky herbage to the watershed fence and hand-gate. Pass through the gate, bearing left, and negotiate the marsh to reach firm ground rising to the short north–south summit ridge.

Via High Tove 320m/1050ft 4.5km/2¾ miles

10 An option when the ground is either bone dry or gripped in frost is to complete the ascent to High Tove by turning south to follow the east side of the ridge fence. This is not an activity upon which one can heap much praise, being reminiscent of a Pennine bog-hopping yomp, with the presence of red grouse adding fuel to the notion!

Sheepfold below the summit to the north looking to Raven Crag, Blencathra, Clough Head and Great Dodd

Summit outcrop with the belle of Bell Crags

THE SUMMIT

Well, yes, it's true – the summit is innominate on all maps. I bestowed the name, elevating it from an outcrop set low down the northern slope. A small cairn rests on the southern top, while a larger outcrop makes a more convincing summit at the northern tip of the ridge. The panorama over the page is taken from this outcrop. On the high shelf, directly beneath the summit to the north, stands possibly the neatest sheepfold in Lakeland. It certainly deserves close inspection – the small compartment appears to have had a roof. Nearby is a further small roofless bothy next to modest evidence of quarrying in the flaky rock. West of the summit find the old metal fence-corner strainer post, in front of the present fence. The fell offers the most marvellous northern prospect – as may be judged from the image on page 11, looking to Blencathra.

SAFE DESCENTS

Join the old bridle path traversing the depression immediately south of the summit. The easiest option is east, and the improving path leads down into the plantation surrounding Harrop Tarn, though Thirlmere at Dob Gill is bereft of services for the wet and weary. Better then the westward line to Watendlath and Borrowdale beyond, though you may have to suffer facing the prevailing wind and no doubt the worst the elements can throw at you!

RIDGE ROUTES

ARMBOTH FELL ↓165m/540ft ↑75m/250ft 1.6km/1 mile

Descend via the grand sheepfold due north, watching for the outcrops. As the slope levels, pass an old cairn and an erratic before fording the feeder-gill to Launchy Gill, then cross the wire fence. Pass through the old wall, proceed up the rough, easier angled slope to the prominent erratic on the brow, and the summit outcrop lies across marshy ground ahead.

HIGH TOVE ↓50m/160ft ↑10m/30ft 3.2km/2 miles

The many energetic souls who innocently set their sights on an end-to-end ridge walk from Great Langdale to Keswick should be under no illusion – the going north of Bell Crags is as wet as it gets on any ridge walk in Lakeland. The only saving grace is the presence of the fence, to which one either clings or bounces. The final rise to High Tove is at least on improving ground, though things degenerate again beyond there as you go towards High Seat.

ULLSCARF ↓30m/100ft ↑210m/690ft 2.8km/1¾ miles

Aim south-west to the fence. Ignore the hand-gate on a clear path which passes a large pool, sliced through by the fence, and head directly for the foot of Standing Crag. The path takes a leftward slant in climbing up through a weakness to the top of the crag. The fence resumes from the very top, a spot worth visiting for the fine view. The path keeps close company with the fence to the acute corner, where you bear south on the grassy plateau following the line of old fence stumps and proceed to the summit cairn.

PANORAMA

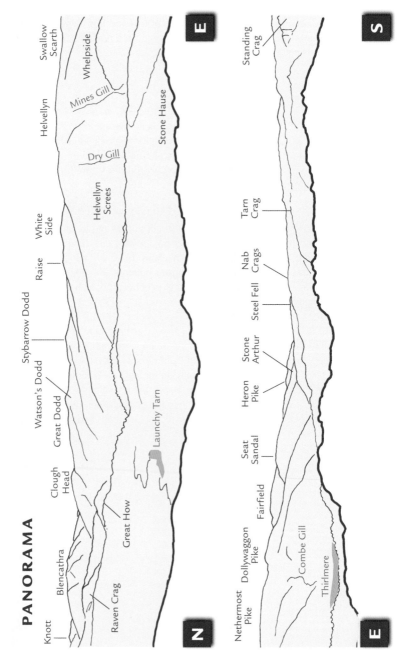

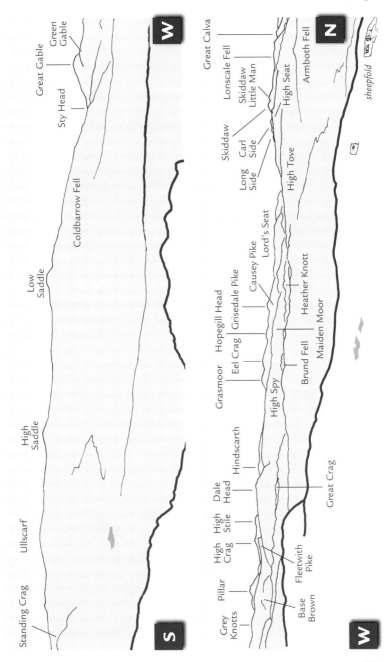

W

Green Gable
Great Gable
Sty Head
Coldbarrow Fell
Low Saddle
High Saddle
Ullscarf
Standing Crag

S

N

Great Calva
Lonscale Fell
Skiddaw Little Man
High Seat
Armboth Fell
Skiddaw
Carl Side
Long Side
High Tove
Causey Pike
Lord's Seat
Grisedale Pike
Hopegill Head
Eel Crag
Grasmoor
Heather Knott
Maiden Moor
Brund Fell
High Spy
Hindscarth
Great Crag
Dale Head
High Stile
High Crag
Fleetwith Pike
Pillar
Base Brown
Grey Knotts

sheepfold

W

35

3 BLEABERRY FELL *(589m, 1932ft)*

The fell forms a convincing northern culmination to a range of, admittedly, modest and greatly be-marshed tops stemming from the central plateau of High Raise. To east and west stirring crags command valley views. When seen from across the Naddle valley or Castlerigg Stone Circle it projects a striking headland, strengthened by Dodd Crag and the shy cliffs of Shoulthwaite Gill. Walkers lured to explore this eastern aspect are seldom disappointed, especially as the climb to the summit is rewarded with a rapturous panorama of famous fells.

The fell bears little physical likeness to the adjacent Clough Head, though they both offer dry-shod ascents to major range-end viewpoints. When viewed from Brandelhow (see title view above), or from aboard the Derwentwater launch, the domed heather-darkened summit stands proudly aloft. From here onwards the Central Fell range falters in graceful stages into the Greta gap, forking either side of Brockle Beck – going westward to Walla Crag and eastward over Dodd and Pike. The two-tiered competitive climbing walls of Falcon Crag, facing over Derwentwater and warmed by late afternoon sunshine, have long attracted climbers; while to the east the inevitably shaded and seldom-tried cliffs of Dodd, Goat and Iron Crags bear down on the little-visited wilds of the Shoulthwaite valley, a backdoor to the fell to be treasured.

Falcon Crag

ASCENT FROM KESWICK (10)

Via Springs Road and Brockle Beck   512m/1680ft   5.7km/3½ miles

1 From the Moot Hall leave the town centre via St John's Road, which becomes Old Ambleside Road. Just before this road pitches uphill, fork right into Springs Road. Continue by Springs Farm yard, keeping close company with the wooded ravine, the path in its later stages running beside pasture fencing. Note that the fenced path bearing right can be used to access Great Wood and gain a more direct ascent of Walla Crag. The easier course continues uphill, passes through a kissing-gate, dips into the dell again and crosses a footbridge to join the minor road at a hand-gate. Go right, forking right at the approach to Rakefoot Farm. Cross the footbridge and rise to a stile (and padlocked field-gate).

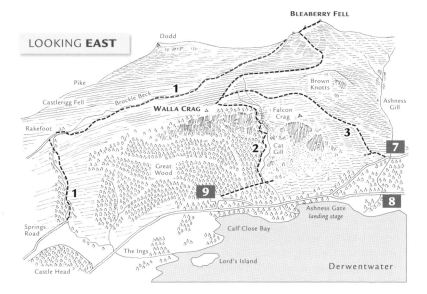

LOOKING **EAST**

BLEABERRY FELL

Dodd

Pike

Brockle Beck

Castlerigg Fell

1

WALLA CRAG

Brown Knotts

Ashness Gill

Falcon Crag

Rakefoot

3

Cat Gill

2

7

Great Wood

9

1

8

Ashness Gate landing stage

Springs Road

Calf Close Bay

The Ings

Lord's Island

Derwentwater

Castle Head

A clear track ascends and forks, the path by the wall being the direct way to Walla Crag. However, for the purist intent on Bleaberry Fell, keep to the less well-trod track leading straight on, and as this bears up right again, continue on the grass path (little more than a sheep trod), which advances to the fenced sheepfold and ruined shepherd's dwelling. This was destroyed when used for heavy tank-firing practice in the Second World War. From this damp hollow on Low Moss, traipse through quite dense heather tracing the diminishing Brockle Beck ('stream associated with badgers'). With increasing vagueness the path leads on by a fold into a shallow combe. Angle up to the right onto the natural scarp shelf, now with evidence of a path, and continue to reach the large cairn at the top of the steep section of the popular path from Walla Crag. The worn trail trends up left, via an intermediate cairn, to the summit.

Old fold beside Brockle Beck

ASCENT FROM GREAT WOOD (9)

Via Cat Gill   509m/1670ft   3.2km/2 miles

2 Walkers frequently choose to include Walla Crag in their adventure. The reasoning is flawless – it offers two exceptional viewpoints, on a rising tide of visual delight. Two main routes are available to Great Wood. Either include Castle Head, a wooded thimble of a hill fashioned from the core of a volcano, following the segregated path beside the valley road; or, much better, join the lakeside path via Friar's Crag, The Ings alder carr (wooded marsh) and Calf Close (consult WALLA CRAG page 287 for all the options).

From the National Trust car park (pay and display) follow the woodland path south to the footbridge spanning Cat Gill. However, do not cross, but instead pass up through the hand-gate and climb steeply beside the confined gill. A further hand-gate is encountered on the beautifully engineered and stepped path climbing to the scarp-top. One may cross the first wall-stile on the left into the wooded scarp-edge enclosure, or continue more easily upon the green sward to a stile much closer to the top. The summit cairn stands back from the edge on a bare rock plinth. From the brink enjoy quite the best view of Derwentwater, backed by Keswick and Skiddaw. Backtrack over the stile, and join the obvious path shaping to contour above Cat Gill. Be sure to take the left fork, then ford two headstreams on course to round the shoulder of Brown Knotts. Skirting a marsh, climb the newly secured path and rise onto the summit bluff.

Skiddaw from the nick south of Dodd

ASCENT FROM ASHNESS BRIDGE (7)

Via Falcon Crag   430m/1410ft   3.2km/2 miles

3 The top of Cat Gill can be reached on converging paths climbing from Ashness Bridge. Either follow Ashness Gill's north-bank path, traversing to the hand-gate on the left; or take the lower path directly from the bridge, branch right after the stile and climb via the higher fence stile to join the upper path, which rises above Falcon Crag. A spur diversion to the left gives scope to visit the handsomely sited cairn on top of the crag with its fine view of Walla Crag in profile and across the island-dotted lake towards Bassenthwaite and the distant Solway Firth. The continuing path, above the deep re-entrant of Cat Gill, provides another notable scenic moment, before combining with paths from Walla Crag and Cat Gill and turning right bound for the summit.

ASCENT FROM CAUSEWAY FOOT IN THE NADDLE VALLEY (13)

Travellers speeding south from Keswick along the A591 are certain to catch a peripheral glimpse of the craggy edges bearing down upon the Shoulthwaite Gill valley. Walkers looking for new adventures are encouraged to take a closer look, as a trio of intriguing routes climb above the stern facade to attain an inspiring summit panorama. **4** This secretive backstairs approach may begin from the lay-by at Dale Bottom, opposite Causeway Foot Farm, though this involves a roadside out-leg passing beyond the old Vicarage to the ladder-stile on the right, then joining the contouring footpath behind Brackenriggs that connects into the valley.

Dodd Crag from Piper House across the Naddle valley

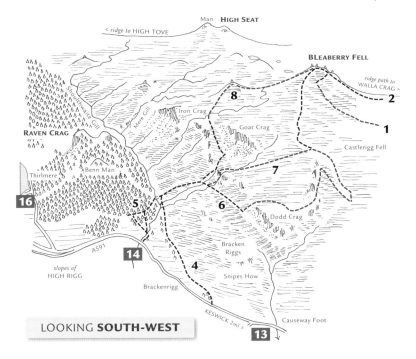

LOOKING **SOUTH-WEST**

ASCENT FROM ROUGH HOW BRIDGE (14)

Via Dodd Crag   445m/1460ft   3.2km/2 miles

5 Perhaps the easier start from the Rough How Bridge lay-by will appeal more. Follow the approach lane (footpath) to Shoulthwaite Farm (Caravan Club site beside the yard). Shoulthwaite is thought to mean 'circular enclosure', suggesting perhaps a lost 'round-house'? Pass through to the kissing-gate entry into the woodland. Branch immediately right up by the internal forest fence to join the forest track, and go right. As the track forks, go right to the tall deer-balking kissing-gate and cross the Shoulthwaite Gill bridge, with an old weir on the upstream side. Follow the winding path up the facing fellside, with the wall to the right, and cross a gill. As the three routes come level with the large erratic, over the wall, they fan their separate ways.

6 Go through the hand-gate and follow the drove way, which contrives to beat back the bracken. It fords then starts to climb. On reaching the brow leave the obvious path and climb the steep slope to the skyline on the left, short of the outcrop. On the face of it this is an apparent folly, but one the author found essential, as the primary path disappears under Dodd Crag and the way beyond is rough and confused. Steep though the climb may appear it is only hampered by bracken.

The grassy fell-top is a blessed relief. Wander to the right to the leading edge of Dodd Crag, a superb viewpoint over High Rigg to Clough Head and Blencathra. Follow the scarp edge south-west towards Bleaberry Fell, but as the working wall (it still serves to pen sheep) has only one wall-stile, this must be sought and climbed. To locate it descend and follow the wall north. As the slope levels encounter the rushy headstream of a gill, and look intently for the through-stones in the wall. Cross this old shepherds' stile with due diligence. Turn back south following the wall up and over the ridge to the junction with a fence. Now go right, all the way to the summit. While not attractive in itself, the resultant summit view definitely compensates.

Via Goat Crags 435m/1430ft 2.7km/1¾ miles

7 This is the most direct, and the easiest route from the Shoulthwaite valley. Go straight up the open bracken-inhibited gill, skirting to the left of the outcrop. Weave up and through a ravine, keeping the rising wall to the right, and continue to the junction with a fence. Pass to the west-side stile/gate and follow the fence left (south) to the summit. **8** On the face of it the more interesting option bears up half-left. Climb, with several guiding cairns, onto the high shelf under Goat Crags via an easy cleft. The rocky edge angles up to pass above a waterfall, better appreciated from the valley floor, though if you already know it from below this moment is all the more impressive. The route turns up the gill and wanders onto the prominent cairned knoll to the south, before traversing north-westward across the damp hollow to the fence corner and stile immediately below the summit.

Dodd Crag

THE SUMMIT

The highest ground is clothed with a ragged mix of heather, bilberry and tough fell grass. Various cairns confirm viewpoints on the rise to the wind shelter and tumbled heap at the top. There is no doubt about its merits as a major viewpoint, and this and Walla Crag are a peerless pair for the greater Derwentwater arena of fells and lakes.

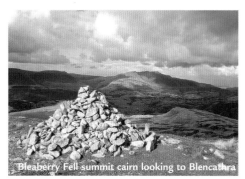
Bleaberry Fell summit cairn looking to Blencathra

Clough Head from Bleaberry Fell summit

SAFE DESCENTS

Follow the main path descending north-westward from the summit – this is the assured way. The fell is lined at a lower level with serious crags, making the course of Brockle Beck to Rakefoot a sure release from potential woes, though it is better to keep to the popular turf trail the whole way.

RIDGE ROUTES

HIGH SEAT	↓50m/160ft	↑30m/100ft	2km/1¼ miles

The ridge path is dubious, dreary and damp. The fence gives some guidance, but is actually better ignored altogether. The usual route leaves the summit, passing a cairn, and weaves a course due south, well to the west of the fence and avoiding excessively wet hollows as best it can. Cross a stile where raw peat gives dry boots their final challenge short of the climb to the summit knoll and old Ordnance Survey pillar.

WALLA CRAG	↓255m/840ft	↑45m/150ft	2km/1¼ miles

Follow the popular path north-west – the steep slope is loose, so take your time. Skirt around a marsh and pass a sheepfold sheltering on the eastern slope of Brown Knotts. The clear path runs downhill, fording two gills above the deep combe of Cat Gill to reach a stile entry into the wooded scarp enclosure.

PANORAMA

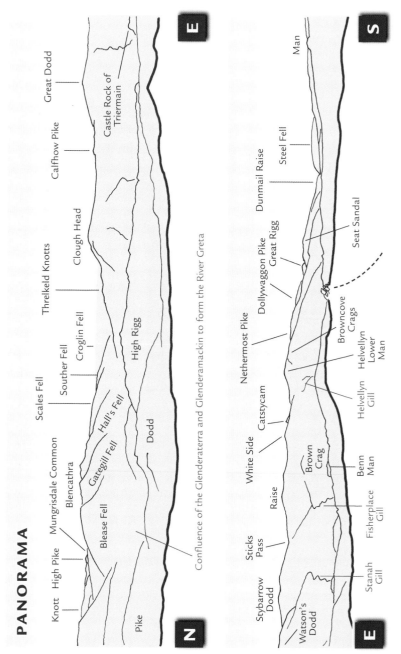

Confluence of the Glenderaterra and Glenderamackin to form the River Greta

N

Knott · High Pike · Mungrisdale Common · Blencathra · Scales Fell · Souther Fell · Threlkeld Knotts · Calfhow Pike · Great Dodd

E

Gategill Fell · Hall's Fell · Croglin Fell · Clough Head · Castle Rock of Triermain

Bleale Fell · High Rigg

Pike · Dodd

E

Stybarrow Dodd · Sticks Pass · White Side · Catstycam · Nethermost Pike · Dollywaggon Pike · Great Rigg · Dunmail Raise · Steel Fell · Man

Watson's Dodd · Raise · Brown Crag · Helvellyn Lower Man · Browncove Crags · Seat Sandal

Stanah Gill · Fisherplace Gill · Benn Man · Helvellyn Gill

S

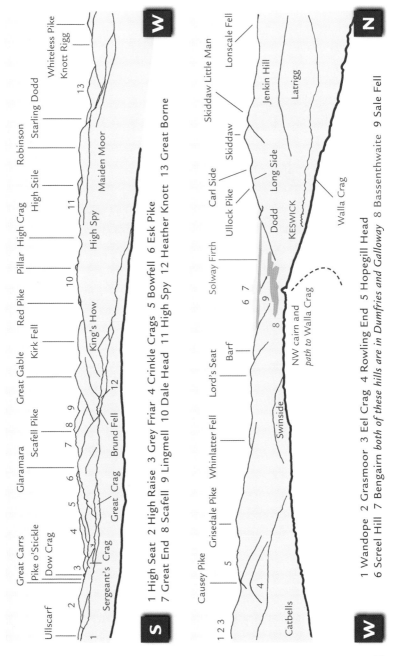

W

Whiteless Pike
Knott Rigg
Starling Dodd
Robinson
High Crag
High Stile
Pillar
Red Pike
Great Gable
Kirk Fell
Scafell Pike
Glaramara
Pike o'Stickle
Great Carrs
Dow Crag
Ullscarf

Maiden Moor
High Spy
King's How
Brund Fell
Great Crag
Sergeant's Crag

13 11 10 9 8 7 6 5 4 3 2 1

12

S

1 High Seat 2 High Raise 3 Grey Friar 4 Crinkle Crags 5 Bowfell 6 Esk Pike
7 Great End 8 Scafell 9 Lingmell 10 Dale Head 11 High Spy 12 Heather Knott 13 Great Borne

N

Skiddaw Little Man
Lonscale Fell
Jenkin Hill
Skiddaw
Latrigg
Carl Side
Long Side
Ullock Pike
Dodd
Solway Firth
KESWICK
Walla Crag
Lord's Seat
Barf
Whinlatter Fell
Swinside
Grisedale Pike
Causey Pike
Catbells

NW cairn and
path to Walla Crag

5
4
6 7
9
8
1 2 3

W

1 Wandope 2 Grasmoor 3 Eel Crag 4 Rowling End 5 Hopegill Head
6 Screel Hill 7 Bengairn *both of these hills are in Dumfries and Galloway* 8 Bassenthwaite 9 Sale Fell

4 BLEA RIGG (556m, 1824ft)

From the curious knob of Sergeant Man, a long arm of fell draws essentially south-east off the high plateau of High Raise. Sustaining a plateau-like character this ridge terminates, after some 5 miles, on Loughrigg Fell above the confluence of the rivers Brathay and Rothay. There are numerous minor named and a few unnamed tops en route, but Blea Rigg and Silver How are the only two that stand out as acknowledged summits. West from Swinescar Hause the ridge livens up as the dependent summits of Blea Rigg take charge; with wet hollows and rocky crests, this section is great fun to explore.

From Great Castle How, Blea Rigg, in dark silhouette, looks every inch a bastion, but from all other viewpoints its individuality is less obvious. To the north Blea Crag forms a solid buttress commanding attention from Easedale Tarn, Tarn Crag and, surprisingly, from high on Sergeant Man. White Crag and Tarn Crag are eye-catching supporting acts to the stirring drama of the Langdale Pikes when viewed from the floor of Great Langdale.

The shortest climbs lead up from Great Langdale, most commonly via Stickle Ghyll, though one may opt for either the shy Swinescar Hause path from near Pye How, or the majestic intimacies of the rock-walls of Whitegill Crag. Easedale approaches

↑ Blea Rigg from the top of Whitegill Crag

from Grasmere have great charm and scenic mix. One may wander up by Blindtarn Moss and the extensive shrubberies of naturally topiaried juniper to Swinescar Hause or, more directly, follow Easedale Beck and Tarn. This latter route provides the greater contrast, from flower meadows to foaming falls, leading the walkers by lapping waters and barren fellsides, and culminating in the steady pull above Blea Crag. Normally a ridge route is the reward for a long and tiresome climb, but walkers may embark from the top of Red Bank and follow the irregularities of the ridge with minimal preliminary ascent. However, even this approach can, and perhaps should, begin from either Grasmere, via Allan Bank, or Chapel Stile, via Meg's Gill (see SILVER HOW page 244).

ASCENT FROM GREAT LANGDALE (32) AND (33)

Choice of car parks: The National Trust Stickle Ghyll or National Park Langdale. There are three basic lines of approach from this dramatic valley setting. In such surroundings scenic adventure must be anticipated even though the subject summit sits well back from the perceived action.

Via Stickle Ghyll	473m/1550ft	3.2km/2 miles

1 Walk up the lane past the New Dungeon Ghyll Hotel. From the gate head straight on through the small enclosures and on beside the tree-shaded beck as it rises to a footbridge. Beyond this, cross a stile to enter the main amphitheatre of this hugely popular ravine. The path, on which much

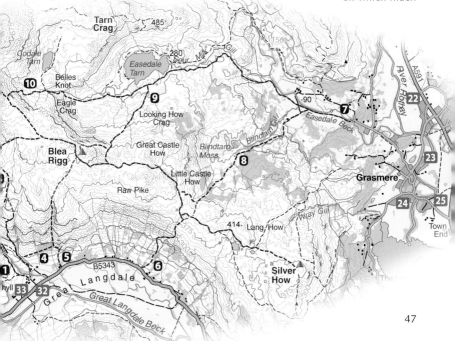

Tarn Crag

attention has necessarily been lavished in recent years, passes up through an old fold and zig-zags via fenced plantings. **2** A path branches right. This is an excellent new path winding up to run impressively under Tarn Crag and reach the outflow of Stickle Tarn. The more popular route which keeps beside the beck all the way is far less comfortable – troops of walkers with heads bent tend to go this way! **3** A far more pleasant and less well-known

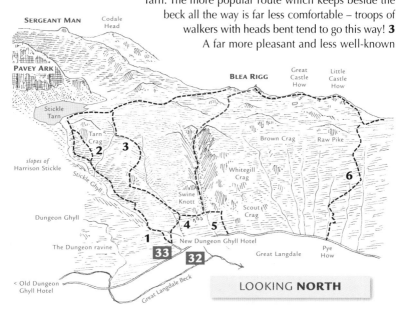

LOOKING **NORTH**

alternative line is recommended. Directly after leaving the New Dungeon Ghyll, cross the footbridge located half-right after the initial gate. The path runs behind Millbeck Farm and enters a lane that rises thereafter onto the bracken ridge, keeping left to avoid outcrop. Either contour onto the main zig-zagging path, climbing off this as it shapes towards Tarn Crag, and wind up to the left of a walled enclosure; or climb, with little initial evidence of a path, in the bracken. On finding a green path skirt the left-hand shoulder of a knoll above an incised gill and traverse the walled enclosure diagonally to join up with the upper section of the old shepherds' path. This then slips over a saddle depression to meet up with the path that runs along the southern shore of the tarn from the outflow. A clear, occasionally cairned path leads north, then east, onto the plateau of Blea Rigg.

Via White Gill	466m/1530ft	2km/1¼ miles

There are two approaches to Whitegill Crag – Route 4, the more direct route up behind the New Dungeon Ghyll Hotel, or Route 5, the climbers' approach to Scout Crag, off the valley road.

4 Pass up by the hotel to the bridle gate, slant right in the triangular enclosure and cross the footbridge. The path rises above Millbeck Farm via a hand-gate with a walled gill gangway. Go through the kissing-gate on the right after 100m, keep the wall to the right and pass through the foot of a larch plantation to cross a low wall into the bouldery ravine.

5 Go to the right along the valley road, passing the entrance to Millbeck Farm to reach a stile/gate with National Trust notice below a field-barn. Pass up above the field-barn to a wall-stile, climbing to the left of the lower buttress, a popular training ground for novice climbers. Cross the ladder-stile, ignore the climbers' path rising right to Scout Crag (which means 'projecting rock'), and instead follow the wall immediately left, with little hint of a path, to enter White Gill. The combined effects of path and gill erosion ensure a loose, clambering way. Above the tree trend to the left for bigger boulder steps and more secure footing. Much of the gill-bed is dry, with subterranean flow. The view out of the ravine is superb, leading the eye across Side Pike to Wetherlam. The natural exit draws into a short, tight

White Gill from the valley road

Lingmoor and the Coniston Fells from White Gill

gully to the right, requiring a spot of mild scrambling; ignore the gill-head itself. The rock walls of Whitegill Crag are hugely impressive and can be best surveyed by wandering onto the open spur to the left once the hard work has been done. The summit of Blea Rigg beckons across undulating cropped out slopes. While there is no evident path, a route is easily concocted, and from this approach the perched summit cairn contrives to look like a bird of prey.

Via Pye How   480m/1570ft   3.2km/2 miles

6 A footpath commences from the valley road midway between Pye How and the Long House. The lack of car parking and apparent plainness of the route ensure that this is more commonly used as a line of swift descent on circular walks from the New Dungeon Ghyll Hotel. It is nonetheless a pleasing path, especially if time is taken for frequent pauses to look back upon the stunning surround of majestic fells.

A kissing-gate gives entry into a pasture, initially keeping the wall to the left. Ascend with half-a-dozen waymark posts as aids and cross broken intermediate walls with much mature scrub colonising the enclosures. A ladder-stile crosses the intake wall at the top. The path, at first stony, becomes a pleasant turf trail, and beyond the solitary, gill-shading holly

Whitegill Crag

winds steadily to the ridge top at Swinescar Hause. Joining the ridge path, track left up from the marshy hollow by the old fold and curious cramped shelter. Traverse Little Castle How and Great Castle How, passing pools adorned with cotton grass and bogbean. From the vicinity of a cluster of quartz rocks admire a splendid view west to the striking dark profile of Blea Rigg, the obvious culmination of the northward-plunging Blea Crag. The summit is confirmed by the presence of a walled rock shelter directly below. Though the ridge path waltzes by to the right, many a head-down fellwalker will miss the summit, erroneously believing the next prominent cairnless outcrop to the west to be the ultimate point.

ASCENT FROM GRASMERE (22–25)

Via Blindtarn Moss   497m/1630ft   4.5km/2¾ miles

Juniper in Blindtarn Moss

7 From the Sam Read bookshop road junction in the midst of the village walk north along Easedale Road via Goody Bridge. A few paces short of the Oak Lodge (teas), cross the Easedale Beck footbridge. A long view of Sour Milk Gill backed by Tarn Crag beckons across lovely flower meadows, the beginning of a fine wild trail. A part-paved path leads past New Bridge, and on reaching a gate (yellow footpath waymark affixed) the first route option begins.

8 Go through this gate, entering a meadow pass, and continue on by open woodland to join the access track at a gate leading to a pair of holiday cottages. Glance by these to a gate. Beyond the gate, the path trends up by the beck and leftward to a footpath waymark post that guides right into the hollow of Blindtarn Moss; the abundance of bushes ensures plenty of bird song during this approach. The term *blind* means 'obscure outflow'. The scene is quite unique, a wild Chinese garden in the fells.

LOOKING **SOUTH**

Ridge path from Great Castle How

The path climbs up through the juniper, and higher up, as the ground steepens, the cairned path is worn to loose stones. Either follow the cairned path to the soggy saddle of Swinescar Hause or, just prior to the top, slant onto the right-hand side to follow the old green zig-zag path which offers sweeter footing to rise onto the westward climbing path above the quaint stone bivvy shelter (see below). The ridge path weaves on, over Little Castle How and under Great Castle How, passing two sheets of water and a prominently perched rock to reach the summit bluff.

Via Easedale Tarn   490m/1610ft   5km/3 miles

9 The popular path to Easedale Tarn leads to the next gate and over the Blindtarn Gill bridge, heading straight across the open meadow (ignore the farm track right to Brimmer Head). Go through a gateway and subsequent kissing-gate. The paved path enters a lane which funnels, then opens, winding up above Sour Milk Gill. The

Blea Crag

best view of the falls is from the base of the sheepfold, though there is no ready path down. Only the upper fall can be easily reached from the path, and its plunge pool can be the scene of much splashing and excited chatter on hot summer afternoons.

The path has received considerable remedial paving, and the final section to the tarn is presently in the course of construction.

Easedale Tarn itself continues to attract walking visitors, many of whom, as has long been the case, are quite content to make it the ultimate point of their

North-east from Great Castle How

walk, backtracking via the Stythwaite Steps footbridge at the foot of Far Easedale. Either side of the tarn, conical drumlins emphasise the glacial origins of this bleak amphitheatre. The domed top of Tarn Crag looms close right, while Blea Crag forms the southern sidewall, with the sub-edge peak of Belles Knott shielding Codale Tarn a little to its right. Follow the path above the tarn, and watch for a small cairn where the Blea Rigg path very evidently branches left. This winds up above the drumlins seeking the natural dip in the ridge. Then one may either continue to the saddle, close to the perched boulder, or angle up right behind Blea Crag via a rake.

Via Belles Knott   500m/1640ft   6.5km/4 miles

10 As a final option, continue on the south side of Easedale Tarn. The path leads up beside the main feeder-gill, with several essentially stepped sections beside the cascades, and is overlooked by the arresting peak of Belles Knott up to the right, a well-respected scramblers' route and object of photographic composition. Above the falls

Pool on Great Castle How

a side-path bears right, fording the gill, to visit the
hanging waters of Codale
Tarn, with its tiny outflow
and picturesque isle set
beneath the great slope of
Codale Head. The main
path zig-zags up to a ridge-
top path interchange, where
you turn left, south-east,
and wander some half a
mile to the summit.

Seat Sandal and Fairfield from Little Castle How

THE SUMMIT

There can be some doubt as to which is the highest point, with several rocky tops
vying for pre-eminence; conventional mapping offers only slack captioning to add to
the confusion. The one sure clue is the presence of a cairn sitting on top of a blade of
rock, directly above the shelter passed on the eastern approach. This is the culmination of the outcrop above Blea Crag, and the high point seen from Great Castle How.
The view is superb, with Pavey Ark and Harrison Stickle the mighty neighbours. The
Helvellyn chain rises invitingly eastward above the serried ridges overlooking
Easedale, and the Coniston Fells tantalise beyond Lingmoor Fell and Side Pike.

Blea Rigg summit outcrop

SAFE DESCENT

With crags close to the northern brink, great care is required in poor conditions. The ridge path is plain enough in most situations, but should the shelter of the valley be urgently required the best bet is to follow the ridge path running east. This leads under the summit by the walled shelter, down to the first depression. Bear left (north), descending north-eastwards through a shallow hollow east

Walled rock-shelter tucked under the summit

of Blea Crag and down to the popular path running close to Easedale Tarn. This path leads by Sour Milk Gill, the safety of the Easedale meadows and into Grasmere.

RIDGE ROUTES

SILVER HOW   ↓205m/670ft   ↑45m/150ft   3.2km/2 miles

The twists and turns of the ridge trail ensure an entertaining march. En route pass two sizable pools and a cluster of quartz stones by the path, prior to crossing Great Castle How; deviate left to its top for a dramatic view of Codale Head, while the opposing and little-visited Raw Pike gives a fine view over Great Langdale. Beyond Swinescar Hause the ridge is of a more rolling nature, though there are more pools, the largest being consumed by weed. The path runs under the higher top of Lang How (by nearly 19m, 62ft) and traverses the headstream of Wray Gill to reach the scarp-top summit.

SERGEANT MAN   ↓15m/50ft   ↑205m/670ft   2km/1¼ miles

The occasional cairn indicates a surprisingly modest ridge trail. Immediately after the fourth mock summit knoll notice a small section of marsh, fenced off to evaluate the effects of non-grazing. A drastic reduction in sheep grazing would allow trees and shrubs to regain their ancient footing. After all, they are only waiting in the wings for the day, though crucial minerals have been leached in the now acid grassland to fur-

Paddy Dillon beside a rock pool near Blea Rigg summit

ther inhibit such a restoration. Just short of the path interchange admire the rock basin; cairns now abound. From here the ridge narrows, with rocky outcrops, including one notable tilted slab. The path forks, then reunites on the steady climb to the outflow of the marsh west of Codale Head. The summit is swiftly attained on the popular and worn final path.

PANORAMA

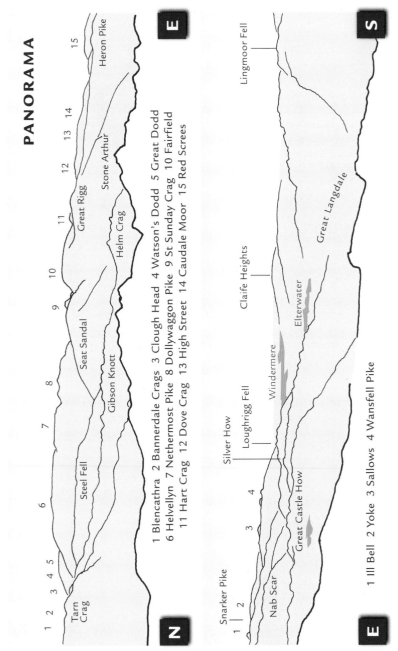

1 Blencathra 2 Bannerdale Crags 3 Clough Head 4 Watson's Dodd 5 Great Dodd
6 Helvellyn 7 Nethermost Pike 8 Dollywaggon Pike 9 St Sunday Crag 10 Fairfield
11 Hart Crag 12 Dove Crag 13 High Street 14 Caudale Moor 15 Red Screes

1 Ill Bell 2 Yoke 3 Sallows 4 Wansfell Pike

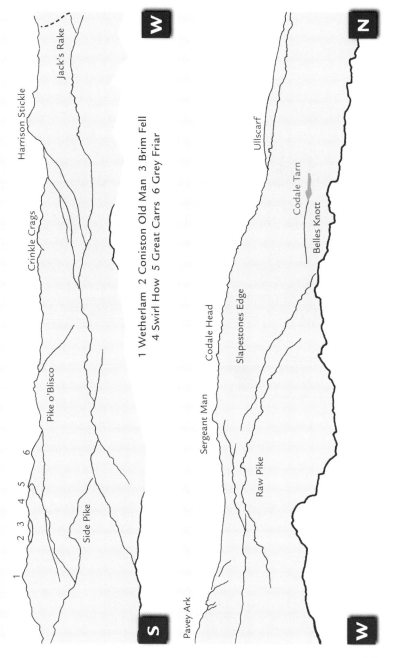

W

N

Jack's Rake

Harrison Stickle

Crinkle Crags

Pike o'Blisco

6
5
4
3
2
1

Side Pike

1 Wetherlam 2 Coniston Old Man 3 Brim Fell
4 Swirl How 5 Great Carrs 6 Grey Friar

S

Ullscarf

Codale Tarn

Belles Knott

Codale Head

Slapestones Edge

Sergeant Man

Raw Pike

Pavey Ark

W

5 CALF CRAG *(537m, 1762ft)*

A curved ridge sweeps north-westward from the of Vale of Grasmere. It begins auspiciously with Helm Crag, probably Grasmere's best-known and best-loved hill, from where it takes a roller-coaster ride over Gibson Knott, climbing over Pike of Carrs to land eventually upon Calf Crag. This distance from valley affairs lends the fell-top a certain lonely mystique; in fact, many fellwalkers may only vaguely remember climbing it once in all their adventures.

The summit forms the pivotal point on the Greenburn Dale horseshoe, which normally begins with a flourish, climbing onto Steel Fell, and finishes with aplomb upon Helm Crag. Though there is a warning for any walker approaching from Steel Fell in misty conditions – the lie of the land makes it all too easy to miss the top, ending up at the pass at the head of Far Easedale. The Far Easedale horseshoe itself runs clockwise, climbing Tarn Crag first, from the vicinity of Easedale Tarn.

The notion of greater Easedale super-highway, combining the skylines of Far Easedale and Easedale Tarn, is something special to contemplate. That would begin with Helm Crag, pass over Calf Crag to climb via Codale Head, and culminate upon

↑ Calf Crag from above Brownrigg Moss

Sergeant Man before heading for Blea Rigg and Silver How. This is a really excellent expedition, which might be made all the more sumptuous with the inclusion of High Raise.

The fell-name, in common with Calfhow Pike and Calf Hole, refers to the presence of red deer does and fawns; these would be a rare, though not an entirely impossible, sighting today. The best view of the fell is from beneath Deer Bield Crag (itself a reference to a place of shelter for the aforementioned deer), its steep southern slopes spilling into the wild depths of Far Easedale. Apart from a moment of crag at the head of Greenburn Dale, the fell drifts soggily northward and merges into the morass of upper Wythburn Dale.

Splintered rock above Brownrigg Moss

516. Nab Crags

Castle Crags

Wyth Burn

Till Gill

❸

Dunmail Raise

The Bog   468

Cat Gill

Steel Fell

Blakerigg Crag

306

57

Calf Crag   Rough Crag

Green Burn

Mere Beck

Carrs

Far Easedale Gill

Gibson Knott

❶

A591

Raise Beck

Town Head

Tongue Gill Force

Ferngill Crag

Deer Bield Crag   ❷

Horn Crag

355   105

Helm Crag

The Lion and the Lamb

Tarn Crag   485

Godale Tarn

280

Sour Milk Gill

Far Easedale Gill

Mill Bridge

21

Belles Knot

Easedale Tarn

Eagle Crag

Looking How Crag

Blea Rigg

556

Great Castle How

224

Blindtarn Gill

Easedale Beck

River Rothay

22

90

Blindtarn Moss

Little Castle How

Grasmere

23

ASCENT FROM THE A591 AT MILL BRIDGE (21)

Via Greenburn Dale   442m/1450ft   3.5km/2¼ miles

1 Greenburn Dale is a beautiful valley, well rewarding a visit, both for its own sake and as a route to Calf Crag. Start either from the bus stop above Town Head or from Mill Bridge, following the minor road down to the bridge where Raise Beck becomes the River Rothay. Go right, passing Ghyll Foot. The two approaches merge as they turn up the drive leading over cattle grids by Helmside and rise to Turn Howe (which means 'the thorn mound') and the subsequent gate onto the fell. Go forward with the green track, leading alongside a wall on the right, then go through a gate into a short lane. This emerges beyond the attractive waterfalls to continue as an unfettered track.

Passing moraine the track bears left and crosses newly set stepping-stones, then goes right to contour past a tidy sheepfold set between boulders. Watch for a cairn marking the point where the path climbs left, up a wet patch, and zig-zags to the saddle. Spot the cairn on the right, which guides onto the clear path climbing Pike of Carrs. Sections of eroded peat intervene en route to the summit.

Swirling surface of a pool in Far Easedale Beck

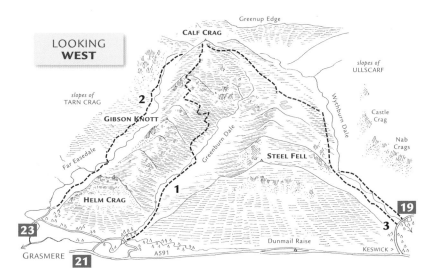

LOOKING **WEST**

Greenup Edge

CALF CRAG

slopes of
ULLSCARF

slopes of
TARN CRAG

2

GIBSON KNOTT

Greenburn Dale

Wythburn Dale

Castle Crag

Nab Crags

Far Easedale

STEEL FELL

1

HELM CRAG

19

23

3

GRASMERE   **21**

Dunmail Raise

KESWICK >

A591

Pike of Carrs from Far Easedale

ASCENT FROM GRASMERE (22–25)

Via Far Easedale   457m/1500ft   5.7km/3½ miles

2 Leave Broadgate opposite Sam Read's bookshop, along Easedale Road. This leads naturally onto the signposted bridle path running into Far Easedale. After crossing Stythwaite Steps footbridge keep right, with the one clear path, which has a few rough sections en route to the saddle at the dale head. The metal stakes are all that remain of an old step-stile. Bear acutely right, bound for the summit outcrop which is already in sight beyond the tarn in Brownrigg Moss.

ASCENT FROM STEEL END (19)

Via Wythburn Dale   380m/1250ft   5.5km/3½ miles

3 (Also consult the STEEL FELL map on page 251). Footpaths lead from either side of the road-bridge spanning Wyth Burn, opposite the Steel End car park. A further path follows a farm track via a lane stemming off the bridleway above West Head, formerly known as Steel End prior to the amalgamation of farm holdings. Negotiate the sequence of ladder-stiles by any of the paths that converge and reach the footbridge beneath Rake Crags, just where the valley begins to constrict. Follow the clear path climbing up the south side of the ravine below Black Crag. When the wind blows up the valley the fuming falls can be most impressive, with the spray flying high. The dale opens, becoming progressively more desolate, and the beck slothfully winds through a gently curving tarn. Leave the obvious path, climb the easy slopes (no path) and skirt to the west of the tarns in the wide, shallow depression of the ridge. Join the ridge path from Steel Fell and head damply south to the summit.

Calf Crag summit cairn

THE SUMMIT

A cairn rests aloft a pronounced up-thrusting outcrop. The steep rock face on the Easedale side is high enough to require walkers to be wary in poor visibility. Being hemmed in by the bulky mass of High Raise and Ullscarf ensures that the best elements of a disappointing view are eastward – to the long, unflattering western wall of Helvellyn and Fairfield. The craggy facade to Tarn Crag, notably Deer Bield Crag, which can be seen across Far Easedale, merits prime attention. As so often occurs, where summits are not prized by all, walkers create 'avoiding paths' around the summits from existing sheep trods; one such example runs below the summit on the southern flank.

SAFE DESCENTS

The ridge path east is reliable, if followed meticulously. However, in very poor conditions it may be prudent to head initially west, by Brownrigg Moss, to reach the saddle at the head of Far Easedale. At this point, turn east to follow the valley path in comparative shelter and, importantly, with the greatest certainty of homing in on Grasmere.

RIDGE ROUTES

GIBSON KNOTT	↓120m/400ft	↑30m/100ft	2km/1¼ miles

The path takes off east, traversing eroded peat, before dipping more steeply off Pike of Carrs to a cairn in the depression. The ridge is sufficiently drawn in to give excellent views, though the path's southern bias tends to make Easedale the focus of attention. Passing a rock chair to the left, the ridge engages in several switchbacks to the summit.

SERGEANT MAN   ↓15m/50ft   ↑210m/690ft   3.2km/2 miles

En route west, to the saddle between desolate Wythburn Dale and the deeply entrenched Far Easedale, the popular path negotiates some damp ground. The ridge path ignores both, marching due south largely in the company of what remains of the metal estate-boundary stakes, leading via several pleasing pools over Codale Head, and rounding a marsh to climb the obvious, and certainly distinctive, summit knoll.

STEEL FELL   ↓70m/230ft   ↑90m/300ft   2.4km/1½ miles

Leave the summit heading north, and the route soon gets decidedly marshy, especially along the old fence-line. The popular path keeps well to the right, and in so doing enjoys the view into Greenburn Dale down to right. Curving north-east, the less well-trod path, near the fence, merges from the left. Saunter on the south side of the two large, oddly nameless tarns. Now going east, follow a fence ascending from the left to the acute corner by the summit cairn.

Deer Bield and Tarn Crag from below Calf Crag summit

PANORAMA

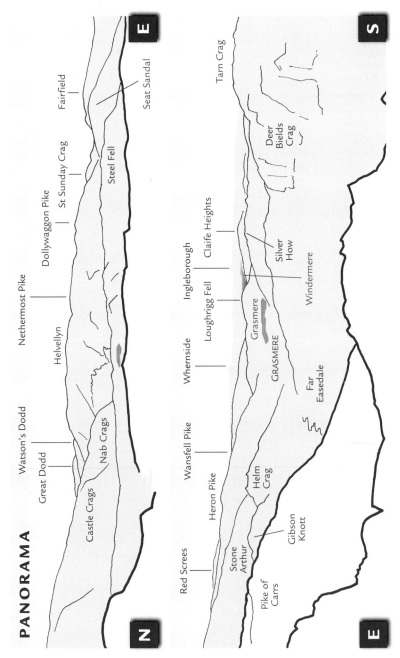

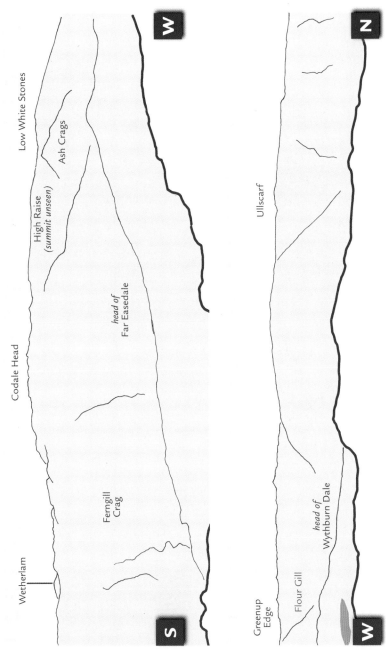

5 Calf Crag

W

N

Low White Stones

Ash Crags

High Raise
(summit unseen)

head of
Far Easedale

Codale Head

Ferngill
Crag

Wetherlam

S

Ullscarf

Greenup
Edge

Flour Gill

head of
Wythburn Dale

W

6 EAGLE CRAG *(520m, 1706ft) (estimated height)*

One can't help but wonder how many travellers venturing through Borrowdale for the first time swing through Rosthwaite, catch a sudden and unsuspected glimpse of Eagle Crag in the corner of their eye and yelp with delight. As the name suggests, it gives the Stonethwaite valley a stunning focal point, a real camera-catcher. Walkers traversing the Central range via Greenup Edge see it much in the same light as Grasmere folk consider Helm Crag – it is a much-loved ingredient in an adorable fell landscape.

The fell marks the termination of an extended limb descending directly from High Raise – a featureless ridge smartly coming to attention upon Sergeant's Crag, en route to this grand finale. There is but one prime ascent and one backdoor route that is best kept for descent, foul weather or not. Chances of spotting golden eagle, held in the fell-name, are nigh on nil. It was documented in 1777 that 'Here is every year an airy or nest of eagles'. They have been persecuted to extinction, the valley folk mighty relieved at their demise. How times and perceptions change!

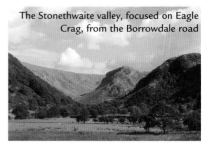

The Stonethwaite valley, focused on Eagle Crag, from the Borrowdale road

↑ Eagle Crag from the bridle path east of Stonethwaite Bridge

ASCENT FROM STONETHWAITE (1)

Direct   427m/1400ft   3.2km/2 miles

1 From the centre of the hamlet, follow the lane signposted 'Greenup Edge' that leads over the Stonethwaite Beck bridge. In winter, when the beck-side trees have lost their foliage, Eagle Crag makes a fine subject. After the gate go right, with the gated bridle track. Cross the footbridge immediately above the confluence of Greenup Gill and Langstrath Beck. Bear left and cross the fence-stile, taking care to keep on the low side of the flush marsh which is abundant in delicate bog flora. The path brushes through bracken of potentially monster proportions; keep parallel with the Greenup Gill fence. Pass through a hand-gate in the down-wall, and while a path continues low beside the wall and gill, continue on the shepherds' path angling gently up the slope to a wall-gap.

At this point the climb proper begins. Keep the partly broken wall to the right, and the path, confirmed by modest cairns of transitory existence, winds up to a fragile stile at the top of the rising wall hugging the undercliff.

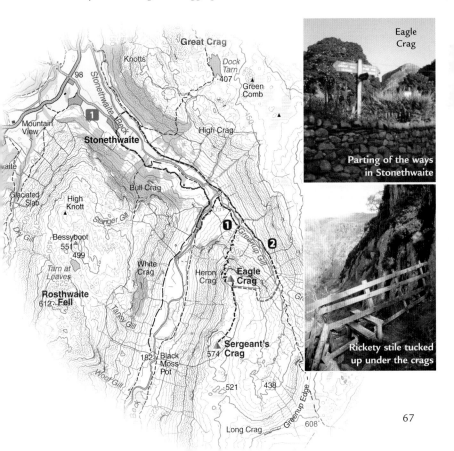

Eagle Crag

Parting of the ways in Stonethwaite

Rickety stile tucked up under the crags

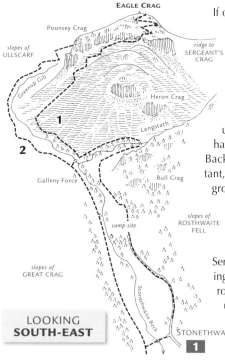

EAGLE CRAG

Pounsey Crag

slopes of
ULLSCARF

ridge to
SERGEANT'S
CRAG

Greenup Gill

Heron Crag

1

Langstrath

2

Galleny Force

Bull Crag

camp site

slopes of
ROSTHWAITE
FELL

slopes of
GREAT CRAG

Stonethwaite Beck

LOOKING
SOUTH-EAST

STONETHWAITE

1

If one's temper has been tested by the sweaty work to this point, prepare for a fell-ecstasy lift-off. Smartly a narrow breach in the craggy defences permits a short stair climb. The way beyond suggests two options, but in reality there is but one. The path leading up left ends abruptly but gives a handsome view of Pounsey Crag. Backtrack to continue – this is important, as there is no safe fellwalking ground further left. The prime route goes immediately right, along the ledge marked with ice-like fragments of quartz, and terminates with a fine full-height view of Sergeant's Crag. Now switch up, making several similar sharp turns to avoid rock bands, with much heather underfoot. The immediate and outward scenery is consistently exciting. Duly, and with no little sorrow for an end to the fun, the tilted summit slab is rounded.

Stonethwaite valley from 50 paces due north of the summit

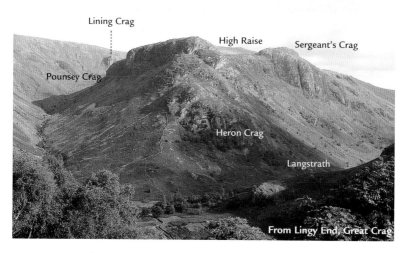

Lining Crag

High Raise

Sergeant's Crag

Pounsey Crag

Heron Crag

Langstrath

From Lingy End, Great Crag

Via Greenup Gill 442m/1450ft 4km/2½ miles

2 The fell has only one other tenable line of ascent for the ordinary mortal, one that is more likely to be used for descent by walkers wisely avoiding the risk of trying to unlock the intricacies of the principal ascent. Ignore the footbridge and continue up the Greenup Gill path via gates. The forbidding presence of Eagle and Pounsey Crags lends drama to the ascent along a bridle route made all the more popular by its inclusion in the Coast to Coast Walk established in 1972. Just short of the moraine branch right, ford the gill and make a steady ascent left, thereby avoiding serious outcrops and quickly beating the bracken. There is no path, but follow the natural line, which turns and contours to the base of the truncated wall above Pounsey Crag. Follow the wall to a ladder-stile crossing the ridge-top wall, and go right to the small rock-step at the wall corner to complete the climb.

THE SUMMIT

A broad, tilted rock outcrop surmounted by a small cairn forms the summit, and heather abounds. A second natural block lies prostrate a few yards to the north. This has the appearance of fallen pillar, though

Key breach gully during direct ascent of Eagle Crag

of course it's nothing of the sort. The view concentrates north-westward, back from whence you came, through the Stonethwaite valley. The best place to see the valley is some 50m north; a thin path leads to the spot – this must not be misconstrued as a line of descent!

Eagle Crag summit cairn

SAFE DESCENTS

Descend south from the summit, via the small rock-step in the wall corner, then cross the ladder-stile a matter of 30m along the ridge wall. Follow the descending wall due east, where the wall abruptly ends above a cliff. Contour right until easier slopes permit you to complete the descent via a steep, open fell-side. There is no hint of path after leaving the wall end. Ford Greenup Gill and join the bridle path leading down into the Stonethwaite valley.

RIDGE ROUTE

SERGEANT'S CRAG	↓10m/30ft	↑60m/200ft	0.8km/½ mile

Descend south, cross the stile to the right of the wall corner and follow the ridge wall. The path is clear enough, and later it drifts half-right up to the summit. Be mindful that cliffs line the near western slopes.

Eagle Crag from the top of Sergeant's Crag Gully

Pounsey Crag

PANORAMA

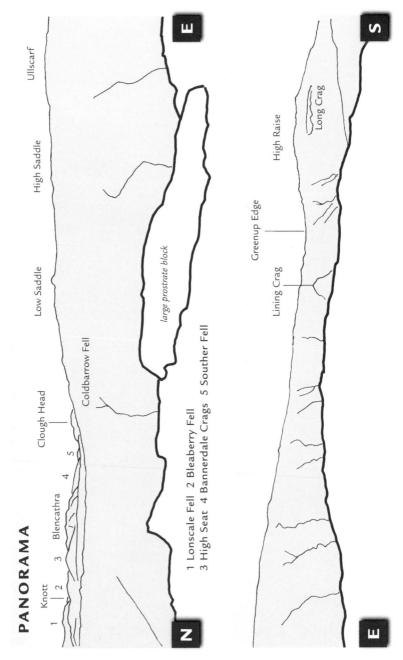

Knott
1 2 3 Blencathra 4 5 Clough Head   Coldbarrow Fell   Low Saddle   High Saddle   Ullscarf

N

E

large prostrate block

1 Lonscale Fell 2 Bleaberry Fell
3 High Seat 4 Bannerdale Crags 5 Souther Fell

Lining Crag   Greenup Edge   High Raise

Long Crag

E

S

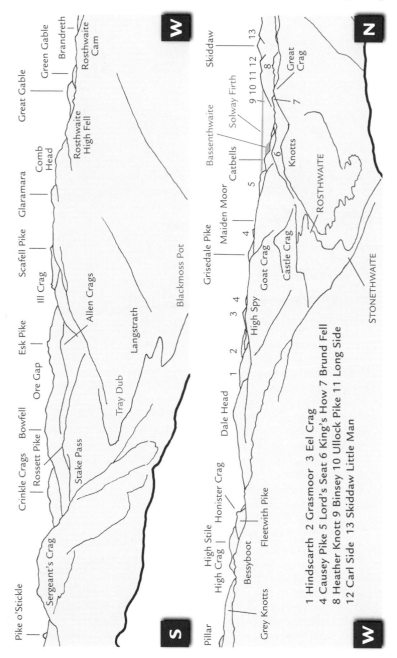

S Pike o'Stickle | Sergeant's Crag | Crinkle Crags | Rossett Pike | Bowfell | Ore Gap | Esk Pike | Stake Pass | Ill Crag | Scafell Pike | Allen Crags | Glaramara | Tray Dub | Comb Head | Langstrath | Rosthwaite High Fell | Blackmoss Pot | Great Gable | Green Gable | Brandreth | Rosthwaite Cam **W**

W Pillar | High Stile | High Crag | Grey Knotts | Bessyboot | Fleetwith Pike | Honister Crag | Dale Head | High Spy | 1 2 3 4 | Goat Crag | Grisedale Pike | Castle Crag | Maiden Moor | ROSTHWAITE | Catbells | 5 6 | Knotts | Bassenthwaite | Solway Firth | 9 10 11 12 | 7 | Great Crag | 8 | Skiddaw | 13 | STONETHWAITE **N**

1 Hindscarth 2 Grasmoor 3 Eel Crag
4 Causey Pike 5 Lord's Seat 6 King's How 7 Brund Fell
8 Heather Knott 9 Binsey 10 Ullock Pike 11 Long Side
12 Carl Side 13 Skiddaw Little Man

7 GIBSON KNOTT *(421m, 1381ft)*

Fells come in many guises – some are solitary summits while others, like Gibson Knott, are characterful components of a greater whole. The greater whole in question is the triple-topped ridge dividing Far Easedale from Greenburn Dale. As a ridge walk it is an undulating roller coaster ride that should put a smile on any fellwalker's face!

The southern slopes are rough and uninviting, with Horn Crag, the one major feature, tucked under the summit. There is but one line of approach from Far Easedale venturing to the Bracken Hause saddle below Helm Crag. From Greenburn Dale, to the north, there are three comfortable lines: the corresponding route to Bracken Hause from the recently installed footbridge above Turn Howe; a pathless route from the stepping-stones close to the moraines of the upper dale; and a later shepherds' path reaching the depression below Pike of Carrs. Greenburn Dale deserves to be better known, and a circuit concentrating on the valley is recommended using any two of these three routes, which can still include Helm Crag there and back from Bracken Hause.

Gibson Knott from Town Head

↑ Gibson Knott from Helm Crag

ASCENT FROM MILL BRIDGE (21)

Via Bracken Hause 335m/1100ft 2km/1¼ miles

1 There is lay-by parking at Mill Bridge (bus stop above Town Head). Follow HELM CRAG Route 3, page 126. Then from the gate above Turn Howe go forward along the level track passing though a gate, with Greenburn Beck close down to the left. Bear left to cross the wooden footbridge above the first waterfall, a vibrant water-moment. The path climbs the pasture to cross the lane via facing hand-gates (the second presently in need of repair), then climbs directly up the short turf slope to Bracken Hause, the saddle depression

Horn Crag

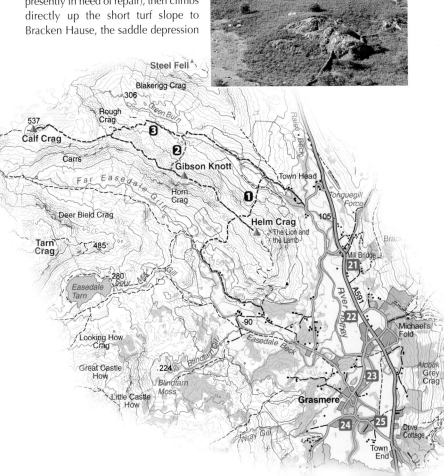

Helvellyn   Nethermost Pike   Dollywaggon Pike

Steel Fell   Seat Sandal

summit

Horn Crag

Easdale Tarn

Gibson Knott ridge from Blea Crag

below Helm Crag. Turn right. The path avoids the early exchanges with the ridge, pre-
ferring to run along the southern flank, with a bird's-eye view over Stythwaite Steps into
Far Easedale, before pitching onto the knobbly crest. Watch for the summit cairn, as the
path turns a 'blind eye' at the critical moment.

Via Greenburn Dale   351m/1150ft   3.2km/2 miles

2 Keep to the track via a second gate and short lane, and pass above a more impressive waterfall, made all the more picturesque by the larch spinney and attendant ice-
smoothed outcrop. The adjacent wall is lost, and the track becomes a little less certain until, breaking through moraine, it encounters the large, shallow basin of

Helm Crag from the ridge

Loughrigg Fell

Grasmere

CALF CRAG

Pike of Carrs

3

GIBSON KNOTT

slopes of
TARN
CRAG

Horn Crag

2

HELM CRAG

Bracken Hause

Far Easedale

1

Greenburn Dale

slopes of
STEEL
FELL

falls

Turn Howe

Town
Head

Raise Beck

Helmside

Ghyll Foot Farm

Dunmail Raise

LOOKING **WEST**

minor road to
Easedale Road,
< GRASMERE

A591

21

Greenburn Bottom. High to the right Blakerigg Crag presides over a lovely wild scene, the hollow once filled by a tarn. Comparable shallow pools adorn the flat ridge that forms the north-western headwall to this truncated dale. The fellwalker seeking peaceful sanctuaries will just love the upper reaches of Greenburn Dale. The path veers left to cross the newly set stepping-stones. Bear left a matter of 30m downstream before bearing right to mount the obvious rounded grassy rigg, without a hint of a path. Climb, avoiding the skyline crags to the left, and join the ridge path at a marshy depression. Go left to reach the top after a tilted slab.

3 Alternatively, from the stepping-stones, bear right on a pleasing green way by an unusual triangular sheepfold built against three large boulders. The casual stroll is interrupted at a very modest six-stone cairn, and from here the path heads uphill. Only after stepping over a marshy patch does the ascent ease onto a weaving trail that rises to the twin-dip saddle on the ridge. Ahead, across Far Easedale, Deer Bield Crag is viewed as a striking cliff feature on the shadowy northern flank of Tarn Crag. While up to the right, the false summit of Pike of Carrs leads the eye westward up the ridge towards Calf Crag. Guided by the left-hand of two cairns, head east along the ridge. After some 100m spot an alcove 'throne' built into a ruckle of rocks to the left of the path.

The ridge is entertainingly rocky, though there is one peaty interlude the path cannot avoid. As the path comes above a small crag watch for the summit cairn close to the left. It is easy to miss when attention is fixed on maintaining a steady step! See HELM CRAG page 125 for the ascent out of lower Far Easedale.

Stone throne on the Gibson Knott ridge

Blakerigg Crag from Greenburn Bottom

THE SUMMIT

Perhaps it is fortunate that the consensus of visitor opinion has chosen a place for the summit cairn, as there are several contending knobby knolls. The view is everything, especially over the wild bowl of Far Easedale. However, there is much else to enjoy – Helm Crag seems lowly backed by the might of the Helvellyn range; to the north rises the craggy face of Steel Fell; and southwards the Coniston Fells lie beyond Blea Rigg. But it is to the rocky bulk of Codale Head that most attention will be given, with Harrison Stickle and Pavey Ark making guest appearances.

Gibson Knott summit looking to Steel Fell and Helvellyn

Steel Fell

Helvellyn

Nethermost Pike

Dollywaggon Pike

Looking south-east along the ridge from Pike of Carrs

SAFE DESCENTS

Hold to the popular ridge path. If the need to leave the ridge is urgent then Bracken Hause to the east provides steep, but sure lines to the foot of either Greenburn Dale for Town Head (north) or Far Easedale for Grasmere (south). There are two further reliable ways into Greenburn Dale – firstly from the first deep depression west of the summit, a pathless grass line down to the stepping-stones; and secondly by the old shepherds' path further west, immediately before the climb to Pike of Carrs.

RIDGE ROUTES

CALF CRAG	↓30m/100ft	↑120m/400ft	2km/1¼ miles

The ridge path is clear cut, only becoming taxing with the climb to Pike of Carrs, and from then swathes of eroded peat lead to the summit outcrop. The views en route, particularly to Deer Bield Crag, are excellent.

HELM CRAG	↓90m/300ft	↑100m/330ft	1.6km/1 mile

The path dips from the summit with the main path trending onto the southern flank, though a slightly more taxing path continues along the ridge proper. If this has virtue, then it is as means of side-stepping the inevitable drudgery of engaging with large walking parties. Helm Crag forms such a wonderful culmination to the ridge (see book cover). The path slips straight across Bracken Hause and climbs directly to the foot of the massive jagged summit outcrop... which only leaves you with the decision whether to climb it or not!

PANORAMA

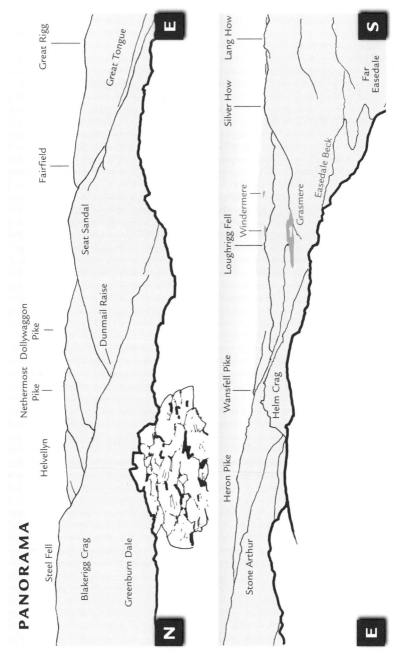

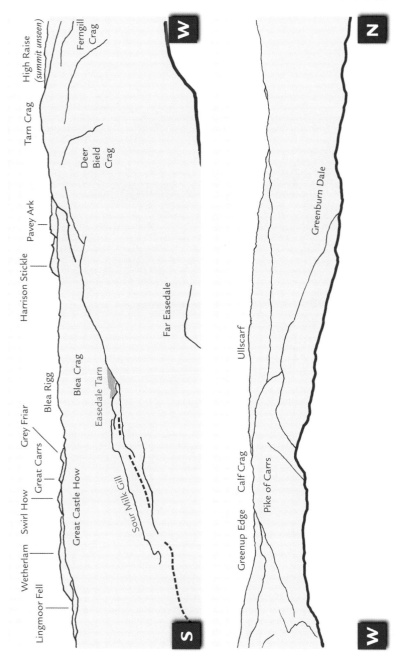

High Raise *(summit unseen)*

Ferngill Crag

Tarn Crag

Deer Bield Crag

Pavey Ark

Harrison Stickle

Far Easedale

Blea Crag

Easedale Tarn

Blea Rigg

Grey Friar

Great Carrs

Swirl How

Great Castle How

Sour Milk Gill

Wetherlam

Lingmoor Fell

Greenburn Dale

Ullscarf

Greenup Edge

Calf Crag

Pike of Carrs

81

8 GRANGE FELL *(416m, 1365ft)*

The long perspective view above gives a strong clue to the rough nature of this tangled fell, which forms the steep verdant eastern cheek to the much adored Jaws of Borrowdale, where Derwentwater gives way to Borrowdale proper. To new eyes it must appear a confusing rocky height, with birch, heather and bilberry clinging tenaciously to this knobbly irregular ridge where three summits vie for individual attention. In terms of elevation and company this is a modest fell. But what Grange Fell lacks in height is more than compensated for by the infusion of the picturesque. Samuel Johnson said 'he who tires of London, tires of life' – and the same may be said of Grange Fell. Climbers have long relished the accessibility and firm holds of Shepherd's, Black, Greatend, Bowder and Gowder Crags, while walkers have found comparable pleasure in unlocking its apparent labyrinth of paths combining the sylvan with a wild heather-scape.

Of the three summits, two are commonly visited – King's How and the actual top, Brund Fell – while the third, Heather Knott, set well to the north, remains little visited, being considered too much of a nuisance to bother with. But walkers who think like that miss out – for the traverse of this northern limb of the ridge from Lodore is delectably intricate. The climb onto the northern top of Brown Dodd deserves to be better known, though the going is tough over the ridge top, where the heather has not been heavily grazed in recent decades and shows what a bit of healthy neglect can do for habitat diversity. The fell-name has a medieval root, being linked to the home farm at Grange-in-Borrowdale, established by the monks of Furness Abbey in 1209.

The Jaws of Borrowdale, of which this fell forms one side, are not some sabre-toothed monster lurking in the shallows of the Derwent below the Bowder Stone. The name derives from the golden age of Romantic Lakeland writing, when the beauty of the constricted valley was recognised and given elegant expression in this phrase. Only on the west side of the River Derwent is there a consistent path to follow through the sylvan 'Jaws', made all the more delightful by the clear waters chattering over the pebbly riverbed.

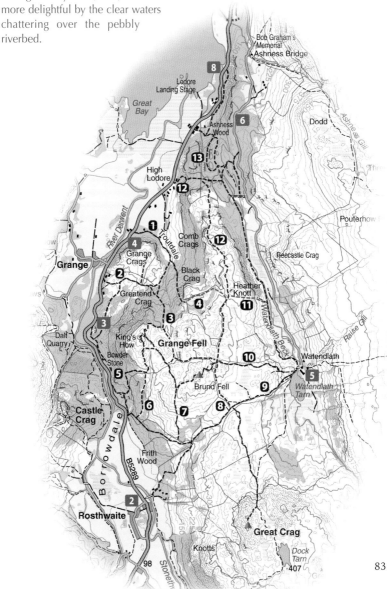

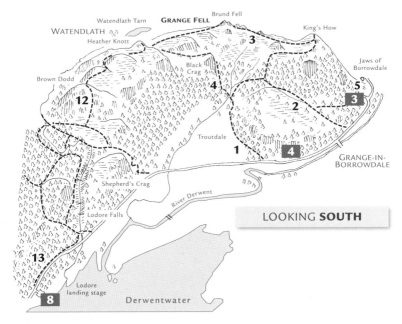

BRUND FELL   416m/1365ft

This is the actual top of Grange Fell. Seen either from the Great Crag or Heather Knott, it is identified by its bristly skyline. Two neighbouring outcrops vie for supremacy, with the jaunty sounding Jopplety How a passive onlooker – a shapely pike rarely, if ever, climbed.

South from Comb Crags

Skiddaw and Derwentwater during the ascent by Black Crag

HEATHER KNOTT   415m/1362ft

While merely a metre inferior to Brund Fell, this top attracts far fewer walkers, which is no bad thing for those who do make the effort. It is a real knott, particularly when seen from the south, and makes a splendid objective, especially when combined in a triple-top traverse of the whole fell. The view north over Derwentwater to Skiddaw is marvellous, and looking south-west from here there is a superb view of King's How. The top culminates a tangled knot of heathery fell, running over Brown Dodd, and to the north it is liberally sprinkled with birch, quite a vision of what much of Lakeland could look like given reprieve from sheep grazing. In late summer its bracken slopes harbour massive teeming ant hills, not evident where sheep maraud.

KING'S HOW   392m/1286ft

King's How from Heather Knott

This was named in 1910 as a memorial to King Edward VII, following its purchase by the National Trust. One might consider this the leading component of the Grange Fell massif, a craggy, heavily wooded height, the compulsive objective for a climb out of the scenic wonderland that is the Jaws of Borrowdale. Many a walker who has climbed either via Troutdale or Red Brow has been more than content to leave the rest of the fell well alone. The view from the summit is a rich reward, with the eye being drawn south along the green strath of Borrowdale to the mighty Scafells, north beyond Derwentwater to Skiddaw, and near west to the craggy precipices of Low Scawdel (a name that quaintly meant 'bald head') and over to High Spy.

The three component summits of Grange Fell have dedicated panoramas to instil those vivid scenes in the mind and gnaw at one's desire to return and claim them all.

Path above Red Brow

ASCENT FROM GRANGE-IN-BORROWDALE (4)

Via Troutdale 366m/1200ft 2.5km/1½ miles

1 Embark either from the Grange Bridge bus stop or the small lay-by south of the Leathes Head Hotel. Walk beside the valley road to the bridle lane branching right from behind the hotel. This leads to Troutdale Cottages and through a gate into Troutdale. A clear path runs on towards Comb Gill. Do not ford the gill, but keep right, rising into the woodland above it. The path rises to a hand-gate, where you bear left, fording a gill to rise into the birch-wood shrouding the looming Greatend Crag.

Summit of King's How

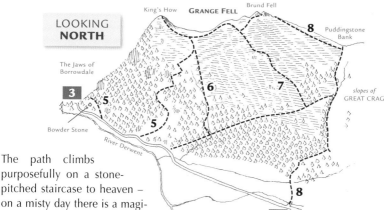

LOOKING **NORTH**

The Jaws of Borrowdale

Bowder Stone

River Derwent

King's How **GRANGE FELL** Brund Fell

8 Puddingstone Bank

slopes of GREAT CRAG

2 ROSTHWAITE

The path climbs purposefully on a stone-pitched staircase to heaven – on a misty day there is a magical sense of being in the dwindling Costa Rican 'cloud forest'. The path winds up to a marshy hollow. Keep right, climbing under a yew tree, and ascend to the high point of the cross-ridge wall: don't be tempted to follow this down as it ends precipitously above Bowder Crag. Go left, joining the narrowing heather ridge winding up to the summit of King's How.

Grange-in-Borrowdale from Grange Crags

ASCENT FROM QUAYFOOT NATIONAL TRUST CAR PARK (3)

Via King's How direct   2.5km/1½ miles

There is a choice of two routes leading either north or south. **2** The more direct heads north. A hand-gate in the bounding fence marks an exit to the car park at its upper end. A minor path crosses the gill depression, passes a large erratic and slips through an old slate quarry to join the green bridle path. This contours directly ahead above a damp slope, before climbing onto the ridge to reach a hand-gate in the saddle. (Note: a spur path can be followed on the left, just prior to the hand-gate. It crosses a ladder-stile heading north to approach the birch-fringed brink of Grange Crag: a little-visited and quite enchanting viewpoint, especially notable for its bird's-eye view of Grange Bridge. Backtrack to continue.) Beyond the hand-gate in the saddle, there is a handsome view of Greatend Crag with an erratic in the foreground. Advance until a path is spotted forking right, short of the next wall hand-gate, and here join Route 1. **3** The 'stairway to heaven' from Troutdale outlined in Route 1 can side-step King's How and progress directly to Brund Fell. Having completed the major stepped ascent, cross the fence stile on the left. The path runs up a shallow side-valley with a wall on the left, and in its later reaches curves right to join the direct path from King's How. Cross the ladder-stile to the left and rise to the next brow where the path bears acutely left to climb to the top of Brund Fell.

Via Heather Knott   350m/1150ft   1.5km/1 mile

4 A beautiful approach to Heather Knott, based upon the path established by climbers to reach Black Crag and the famous Troutdale Pinnacles. Follow the path from Troutdale Cottages as in Route 1, only this time stride across Comb Gill, climbing purposefully into the natural woodland on a well-made path to the base of Black Crag. A loose trail works up beneath the towering pinnacles to a notch beside a gill. Cross the fence tight by the rock. One may clamber left over the adjacent outcrop to discover a superb, if perilous, view down into Troutdale. The primary way follows the wall left beside Bleacrag Moss, curving up the rough valley head to the hand-gate, where the ridge path below Heather Knott is joined.

Via the Jaws of Borrowdale   390m/1280ft   2.5km/1½ miles

5 Follow signs to the Bowder Stone and pass a fenced quarry via a gate on a popular surfaced pathway. Find the massive tilted boulder in a glade – the nearside is angled sufficiently to give climbers scope for wet-weather bouldering practice. It lies here not because it tumbled from the crag above, like so much of the rock in the vicinity, but rather was transported by the random

The Bowder Stone

High Spy
Low Scawdel
Goat Crag
Nitting Haws
Castle Crag
The Jaws of Borrowdale from the southern slopes of King's How

Jopplety How

haul of a glacier – an Ice Age erratic. No prehistoric rock art has been recognised here, though that is not to say that it does not exist. A flight of wooden steps gives access to the naturally notched top. Countless visitors have made the rock slick, and cautious visitors do not venture too far beyond the security of the handrails!

The path, a former quarry-extraction track, continues and declines to a hand-gate at the road. Follow the roadside verge path until a footpath sign and stile indicate the beginning of a path to the left. A clear path ascends through the bracken, first onto the low rigg on the right, then curves left up through the bracken to slip under a yew tree, climbing to go through a broken wall then winding up the steep, lightly wooded fellside. The views improve as height is gained, particularly after coming above a wall, where they open to the south over the meadows of Borrowdale backed by the highest hills in England.

This point can be reached by **6**, an unusual and intriguing modern invention. It begins a little further along the valley road at Red Brow, identified by the recessed lay-by, just where the road opens to the Borrowdale meadows. Go through the gate, ascend the bridle path, and a few yards short of a tiny gill ford bear sharp left up the bank. An evident path leads uphill. Ignore the early footpath right as it quickly becomes consumed by bracken, having fallen from favour. Continue climbing the wooded edge. The path persists to a wall gateway, where you link up with Route 5 to climb the final open section of the south ridge to the top of King's How.

7 Continue up the bridle path on a delightful woodland way and ascend to a hand-gate. The path traverses a bracken fellside, passing the cluster of rocks known as the Resting Stones. From here there is a lovely view down on the green Rosthwaite vale. Watch for the ladder-stile left before the conifer copse. One may continue to a

Brund Fell from King's How

kissing-gate to join the Puddingstone Bank path or cross this ladder-stile, climbing the slope beside the plantation, slanting left on a pronounced path. As King's How duly comes into view the path forks. Go right and climb to Brund Fell, the summit of Grange Fell.

ASCENT FROM ROSTHWAITE (2)

Via Puddingstone Bank   351m/1150ft   2km/1¼ miles

8 The popular bridle path over Puddingstone Bank to Watendlath provides the ideal springboard for an ascent from Rosthwaite. Rosthwaite serves the visitor well, and especially welcome is the Flock-in tearoom. The village name is thought to mean 'the enclosure surrounding a cairn' – the stone piles engulfed by the jigsaw of walled enclosures in upper Wasdale being an elaborate expression of the same. Cross the Stonethwaite Beck bridge north of the post office and fork left, facing the entrance to Hazel Bank Hotel. Pass above Dinah Hoggus camping barn; converted from a field hog-house (originally winter housing for sheep), this is an aesthetically pleasing

Heather Knott

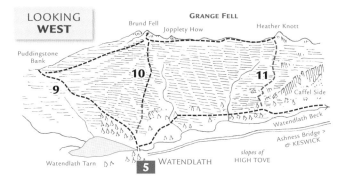

piece of farm diversification. The lane winds up to a gate. An open trail that has received some restorative treatment leads up the slope. Take opportunities to look back from time to time, as the view over upper Borrowdale improves with every stride and is quite superb. Two gates on, the track levels as it approaches the watershed. Bear left after the second gate, keeping the wall to the left. Reach the low ladder-stile over the wall, which you duly cross, and wind up to the summit outcrop.

ASCENT FROM WATENDLATH (5)

Via Puddingstone Bank   168m/550ft   2km/1¼ miles

9 The easiest route of all strides out upon the bridle path traversing Puddingstone Bank. From the National Trust car park (with adjacent toilets and farmhouse tearoom) walk through the hamlet to cross the packhorse bridge at the outflow of Watendlath Tarn. Take the main path, left, via the hand-gate signposted to Rosthwaite, observing

Heather Knott and the Watendlath valley from the knoll west of the hamlet

the antics of ducks and fly-fishermen afloat on the tarn. The track climbs steadily, with lovely views back upon the hamlet and tarn. Just short of the gate at the pass go right, accompanying Route 8 to the top. Keeping the wall to the left, one may either cross the first ladder-stile on the left and ascend the pathless slope direct to the summit or, probably better, keep with the wall to the low ladder-stile at the top.

Direct	168m/550ft	1.5km/1 mile

10 This route avoids the walking traffic on the Puddingstone Bank bridle path. An early branch right, just above the tarn shore, leads up the bank, with a fine view down the Watendlath Beck valley towards Skiddaw. A narrow path leads through a hand-gate. Ascend with a wall over to the right and sporadic evidence of a path. With some wet ground on the rise to the wall junction, go left along the ridge path, rounding the wall on the right to the low ladder-stile.

Via Heather Knott	190m/620ft	2.5km/1½ miles

11 This unusual line of ascent to Brund Fell will inevitably turn into a circular walk, as it first claims Heather Knott, a summit strikingly in view from Watendlath above the rugged Caffel Side. Go through the gate, first right after the packhorse bridge, and follow the path down the valley. Immediately before the second hand-gate and before the short flight of steps, go left to clamber up the pathless rough fellside, en route peering over the craggy ramparts of Caffel Side ('red deer calf's fellside'). Climb with a wall, then fence to the right, onto the upper slopes to reach the ridge-top stile at the fence junction to join the ridge path from Brund Fell. Cross the stile and work left, round and up the tough herbage to the summit of Heather Knott.

Retrace your steps to the stile at the fence junction and head south, keeping the fence to the right. Ignore the hand-gate on the right in the dip, where Route 4 joins from Bleacrag Moss. The undulating ridge is not only rough but very wet, a major contributory factor in the isolation of Heather Knott. Continue beside the fence, negotiating marshy patches, to a wall junction where there are two stiles. Cross the left-hand stile, keeping the wall to the right. Go round the right-hand corner to a low ladder-stile, which you cross and climb onto Brund Fell.

ASCENT FROM SURPRISE VIEW (6)

One may use either the Surprise View or Ashness Bridge (7) car parks as starting points for expeditions into the Watendlath valley. For the climb onto Brown Dodd, avoid road walking by passing through Hog's Earth wood to the footbridge at the foot of the upper valley meadows. Visitors to the Surprise View

Walkers converse at Surprise View

High Lodore and Shepherd's Crag

Shepherd's Crag

are both encouraged to revel in the view and given warning that it is the brink of a raw mountainside bereft of protection. It overlooks the great marsh running out into Derwentwater backed by Catbells and Skiddaw, a sumptuous scene, always rewarding and never the same, with ever changing lighting and fell colour textures.

Via Brown Dodd   189m/620ft   3.3km/2 miles

Daffodils at High Lodore Farm

12 There is a choice of two routes here. One may follow the Watendlath road south through Ashness Wood, taking the first obvious track slip-off right, through the woodland, and dipping to a hand-gate adjacent to the Watendlath Beck footbridge. Alternatively, keep with the road past the finger of rock to the cattle grid, then turn immediately right, going via the stile and steps descending to the footbridge. Spot the direction plate set in the ground at your feet on the western side. Keep the wall on your right, as to 'Lodore', but after 50m, before the next hand-gate, go left, keeping the enclosure wall right. Go round the right-hand corner to reach a hand-gate where walls converge. Beyond, the footpath treads a small causeway. At the end turn acutely left.

This point can be reached on a more direct approach from High Lodore Farm (reached from starting point 8). High Lodore Farm is quite a focus, particularly for

Watendlath, as seen during the ascent of Brund Fell

rock climbers, and the byre café is used year-round by agile crags-men and women fresh from their routes on Shepherd's Crag. There is no casual parking in the vicinity, and it is imperative to seek approval from the farm to use the farmyard for this purpose. Pass up the track behind the farm. Keep right, off the climbers' path, via a seat, then ascend to the saddle, from where paths radiate. Down to the left spot a dam at the head of the Lodore Falls gorge. The name Lodore actually describes this 'door', the main gorge of Watendlath Beck, while High Lodore relates to the saddle you are standing on, the 'high low door'. One may continue, via the hand-gate, into the wood beside the tumultuous beck. Cross a fence-stile to venture to the Watendlath Beck footbridge or go directly right, first with the wall on the right, then curve left and skip over a tiny gill to reach the neat wall running beside the causeway path.

The north ridge begins here. Don't be under any illusion – while this is a fine route, it is reminiscent of the Harlech Dome in Snowdonia, ankle-twisting stuff. Reford that little gill and advance to a loose hand-gate in a wall. The path drives on through bracken, aiming for the dip in the skyline between outcrop and the view back over Derwentwater to Skiddaw from near the top makes a fine excuse for a brief breather! Once up, bear half-left to thread through another outcrop gap. Again the path drifts left through the bracken and heather, passing around a bluff and contouring by a tiny combe to reach a marshy tussocky hollow. Go forward to meet up with the wall and accompany this to where it curves right. Now bear left up a groove to follow the ridge-top path on Brown Knoll. Again keep a left-hand bias over rank heather, avoiding the second knoll, to reach a dip before the final pull to the top of Heather Knott via its western slope.

Maps persist in naming this peak Ether Knott, reflecting local dialect. In Greek mythology 'ether' was the upper atmosphere where heaven resided and, given the season and best of conditions, surely no more divine place exists!

ASCENT FROM KETTLEWELL (8)

Via Gowder Crag   366m/1200ft   3.5km/2¼ miles

Gowder Crag above Lodore Falls

13 Searches for a boiling spring will be in vain in spite of the name Kettlewell, which is delightfully situated on the south-eastern shores of Derwentwater. Cross the main road and follow the path to the right, weaving through the woods at the base of the Surprise View cliffs. This path meets up with right-of-way at the back of the Hilton Keswick Lodore Hotel. Signed off the road 'To Lodore Falls', it leads through the backyard (akin an industrial works), passing the indoor swimming pool and going over a footbridge. You might enjoy clambering into the chaos of boulders to view the 'fuming falls' – by comparison with many they are a modest exhibition. The path climbs purposefully up the woodland bank, and the first turn/s are the result of rock climbers hastening down from Gowder Crag.

However, one may take a half-right branch to join the path leading up beneath the crag and ascending above the gorge to a fence-stile. The same fence-line can be reached by continuing the initial ascent. The path switches right to cross a stile on the

Derwentwater from Brown Dodd

Brund Fell summit outcrop

brink, all within woodland. This path continues forward to meet up with the Gowder route on a gentle curving path, by which means many strollers make a simple loop back. If the beck is low, and only then, one may venture to balance on the irregular stones to ford Watendlath Beck down to the right. Otherwise go left, south-east, through Hog's Earth (which means 'the shelter of over-wintering hoggets'), and exit the woodland at a hand-gate, joining Route 12 to go right to cross the footbridge over Watendlath Beck.

BRUND FELL SUMMIT

A question mark hangs over the summit – which of the two contending outcrops can claim superiority? The summit adopted by walkers is abrupt and only large enough to form a base to a small cairn. The irregular outcrop features several intriguing igneous medallions which take on artistic shapes, looking as if they could have been chiselled. Old survey maps lead to the view that the outcrop a little to the west is 1ft higher (hence the Brund Fell panorama is taken from that spot).

SAFE DESCENTS

The roughness and confusing terrain of the upper fell may be a concern in misty conditions. The easiest line of escape is east. Cross the low ladder-stile and from thereon aim south, beside the descending wall, to the top of Puddingstone Bank. On meeting the track, either go right (west) to Rosthwaite, 1 mile, or left (east) to Watendlath, ½ mile.

RIDGE ROUTE

GREAT CRAG	↓90m/300ft	↑40m/130ft	2km/1¼ miles

Begin upon the route to the top of Puddingstone Bank just described. A continuing path leads south, via the hand-gate, winding across intermittently marshy ground with patches of bog myrtle to a further hand-gate in a cross-ridge wall. The path bears slightly left to link up with the path rising from the lane on the west side of Watendlath Tarn. Now bear right, skirting the marsh to a hand-gate. Thereon the path climbs towards Dock Tarn, take the first clear turn right before the tarn to up to the top.

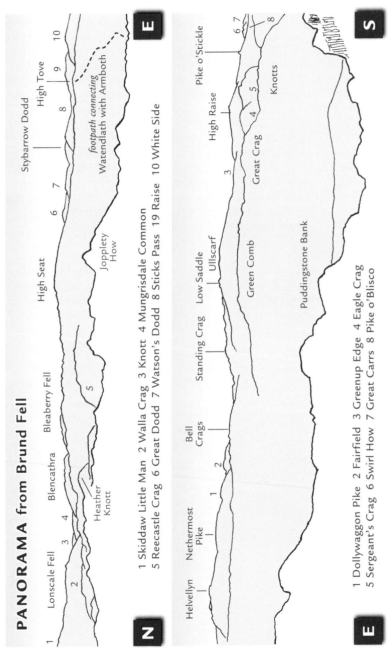

PANORAMA from Brund Fell

N (top section)

Lonscale Fell · Blencathra · Bleaberry Fell · High Seat · Stybarrow Dodd · High Tove

Heather Knott · Jopplety How

footpath connecting Watendlath with Armboth

E

1 Skiddaw Little Man 2 Walla Crag 3 Knott 4 Mungrisdale Common
5 Reecastle Crag 6 Great Dodd 7 Watson's Dodd 8 Sticks Pass 19 Raise 10 White Side

E (bottom section)

Helvellyn · Nethermost Pike · Bell Crags · Standing Crag · Low Saddle · Ullscarf · Green Comb · Great Crag · High Raise · Pike o'Stickle

Puddingstone Bank · Knotts

S

1 Dollywaggon Pike 2 Fairfield 3 Greenup Edge 4 Eagle Crag
5 Sergeant's Crag 6 Swirl How 7 Great Carrs 8 Pike o'Blisco

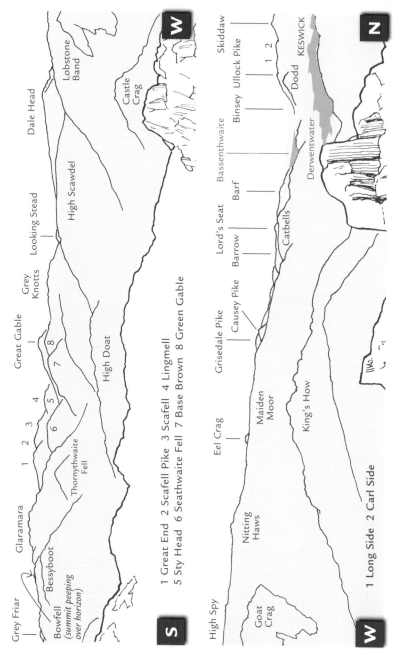

W

Lobstone Band

Dale Head

Castle Crag

Looking Stead

High Scawdel

Grey Knotts

Great Gable

8
7
5 6
4
1 2 3

Glaramara

High Doat

Thornythwaite Fell

Grey Friar

Bessyboot

Bowfell (summit peeping over horizon)

S

1 Great End 2 Scafell Pike 3 Scafell 4 Lingmell
5 Sty Head 6 Seathwaite Fell 7 Base Brown 8 Green Gable

N

Skiddaw

Binsey Ullock Pike

1 2

Dodd

KESWICK

Bassenthwaite

Derwentwater

Lord's Seat

Barf

Barrow

Catbells

Causey Pike

Grisedale Pike

Eel Crag

Maiden Moor

King's How

High Spy

Nitting Haws

Goat Crag

W

1 Long Side 2 Carl Side

99

Central Fells

PANORAMA from Heather Knott

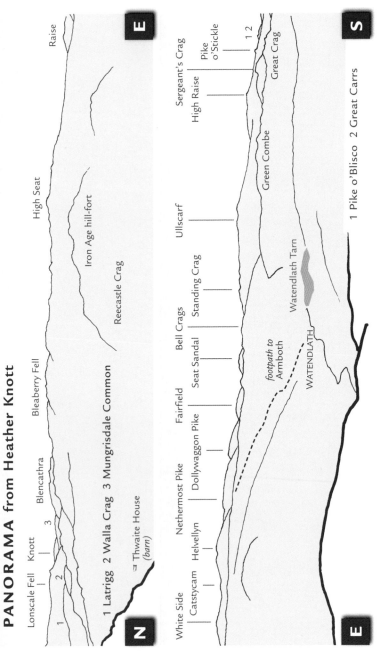

E

N

Raise

High Seat

Bleaberry Fell

Blencathra

Knott

Lonscale Fell

Iron Age hill-fort

Reecastle Crag

3

2

1

1 Latrigg 2 Walla Crag 3 Mungrisdale Common

Thwaite House
(barn)

S

E

Sergeant's Crag

Pike o'Stickle

Great Crag

High Raise

Green Combe

Ullscarf

Watendlath Tarn

Standing Crag

Bell Crags

Seat Sandal

Fairfield

Dollywaggon Pike

Nethermost Pike

Helvellyn

Catstycam

White Side

footpath to Armboth

WATENDLATH

1 2

1 Pike o'Blisco 2 Great Carrs

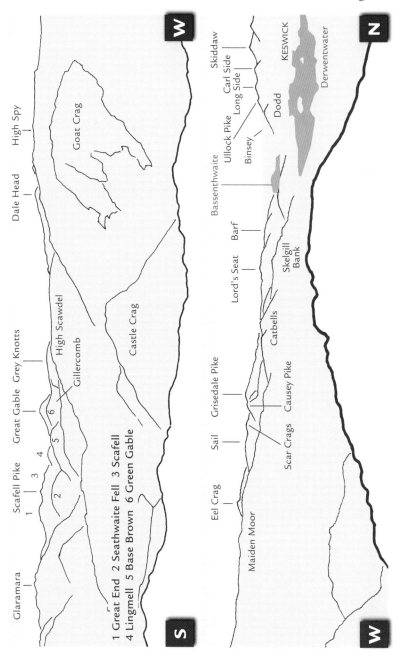

W

Glaramara Scafell Pike Great Gable Grey Knotts Dale Head High Spy

1 3 4 5 6

High Scawdel

Gillercomb

Goat Crag

Castle Crag

1 Great End 2 Seathwaite Fell 3 Scafell
4 Lingmell 5 Base Brown 6 Green Gable

S

N

Skiddaw Carl Side Long Side Ullock Pike Bassenthwaite

KESWICK Derwentwater Dodd Binsey

Barf Lord's Seat Skelgill Bank Catbells

Grisedale Pike Sail Eel Crag Causey Pike Scar Crags Maiden Moor

W

PANORAMA from King's How

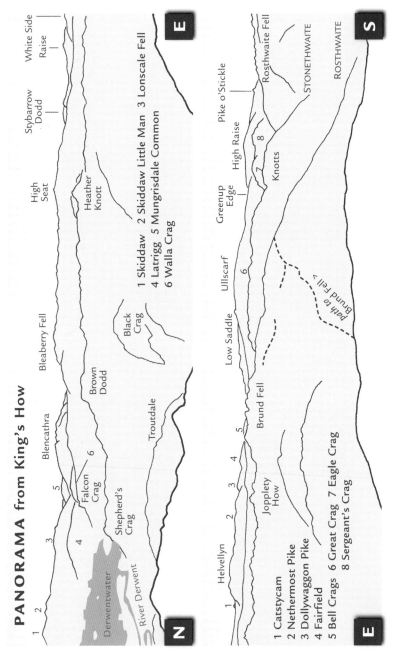

N

White Side Raise

Stybarrow Dodd

High Seat

Bleaberry Fell

Blencathra

Heather Knott

Brown Dodd

Black Crag

Falcon Crag

Shepherd's Crag

Troutdale

Derwentwater

River Derwent

E

1 Skiddaw   2 Skiddaw Little Man   3 Lonscale Fell
4 Latrigg   5 Mungrisdale Common
6 Walla Crag

S

Rosthwaite Fell

Pike o'Stickle

High Raise

Greenup Edge

Ullscarf

Low Saddle

Brund Fell

Knotts

STONETHWAITE

ROSTHWAITE

path to Brund Fell

Joplety How

Helvellyn

E

1 Catstycam
2 Nethermost Pike
3 Dollywaggon Pike
4 Fairfield
5 Bell Crags   6 Great Crag   7 Eagle Crag
8 Sergeant's Crag

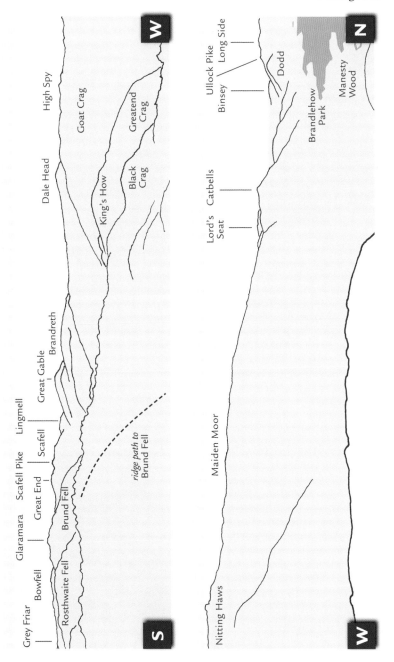

W

High Spy

Goat Crag

Greatend
Crag

King's How

Black
Crag

Dale Head

Brandreth

Great Gable

Lingmell

Scafell

ridge path to
Brund Fell

Grey Friar

Bowfell

Glaramara Scafell Pike

Great End

Brund Fell

Rosthwaite Fell

S

N

Ullock Pike Long Side

Binsey

Dodd

Brandlehow
Park

Manesty
Wood

Lord's Catbells
Seat

Maiden Moor

Nitting Haws

W

9 GREAT CRAG *(452m, 1483ft)*

Observed from Stonethwaite the fell appears to be a mass of trees, a gloriously pleated deciduous skirt (such sylvan tapestries deserve to be revived elsewhere for the benefit of whole-fell diversity). Hidden from view are its roughly textured upper slopes, luxuriant with heather, marsh and volcanic rock. Paths are few. Indeed, apart from the north–south traverse by Dock Tarn and sundry minor diversions to the summit, the fell is bereft of confidence-giving trails, and the fellwalker must rely mostly on the instinctive twists and turns of sheep for any comfort.

Tree roots and bedrock on path exiting woodland above Willygrass Gill

The fell forms an intriguingly rough bridge between Grange Fell and the high central plateau of Ullscarf, and is a back-drop to the much-loved lake-end scene at Watendlath. If your idea of a good time on the fells includes a spot of intense tangle-foot exploration, then this is your kind of top. It attracts few visitors, and most actually ignore the summit, content with the shy charm of Dock Tarn on the lovely path between Stonethwaite and Watendlath. The tarn has irregular shores and is resplendent with reeds and one massive fairy circle of water lilies over on the eastern side: the origin of the tarn name – from the Old English *docce* ('lily pool'). An unusual yet fascinating excursion, when the heather is at its best, is to wander around the ring of little tops surrounding Dock Tarn, by High Crag, Green Comb, Black Knott and Great Crag (no path).

Great Crag offers one more anomaly within Lakeland fell definition among lower 'summits', as it has higher companion parts (hence the cairn on Green Comb is proud of Great Crag's summit by the considerable margin of 28m, 92ft). Green Comb offers superior views into the Watendlath valley and upon Ullscarf, to which it might strictly be thought to belong, though by character it rests fair and square in this chapter. Down to the south-west of the summit, the lower tier ridge of Knotts might attract the attention of explorers. They will do well to resist the temptation, for this area is well defended by bracken and is inferior to the main summit as a viewpoint.

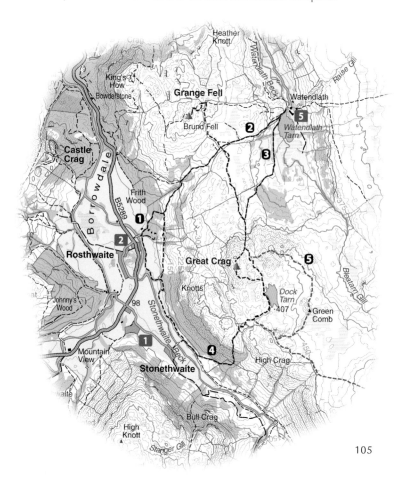

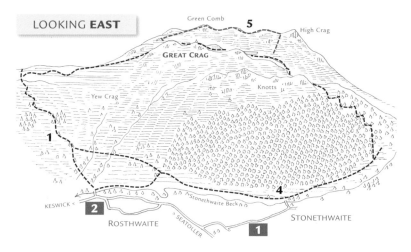

LOOKING **EAST**

Green Comb

5

High Crag

GREAT CRAG

Knotts

Yew Crag

1

4

KESWICK <

2

ROSTHWAITE

SEATOLLER

Stonethwaite Beck

STONETHWAITE

1

ASCENT FROM ROSTHWAITE (2)

Via Puddingstone Bank   357m/1170ft   2.7km/1¾ miles

1 The perennially popular path over Puddingstone Bank to Watendlath provides the ideal springboard for an ascent. Cross the Stonethwaite Beck bridge north of the Post Office and fork left facing the entrance to Hazel Bank Hotel. Passing above Dinah Hoggus camping barn, the lane winds up to a gate. An open trail leads up the slope – take opportunities to look back from time to time as the view over upper Borrowdale is quite superb. Two gates on, the track levels as it approaches the watershed. Bear right, off the bridle path, to the kissing-gate, then wind across intermittently marshy ground with patches of bog myrtle to a further kissing-gate in a cross-ridge wall. The path bears slightly left to link up with the path rising from the lane on the west side of Watendlath Tarn. Now bear right, skirting the marsh to a hand-gate. From here the path climbs towards Dock Tarn. Take the first clear turn right before the tarn to up to the top.

Dale Head

High Scawdel

**Dale Head and Dock Tarn
from Green Comb**

ASCENT FROM WATENDLATH (5)

Via Puddingstone Bank   195m/640ft   2km/1¼ miles

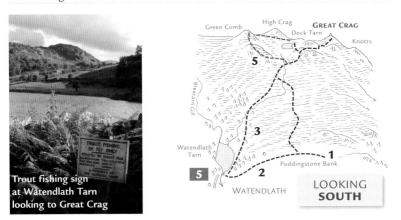

Trout fishing sign
at Watendlath Tarn
looking to Great Crag

*(map labels: Green Comb, High Crag, **GREAT CRAG**, Dock Tarn, Knotts, Bleatarn Gill, 5, 3, Watendlath Tarn, 1, Puddingstone Bank, 5, 2, WATENDLATH, LOOKING **SOUTH**)*

2 From the National Trust car park, behind the farmhouse tearoom, cross the pack-horse bridge at the outflow of the tarn. Here, follow either the main path or see Route 3, below. The main path goes up to the watershed, then branches south via the afore-mentioned kissing-gate. Continue along a clear path over boggy ground with a con-siderable growth of bog myrtle, which is noted for its midge-deterrent properties. At another kissing-gate the trail drifts left to meet up with the path climbing direct from Watendlath Tarn. **3** Alternatively, from the fork in the track beyond the initial gate after the packhorse bridge, follow the gated lane rising above the tarn, and finally wind up a pasture via gates onto marshy ground and meet up with the former ridge-top path. One path leads on via yet more marsh, curving right to a wall-stile and climbing through a weakness in the Great Crag facade. The main thrust of the path wanders on towards the western shore of Dock Tarn. Watch for the cairned branch path to the right, climbing onto the first top; the second is the true summit.

Water-lily ring on Dock Tarn

ASCENT FROM STONETHWAITE (1)

Via Lingy End 354m/1160ft 2km/1¼ miles

4 Park your car along the approach road, not in the hamlet please! Entering the community bear left at the kiosk, signed 'Greenup and Grasmere'. Cross Stonethwaite Bridge to a gate and join the main valley bridle path, co-incident with Wainwright's Coast to Coast Walk. Go right, via the gate. After the sheepfold, which forms a delightful foreground to views of Eagle Crag, the lane dips. At the low wall opening, after some 50m, bear half-left and rise up the pasture on a turf trod between swathes of bracken to a wall-stile. The path goes left, rising to a wall-stile. From here the path climbs purposefully through the deciduous woodland on a stony staircase, switching away from Willygrass Gill. The coppice trees are of comparable age, which suggests that they were largely clear-felled within the last 100 years – oddly the wood is nameless.

Emerging from the canopy take an approving view south to Eagle Crag and Sergeant's Crag, dramatically seen at their very best. Rising onto the appropriately named Lingy End, climb by the heather banks and ruined shepherd's shelter. Skirt round the re-entrant of Willygrass Gill, and the view is of the inaccessible High Crag above the eastern fork of the cascading gill. Cross over the wall-stile and continue to the shores of Dock Tarn, seeking the path leading left at the northern end of the tarn. On this path wind north-westward to the summit.

5 An absorbing time can be had in an indulgent 2km (1¼ mile) circuit of the arc of tops east of Dock Tarn, culminating on Green Comb. Branch from the Lingy End route where the ridge route to Ullscarf fords Willygrass Gill, following the ascending wall. Branch onto the pathless ridge and wind north-east to the cairned top. Continue naturally in a westward arc, with lovely patterned rock to inspect en route to fording a gill and uniting with the path from Puddingstone Bank.

Eagle and Sergeant's Crags from the ruined bothy on Lingy End

Watendlath from Great Crag summit

Great Gable and upper Borrowdale from the summit

THE SUMMIT

Heather, sadly deficient on so many fells, makes repose in this vicinity quite delightful, notably when in full late-summer bloom. To the north, beyond a

Igneous rings on Black Knott

short depression, a large cairn rests on a rock-step. Further cairns mark a subsidiary top, blessed with a superior northward prospect towards Grange Fell and Skiddaw.

SAFE DESCENTS

The consistent path running alongside Dock Tarn gives security for descents to Watendlath 1¼ miles, Rosthwaite (north) 2 miles or Stonethwaite (south) 1½ miles, so head east from the summit to join it.

RIDGE ROUTES

GRANGE FELL	↓40m/130ft	↑90m/300ft	2km/1¼ miles

A path leads north over an adjacent cairned top then bears right, dropping north-east to join the path from Dock Tarn. This now continues down to a wall-stile, and bearing half-right avoids marshy ground resplendent with bog myrtle. At the path fork go half-left to a kissing-gate, and more marshy ground is crossed en route to a second kissing-gate. Cross the Puddingstone Bank track, ascending with the wall to your left to a low ladder-stile. Cross it and wind up to the summit, which is the second top after the apparent summit, marked by a cairn on a sharp pike.

ULLSCARF	↓15m/50ft	↑400m/1300ft	4.3km/2¾ miles

To minimise rough and seriously boggy ground head south-east to follow the main path beyond the outflow of Dock Tarn. Where a wall is seen rising left, bear off, ford the outflow gill, ascending with the wall to the right, and cross the saddle, to the left of High Crag. As you descend, enjoy the marvellous views of Eagle and Sergeant's Crags, as well as the long view up Langstrath to Bowfell. The wall dips right; contour to pick up the wall again along the edge above Greenup Gill. As the wall rises and falls like some latter-day Hadrian's march, follow it until you round a knoll. One may spin off east climbing the fellside to Low Saddle and, picking up the ridge path, continue south-south-east to High Saddle and the ridge fence. Cross the flimsy stile near the acute corner to reach the summit.

PANORAMA

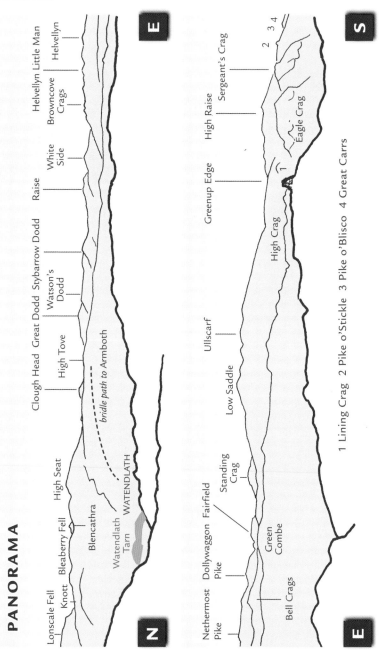

N

Lonscale Fell
Knott
Bleaberry Fell
High Seat
Blencathra
Watendlath Tarn
WATENDLATH

bridle path to Armboth

Clough Head
Great Dodd
Watson's Dodd
Stybarrow Dodd
Raise
White Side
Browncove Crags
Helvellyn Little Man
Helvellyn
High Tove

E

E

Nethermost Pike
Dollywaggon Pike
Fairfield
Bell Crags
Green Combe
Standing Crag
Low Saddle
Ullscarf
High Crag
Greenup Edge
High Raise
Sergeant's Crag
Eagle Crag

2 3 4

S

1 Lining Crag 2 Pike o'Stickle 3 Pike o'Blisco 4 Great Carrs

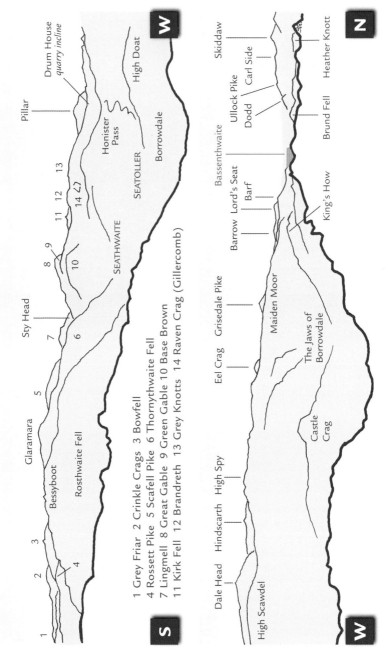

W

Pillar

Drum House
quarry incline

High Doat

Honister
Pass

SEATOLLER

Borrowdale

Sty Head

13

11 12

14

8 9

10

SEATHWAITE

Glaramara

5

Bessyboot

Rosthwaite Fell

3

2

4

1

S

1 Grey Friar 2 Crinkle Crags 3 Bowfell
4 Rossett Pike 5 Scafell Pike 6 Thornythwaite Fell
7 Lingmell 8 Great Gable 9 Green Gable 10 Base Brown
11 Kirk Fell 12 Brandreth 13 Grey Knotts 14 Raven Crag (Gillercomb)

N

Skiddaw

Ullock Pike

Carl Side

Dodd

Heather Knott

Bassenthwaite

Lord's Seat

Brund Fell

Barrow

Barf

King's How

Eel Crag Grisedale Pike

Maiden Moor

The Jaws of
Borrowdale

Dale Head Hindscarth High Spy

Castle
Crag

High Scawdel

W

10 HARRISON STICKLE *(736m, 2415ft)*

In the title view above notice the figure in the foreground is bouldering on the Copt How erratics. This practice should be reconsidered in the light of the recent discovery of 6000-year-old rock art at this precise spot, probably allied to the stone axe factory on Pike o'Stickle.

The Langdale Pikes are up there with Skiddaw and Great Gable as Lakeland landscape icons. When travelling along the winding road up Great Langdale one turns the corner out of Chapel Stile suddenly to comprehend the majesty of the Langdale Pikes. It's one of the most marvellous mountain moments any visitor can have. Harrison Stickle is central, lord and master of a noble group of highly individual fells. The company is composed of the four 'pikes' – Loft Crag, Pike o'Stickle and Pavey Ark, with Thunacar Knott as back-stop. An expedition to any one will turn into a four-top trip – they have that effect. Why resist such a heady cocktail of thrilling situations? The craggy head of Harrison Stickle throws down steep slopes to Stickle Tarn, a tendril ridge reaching down to the valley held tight in the vice by Dungeon and Stickle Ghylls. This rigg has its own moment of exuberance in the little peak of Pike How. Although it always seems such an obstacle from the valley floor, it melts away into insignificance once height is gained; then the real contenders are faced.

ASCENT FROM NEW DUNGEON GHYLL (32–33)

Via Stickle Ghyll   640m/2100ft   2.5km/1½ miles

The ultra-popularity of the Langdale Pikes has ensured a plethora of paths, the line of every desire expressed as a trail of some sort or other.

1 Go either directly up the bridle path from the hotel or ascend from Stickle Ghyll car park information shelter. The paths meet up by the fenced gap and follow the paved path beside Stickle Ghyll. Cross the footbridge and rise to a stile. Keep to the right-hand side of the valley, winding through a fenced area shielding the slope from erosion. The fencing has been compromised by sheep, thus minimising any benefits of grazing relief.

The path forks, with pitching on both right and left paths. The popular route

Harrison Stickle from the Millbeck Farm lane

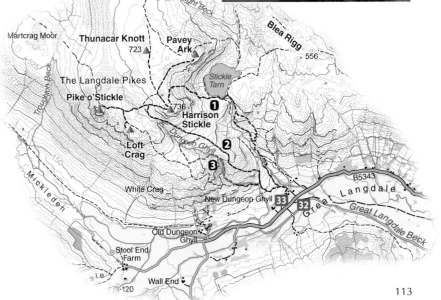

HARRISON STICKLE

PAVEY ARK

Thorn Crag

1

Stickle Tarn

Tarn Crag

2

3

Dungeon Ghyll

1

Pike How

Stickle Ghyll

LOOKING **NORTH**

2

Mark Gate

1

Dungeon Force

3

Millbeck Farm

Great Langdale

33

32

Old Dungeon Ghyll
Hotel & Little Langdale <

New Dungeon Ghyll Hotel
& Sticklebarn Tavern

keeps left above the gill; higher up, after mounting a rock step this path fords the gill and arrives at the dam before Stickle Tarn. The right-hand variant path zig-zags as a stone stair to a further fork, where it bears up left and climbs over the shoulder of the intermediate outcrop below Tarn Crag, thereby linking with the Stickle Ghyll path and completing the ascent to the tarn.

Ahead is the massive crag of Pavey Ark frowning down on the cool, dark waters of Stickle Tarn, and high to the left rises Harrison Stickle. Go left on the obvious path, which has received some restorative paving, though more is needed. Work up the slope to the right of the buttresses. On meeting the contouring path from Pavey Ark, head left, with two optional paths, to the very top; the left-hand path is marginally easier.

Via Pike How   640m/2100ft   2.5km/1½ miles

2 The Pike How route leads off left from the fence gap, rises to a hand-gate and turns right, passing a seat to a stile. Keep the wall on your right, and do not ford Dungeon Ghyll. The well-marked path bears left mounting the steep slope in steady stages. Much of it has been re-engineered to cope with the inevitable heavy foot traffic. Many walkers use this as their return leg after the ascent via Stickle Ghyll, though they would be better resorting to the Mark Gate path off Loft Crag, as it has the best

Bogbean in Harrison Combe

Northern aspect of Harrison Stickle

base. Climbing up to the saddle behind Pike How, make the move right to stand on top; it is a super viewpoint. (Note: a minor path advances north from Pike How along the rim of the slope on a right-hand curve to reach the Stickle Tarn dam. This path might appeal to walkers as an honourable retreat, having ascended Stickle Ghyll only to find the higher fells consumed in threatening cloud.)

The main path proceeds across the open pasture aiming west-north-west for the high shoulder above the deep upper gorge of Dungeon Ghyll. The aggressive slope beneath Harrison Crag affords the path little room, so take your time and watch your footing, as there is loose ground to negotiate. On entering Harrison Combe come to the path junction above the peat-hopping stepping-stones. Either turn sharp right – this route has a rock-step half-way up – or curve round to the right to approach the summit from the north-west without such an obstacle.

Via Dungeon Ghyll   640m/2100ft   2.7km/1¾ miles

3 For those attuned to wild ravines Dungeon Ghyll has an aura that is at the same time forbidding and fabulously attractive. The lower section, shrouded in bracken and trees, is a tight gorge, wherein lurks the actual dungeon. There is no way through – not even the most agile, aquatic gill-scrambler can force their way through.

The route begins by fording Dungeon Ghyll on the recently re-engineered path on course for Loft Crag. However, at the next easing of the ravine above Dungeon Ghyll Force one may cautiously enter, being careful not to trip on tree roots as you do. Scramble over the mid-gill rocks to follow the

Dungeon Ghyll

right bank up to the first mare's-tail waterfall. Scramble dexterously up the right-hand outcrop. The scenery is superb. Keep to the right bank until forced onto the left side, and climb up through the large boulders to reach the baulking upper fall. Here is a thunderous scene, the water crashing into a pool before finally spilling to the gill floor. The exit is the unlikely looking sinister (left-hand) gully, but a simple, safe scramble leads onto the tame fell pasture. Hold to the trod bearing right from the popular path to Loft Crag and angle gently down to ford Dungeon Ghyll in this tame intermediary phase. The path quickly joins Route 2. Alternatively, continue across the slope to Stickle Tarn and link with Route 1, and by either route round the apparently fiercesome and craggily overbearing fell.

THE SUMMIT

Given good visibility it would be hard not to enjoy a visit to this place. Being part and parcel of one of England's finest landscapes does ensure it quite some dignity. There are cairns on the north and south tops, the former being the actual summit. Rock abounds, with the most threatening on the southern rim, so be wary. The view should make you linger and look long and hard. Pavey Ark is subservient but no less impressive, and its relationship to Stickle Tarn seen

Harrison Stickle summit cairn

Harrison Stickle and Tarn Crag

here at its best. The blue ribbon of Windermere draws the eye east – can you spot Low Wood Hotel gleaming white on its far shore? Its is a wonderful spot to witness how the fells rise from the Silurian south and east to a heroic volcanic girdle of high fells crowding above Great Langdale.

SAFE DESCENTS

Just make sure you leave the summit on a northern bias – there is nothing but peril to the south. Paths are well enough marked by constant use. The steep, rough descent to Stickle Tarn is sheltered from a western breeze. The easier route takes the path trending north, as if to Thunacar Knott, and follows a left-curving line from west to south into Harrison Combe. The narrow trod above the upper gorge of Dungeon Ghyll demands care. Beyond, the way is simple, heading south-east to round Pike How to the right.

RIDGE ROUTES

LOFT CRAG	↓105m/345ft	↑60m/200ft	0.4km/¼ mile

Two popular paths lead either west, with a rock-step to carefully negotiate, or north, curving left over easier slopes down to the stepping-stones. Cross the large boulders to help avoid further erosion in the peaty hollow of Harrison Combe. Take the first path left, then angle right on the path mounting the prominent ridge to the cairn.

PAVEY ARK	↓60m/200ft	↑12m/40ft	0.8km/½ mile

Either slip down the north-east path which contours just below the edge over rough ground, or keep to the ridge via the north path, passing a rock tor before drifting right

Pavey Ark   Sergeant Man   Helvellyn

The Langdale Pikes from Chapel Stile

to join a more definite path. The coarse rocks, obviously abrasive, are a fascinating feature of this locale and may tempt many a photographer to reach for his or her camera, seeking to use the textured rocks as foreground subjects. Cross the wall to reach the cairnless summit.

PIKE O'STICKLE ↓105m/345ft ↑75m/250ft 0.8km/½ mile

From the stepping-stones in Harrison Combe, continue west on the worn path to the base of the summit stack. It's hands-on-rock all the way to the top – a compulsive climb to a stunning, scenic station.

THUNACAR KNOTT ↓60m/200ft ↑45m/150ft 0.8km/½ mile

Take the north path, dipping to skirt to the left of the rock tor. Not being on a main ascent route the path is less than convincing. The first cairn is the summit, and the cairn beyond the pool, elsewhere cited as the summit, is several feet lower.

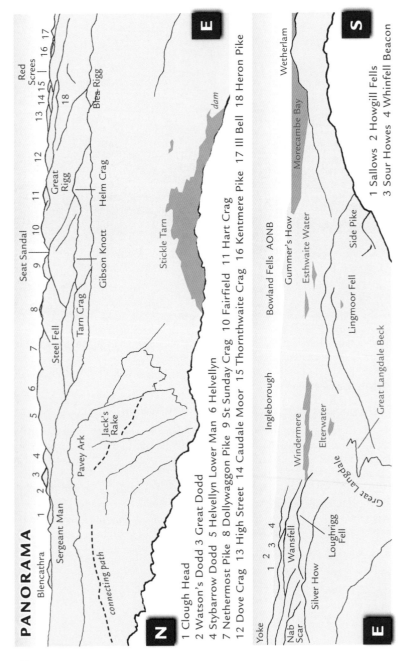

PANORAMA

Blencathra

Sergeant Man

Pavey Ark

Jack's Rake

connecting path

Steel Fell

Tarn Crag

Gibson Knott

Seat Sandal

Great Rigg

Helm Crag

Red Screes

Brea Rigg

Stickle Tarn

dam

1 Clough Head
2 Watson's Dodd 3 Great Dodd
4 Stybarrow Dodd 5 Helvellyn Lower Man 6 Helvellyn
7 Nethermost Pike 8 Dollywaggon Pike 9 St Sunday Crag 10 Fairfield 11 Hart Crag
12 Dove Crag 13 High Street 14 Caudale Moor 15 Thornthwaite Crag 16 Kentmere Pike 17 Ill Bell 18 Heron Pike

Wetherlam

Morecambe Bay

Gummer's How

Esthwaite Water

Side Pike

Bowland Fells AONB

Lingmoor Fell

Great Langdale Beck

1 Sallows 2 Howgill Fells
3 Sour Howes 4 Whinfell Beacon

Ingleborough

Windermere

Elterwater

Great Langdale

Yoke

Nab Scar

Wansfell

Silver How

Loughrigg Fell

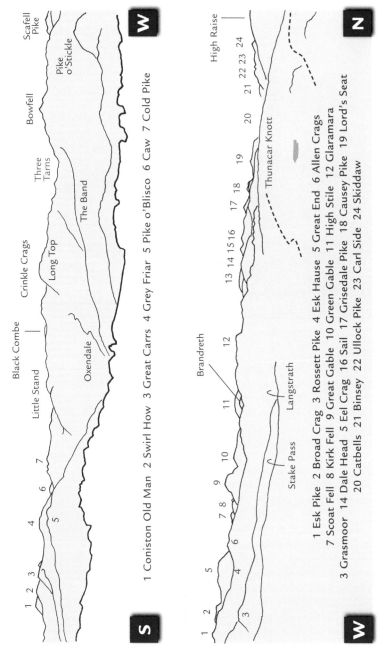

W

Scafell Pike
Pike o'Stickle
Bowfell
Three Tarns
Crinkle Crags
Long Top
The Band
Black Combe
Little Stand
Oxendale
7 6 5 4 3 2 1

S

1 Coniston Old Man 2 Swirl How 3 Great Carrs 4 Grey Friar 5 Pike o'Blisco 6 Caw 7 Cold Pike

N

High Raise
24 23 22 21
20
Thunacar Knott
19 18 17 16 15 14 13
12
11
10 9 8 7
Brandreth
Langstrath
Stake Pass
6
5
4
3
2
1

W

1 Esk Pike 2 Broad Crag 3 Rossett Pike 4 Esk Hause 5 Great End 6 Allen Crags
7 Scoat Fell 8 Kirk Fell 9 Great Gable 10 Green Gable 11 High Stile 12 Glaramara
3 Grasmoor 14 Dale Head 5 Eel Crag 16 Sail 17 Grisedale Pike 18 Causey Pike 19 Lord's Seat
20 Catbells 21 Binsey 22 Ullock Pike 23 Carl Side 24 Skiddaw

11 HELM CRAG *(405m, 1329ft)*

This crag is intrinsic to the Vale of Grasmere. Although the greater bulk of surrounding fells may more regularly lose their heads in cloud, it is this modest height that is known as the cloud-capped hill. And it is not surprising. People have travelled over Dunmail Raise – the main north–south road through the wild fells of Cumbria – for countless centuries, with all eyes turning in recognition to this one knobbly fell. It was always a landmark, the one fell everyone knew by sight, so if lost in mist, with its head in the clouds, it was considered 'helmeted'.

In more recent centuries those travellers have been tourists, who found irresistible the comparison (taken from the Bible) of the summit rocks to a lion lying down with the lamb. The rocks on the southern skyline join in the fun and games by giving observers from the village a second, perhaps even more convincing, leonine profile. How many visitors have thought they were looking at the same group of rocks they saw on their journey

Far Easedale seen during the ascent of Helm Crag

↑ Helm Crag from above The Hollens

south into the valley upon the A591? At a casual glance the fell appears isolated, but fellwalkers know its connectedness with the delightful roller-coaster ridge running over Gibson Knott to Calf Crag, ending at the saddle at the very top of Far Easedale.

ASCENT FROM GRASMERE (22–25)

Direct   341m/1120ft   2.5km/1½ miles

Popular ascents begin from Grasmere village via Easedale Road. **1** Follow either the road or adjacent fenced path beside the hay meadow to cross Goody Bridge – a name that comes from the personal name 'Guddy', recorded in 1586. Now enter Easedale, derived from the Viking name 'Asi', first mentioned in 1332. Beyond Oak Lodge (refreshments) the road leads via a gate through the midst of a meadow, and becomes confined once more at Little Parrock ('the little paddock'). Keep right, facing the lane approach to Brimmer Head Farm, signposted

Helm Crag from Far Easedale

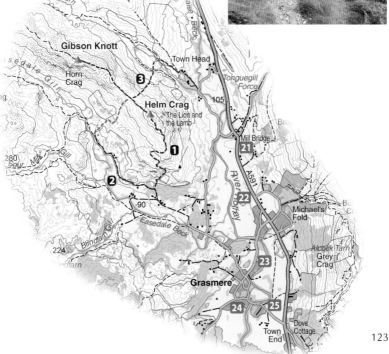

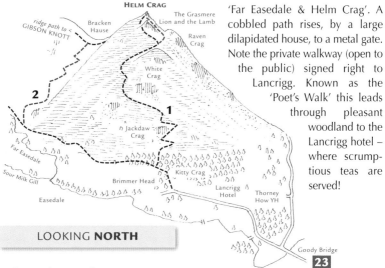

HELM CRAG

ridge path to <
GIBSON KNOTT

Bracken
Hause

The Grasmere
Lion and the Lamb

Raven
Crag

White
Crag

2

1

Jackdaw
Crag

Far Easedale

Sour Milk Gill

Brimmer Head

Kitty Crag

Lancrigg
Hotel

Thorney
How YH

Easedale

Goody Bridge

23

GRASMERE

LOOKING **NORTH**

'Far Easedale & Helm Crag'. A cobbled path rises, by a large dilapidated house, to a metal gate. Note the private walkway (open to the public) signed right to Lancrigg. Known as the 'Poet's Walk' this leads through pleasant woodland to the Lancrigg hotel – where scrumptious teas are served!

From the metal gate two routes diverge. Trend right, through the short lane flanked by woodland, taking the waymarked path which climbs via zig-zags directly ahead above an old quarry. Note that older guides and maps indicate a path taking a right slant; this has been rested. Time, toil and no little funds went into engineering a new 'popular' path up the fell. This path is an excellent piece of rethinking, and in fact a better route than the old way, which enjoys superb views into Far Easedale. It ascends

Helm Crag from above Winterseeds

Western aspect of the Howizter, the summit outcrop on Helm Crag

Lines of ascent

over bare rock at one point before switching right on turf to a saddle (where the old route joined the ridge proper). Head north up the ridge and scramble over the southernmost skyline lion outcrop en route to the summit – which, for most walkers, will be the base of the summit 'howitzer'. Immediately to the east an ancient land-slipped sub-tier gives scope for a spot of exploration. Even if you feel making it to the very top is not your cup of tea, this rough slope will give you a sense of elation and adventure, as not too many visitors venture away from the ridge proper.

Via Bracken Hause   340m/1120ft   3.5km/2¼ miles

2 Go left with the bridle path, again initially flanked by woodland. This track-cum-lane is the age-old pony trail up Far Easedale, destined for Borrowdale via the high watershed of Greenup Edge. The profile of the route was elevated in recent years when Alfred Wainwright created his Coast to Coast Walk and brought it this way. The rough, tracked lane passes a vernacular barn en route to come alongside Far Easedale Beck. As the right-hand wall bears up to the right, follow suit. There is little early evidence of a path, but one does materialise, winding up onto a knoll to mount the steep bracken slope. Pass a lone thorn at a spring to reach the saddle of Bracken Hause – what an appropriate name! Go naturally right with the ridge path to the top.

Greenburn Beck

Helm Crag from Greenburn Dale

ASCENT FROM MILL BRIDGE (21)

Via Bracken Hause   317m/1040ft   2km/1¼ mile

This is the nippy route, catching the fell unawares! **3** There is a bus stop on the A591 above the Town Head Farm, or use the Mill Bridge verge parking space and follow the minor road down over the Rothay, bearing right by Ghyll Foot to reach the drive access to Helmside. Ascend the metalled lane, via its cattle grids, to the gate beyond Turn Howe. Go forward along the level track, passing though a gate, with Greenburn Beck close down to the left. Bear left to cross the wooden footbridge above the first water-fall. The path climbs the pasture to cross the lane, via facing hand-gates, and climbs directly up the steep, short turf slope to Bracken Hause.

HELM CRAG

The Grasmere Lion and the Lamb

Bracken Hause

Raven Crag

3

Goody Bridge

falls

Greenburn Dale

Ghyll Foot

River Rothay

Helmside

Turn Howe

< GRASMERE

slopes of STEEL FELL

Mill Bridge **21**

A591

Town Head

Raise Beck

Dunmail Raise >

LOOKING **WEST**

THE SUMMIT

The ordinary mortal might feel cheated, having struggled up the confounded hill only to find that someone has built an unassailable fortress on top, complete with a deep, dry, stony moat! Steady-headed scramblers will think nothing of the 7m (24ft) climb, with either a rib to the

The Howizter summit outcrop on Helm Crag

south or the north-west groove as their chosen line of ascent; the author has made it to the top on three occasions, each time via the latter line. Console yourselves, there is little extra merit in the ultimate view, though the author's panorama is concocted from a composite of images taken from the actual top.

SAFE DESCENTS

Both conventional lines of ascent give secure footing. The route north from Bracken Hause to the footbridge spanning Green Burn is steep but mostly free of rock hazard.

RIDGE ROUTE

GIBSON KNOTT	↓100m/330ft	↑90m/300ft	1.6km/1 mile

Descend north-west to the saddle depression of Bracken Hause. The ridge path does not always follow the ridge, but keeps a southern bias, though one may tackle the ridge proper with no hazard.

The Grasmere Lion and the Lamb

PANORAMA

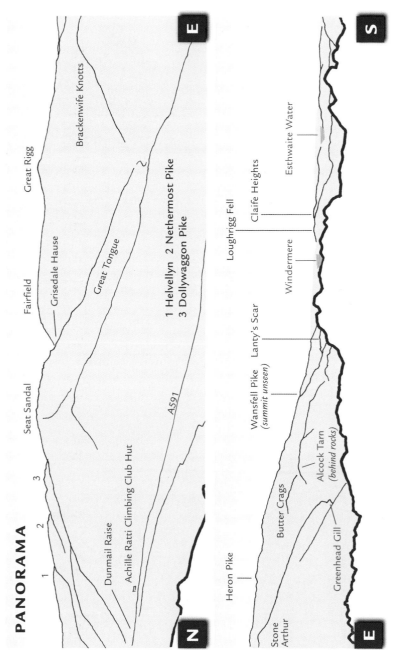

E

S

N

E

Great Rigg

Brackenwife Knotts

Fairfield

Grisedale Hause

Great Tongue

Seat Sandal

1 Helvellyn 2 Nethermost Pike
3 Dollywaggon Pike

Dunmail Raise

Achille Ratti Climbing Club Hut

A591

3

2

1

Loughrigg Fell

Claife Heights

Esthwaite Water

Windermere

Lanty's Scar

Wansfell Pike
(summit unseen)

Alcock Tarn
(behind rocks)

Butter Crags

Greenhead Gill

Heron Pike

Stone
Arthur

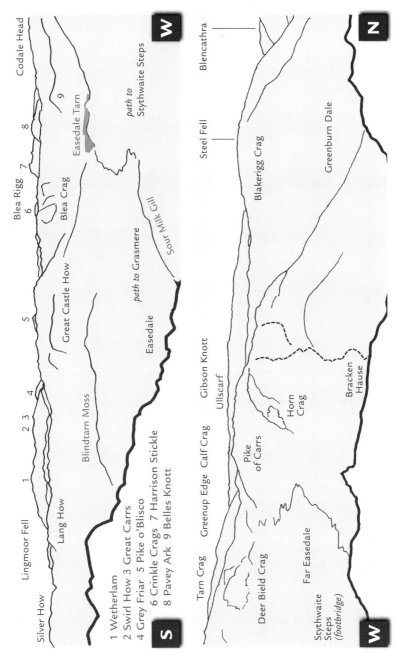

W

Codale Head

9

Easedale Tarn

8

7

Blea Rigg

6

Blea Crag

path to
Stythwaite Steps

Great Castle How

5

path to Grasmere

Sour Milk Gill

Easedale

Blindtarn Moss

4

3 2

1

Lang How

Silver How

Lingmoor Fell

S

1 Wetherlam
2 Swirl How 3 Great Carrs
4 Grey Friar 5 Pike o'Blisco
6 Crinkle Crags 7 Harrison Stickle
8 Pavey Ark 9 Belles Knott

N

Blencathra

Steel Fell

Blakerigg Crag

Greenburn Dale

Bracken
Hause

Horn
Crag

Ullscarf

Pike
of Carrs

Gibson Knott

Calf Crag

Greenup Edge

Tarn Crag

Deer Bield Crag

Far Easedale

Stythwaite
Steps
(footbridge)

W

12 HIGH RAISE *(762m, 2500ft)*

The name of Rosthwaite, in the depths of Borrowdale, meant 'the raise or cairn within an enclosure'. From the village the distant cairn on the south-eastern skyline would be the high cairn, hence High Raise. The main body of the fell has a simple symmetry, content with its role as a range-top, scarp-top viewpoint, and reserving all flamboyance for its ancillary parts. It lies unabashed at the solar plexus of mountain Lakeland, surrounded by far finer specimen heights, its rather plain broad plateau pasture bursting into momentary life on the brink above Langstrath. Given half-decent visibility, High Raise performs a noble duty as a major panoramic station. The view in the western arc beyond Langstrath and Glaramara features Bowfell, Scafell Pike and Great Gable, with the consistently high switchback skyline of the Helvellyn and Fairfield range forming the eastern horizon.

Invariably visitors make this the turning point of their day's walk, a chance to lengthen the stride after a tough pull onto any one of the Langdale Pikes, backtracking to Sergeant Man or Thunacar Knott. By its nature and superior situation it gives a solid reason for any number of radial approaches and circuits – a natural crescendo, drawing out a walk that may otherwise have timidly turned, thus forfeiting a precious hour on the roof of the range. High Raise is a reward, not an irksome addition, and for seasoned fellwalkers this is an oft-repeated royal balcony.

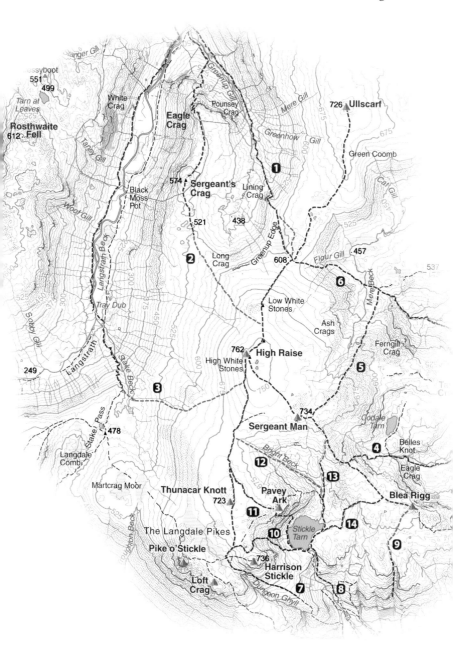

ASCENT FROM STONETHWAITE (1)

Via Greenup Edge 671m/2200ft 6.5km/4 miles

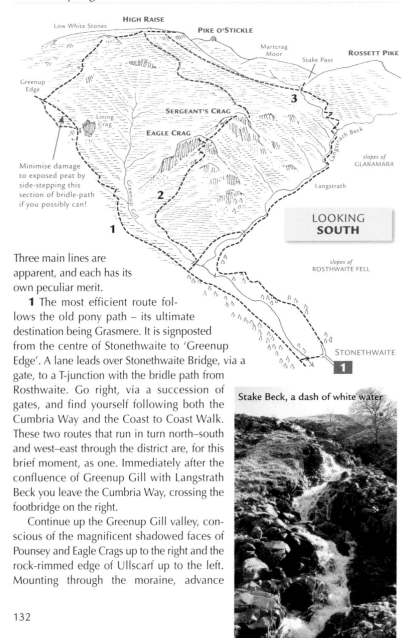

LOOKING **SOUTH**

Minimise damage to exposed peat by side-stepping this section of bridle-path if you possibly can!

Three main lines are apparent, and each has its own peculiar merit.

1 The most efficient route follows the old pony path – its ultimate destination being Grasmere. It is signposted from the centre of Stonethwaite to 'Greenup Edge'. A lane leads over Stonethwaite Bridge, via a gate, to a T-junction with the bridle path from Rosthwaite. Go right, via a succession of gates, and find yourself following both the Cumbria Way and the Coast to Coast Walk. These two routes that run in turn north–south and west–east through the district are, for this brief moment, as one. Immediately after the confluence of Greenup Gill with Langstrath Beck you leave the Cumbria Way, crossing the footbridge on the right.

Continue up the Greenup Gill valley, conscious of the magnificent shadowed faces of Pounsey and Eagle Crags up to the right and the rock-rimmed edge of Ullscarf up to the left. Mounting through the moraine, advance

Stake Beck, a dash of white water

Pool on the High Raise plateau

beyond the site of an ancient tarn to clamber up the rock-staircase to the left of Lining Crag (how did pack-ponies hoof this?). The summit of the crag is frequently visited as a kind of reward for the effort, and the view down the valley towards now distant Borrowdale is certainly rewarding.

The bridle path to Greenup Edge crosses some particularly bad peat marsh. It is recommended that walkers give it a total miss – both in the interests of their own dry feet and for the welfare of the terrain – by climbing directly up to the ridge top from Lining Crag (no path), then going right. The line of metal fence posts act as guides on the ridge path off Ullscarf, crossing the Greenup Edge depression bound for Low White Stones. The climb includes some further peaty ground and an interim rocky ledge before arrival at the Stones gives renewed elation, for it is but a short traverse of the easily angled plateau to gain the summit.

Via Eagle Crag and Sergeant's Crag	686m/2250ft	6km/3¾ miles

2 This is the adventurer's route, full of drama in the preliminary climb, tailing off on the final pull to the ultimate top. Follow the descriptions EAGLE CRAG Route 1 (page 67) and the ridge routes to SERGEANT'S CRAG (page 70), then those subsequently to HIGH RAISE (page 237).

Via Langstrath	670m/2200ft	7.5km/4¾ miles

3 This accompanies the Cumbria Way. From the footbridge at the confluence with Greenup Gill wend up the long Langstrath valley via Blea Rock, a startling upstanding rock beneath the slabs of Sergeant's Crag and Black Moss Pot (stile). The beck intersperses meandering shingle beds with water shoots and rocky channels on an eventful journey upstream to the footbridge at the foot of Stake Beck. Cross the bridge and zig-zag up the old pony route, witnessing some quite amazing water cascades close to the path. As the path eases, branch off left at will to follow a gill east-south-east. As it is eventually lost make for the skyline and join the path from Thunacar Knott, going left to the summit.

133

ASCENT FROM GRASMERE (22–25)

Via Sergeant Man or Far Easedale   670m/2200ft   6.5km/4 miles

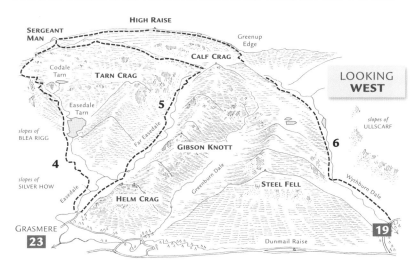

The high plateau is hidden from the east by the headwall of Codale Head, which appears to be the conclusive termination of the high ground above Easedale Tarn. **4** Sergeant Man, perched over the shoulder from Codale Head, is the crucial link point, enabling walkers to attain the plateau with minimal difficulty (follow SERGEANT MAN Route 3 (page 226)) and the ridge route. There are several ridge connections to Sergeant Man, via Blea Rigg, Tarn Crag and Calf Crag, but the natural valley alternative, **5**, wanders up Far Easedale, takes a left turn at the saddle, then climbs in the company of the few forlorn metal stakes that once formed a fence marking the Cumberland–Westmorland county boundary. An off-the-beaten track variation to this

Codale Head and Ash Crags from Wythburn Head

for adventurous types is to drop over the saddle into the head of Wythburn Dale and follow the rough courses of either Mere Beck and Deep Slack or Birks Gill directly onto the plateau.

6 In many eyes this is the most dreary route, as it wends up the lonely wastes of Wythburn Dale, linking to the old pony path at Flour Gill, then climbs onto Greenup

Edge. The route contrives to avoid all hint of rocky outcrop, so may appeal as a simple means of reaching the roof of the range. Consult CALF CRAG Route 2 (page 61), though the essence of the High Raise route would keep with the faltering path, up the southern side of the valley, avoiding the worst of the peaty ridge top. Unless, of course, Calf Crag might be thought worthy of inclusion – and it is.

ASCENT FROM GREAT LANGDALE (32–33)

Via Harrison Combe, Stickle Tarn or Blea Rigg   685m/2250ft   4km/2½ miles

The Langdale Pikes are but a front to a massif that has its remote crown on High Raise. In the traditional spirit of fellwalking this should be considered the ultimate point when setting out on any expedition to climb Harrison Stickle, Pavey Ark or even Blea Rigg and Sergeant Man.

As the diagram reveals there are a number of braided routes, though only Route 12 can claim to be exclusive to High Raise. **7** Follow the one path exclusive to HARRISON STICKLE Route 2 (page 114), rising above Dungeon Ghyll and through Harrison Combe onto THUNACAR KNOTT, see Route 1 (page 268), and from there following the ridge route. Route **8** Climbs Stickle Ghyll, though even here there are three lines. The new zig-zag path which draws under Tarn Crag is better than the unflinching gill path, while the green trod climbing on from the zig-zag is an altogether quieter option still. **9** The Whitegill Crag route (see BLEA RIGG Route 4–5, page 49) makes an exciting variant, side-stepping Stickle Tarn.

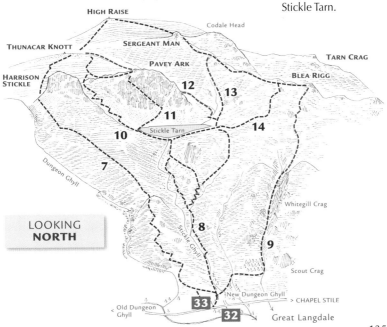

From the shores of Stickle Tarn five routes spring. **10** The eastern approach to Harrison Stickle climbs the scree slope, with evidence of recent path repair (see HARRISON STICKLE Route 1, page 113). As the contouring path from Pavey Ark joins, go straight up onto the saddle. Keep right, rounding a tor to cross the shoulder of Thunacar Knott, now upon the ridge path. **11** Jack's Rake is the route that all true mountaineers take as their royal route to High Raise (see PAVEY ARK, page 200). **12** Either follow Bright Beck from the head of the tarn, through its upper ravine to the broad depression north of Thunacar Knott, or **13** Ford Bright Beck, making for the rounded summit of Sergeant Man. **14** This involves taking the line of least resistance, suitable for those long summer days when one has time to dawdle (see BLEA RIGG Route 3, page 48). Ignore the summit of Blea Rigg and climb left onto the ridge bound for Sergeant Man and the plateau beyond.

THE SUMMIT

This is aptly called High White Stones. Among the pale surface rocks resides a capacious wind-shelter, within which half-a-dozen may huddle when all about is torrid and foul, and a stone-built Ordnance Survey pillar to lean against when fortune brings a balmy sun. This is a place of congregation and expansive scenic pleasure. While some walkers, having gained their bearings, speed on to craggier attractions elsewhere, those who adore just being on top of the world dally long, soaking up this the purest of Lakeland fellscapes, with Glaramara at centre-stage setting the inspirational tone across the obscured depths of Langstrath. On the broad front the fell top has more in common with the Far Eastern Fells, being an almost pancake-flat pasture where sheep wander at will.

OS pillar on High Raise looking west

SAFE DESCENTS

The remote situation carries a price. Innocuous though the broad, peaty-pastured top appears to be, do not be tempted to beeline north as Long Crag is a nasty trap. The surest recourse is to Greenup Edge, joining the well-marked range-crossing pony path. Head slightly east of north for 600m to High White Stones, then north-north-east down to the damp depression. For Grasmere turn right, east, descending initially beside Flour Gill as you cross the rough slope at the head of Wythburn Dale, then fording Mere Beck and rising to the low saddle at the very top of Far Easedale. The path runs securely down this wild dale via the Stythwaite Steps footbridge. For Borrowdale, go left north-north-west, being watchful to keep to the right at Lining Crag. After descending a gully, the path runs down the Greenup Gill valley bound for Stonethwaite, 3¼ miles, and Rosthwaite, 3¾ miles.

The Stake Pass is certainly a safe line for either Borrowdale or Great Langdale, but it almost doubles any journey, and on such grounds should be a last recourse. It is best reached (no path) from the depression at the head of Bright Beck. Southbound routes engage in more tricky terrain, though remember that Sergeant Man is the key for Easedale, as is Thunacar Knott for Langdale, via Harrison Combe and the Pike How route leading down from the head of Dungeon Ghyll.

RIDGE ROUTES

SERGEANT MAN	↓30m/100ft	↑8m/25ft	0.8km/½ mile

Walk south-south-east passing the shallow pools and peaty ground to join the vestige of the metal fence. The summit comes into view as the plateau unfolds.

SERGEANT'S CRAG	↓195m/640ft	↑10m/30ft	2.4km/1½ miles

Advance to Low White Stones, and from here leave the plateau west-north-west on a rough, pathless descent, mindful that Long Crag lurks to the north-west. There is little evidence of a ridge until the reedy depression at the foot of the slope is reached. Then one materialises, as too now does a path, leading to the stile in the summit-embracing wall.

THUNACAR KNOTT	↓85m/280ft	↑50m/160ft	1.6km/1 mile

The main path leads south, gently declining to a broad depression. As the first rocks are encountered along the easy rise, bear off right from the main trail; otherwise the path makes for Pavey Ark.

ULLSCARF	↓155m/510ft	↑120m/390ft	4km/2½ miles

Head north-north-east for 600m to High White Stones, then descend north-north-east to Greenup Edge. Go straight on accompanying the line of metal stakes. Sweep to the right of at least one notable pool before rising onto the drier ridge. Aim north with only the merest of stumps (watch you don't stumble on them) for guides to the solitary summit cairn.

PANORAMA

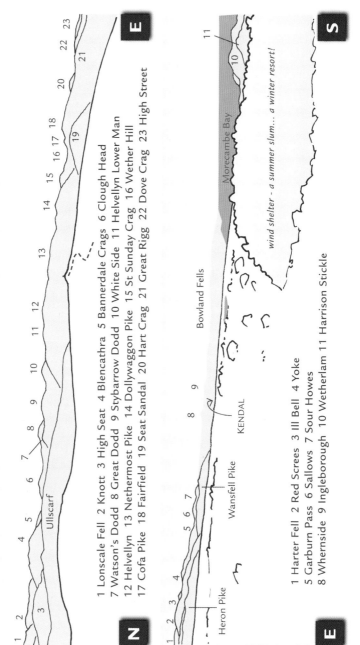

E

1 Lonscale Fell 2 Knott 3 High Seat 4 Blencathra 5 Bannerdale Crags 6 Clough Head
7 Watson's Dodd 8 Great Dodd 9 Stybarrow Dodd 10 White Side 11 Helvellyn Lower Man
12 Helvellyn 13 Nethermost Pike 14 Dollywaggon Pike 15 St Sunday Crag 16 Wether Hill
17 Cofa Pike 18 Fairfield 19 Seat Sandal 20 Hart Crag 21 Great Rigg 22 Dove Crag 23 High Street

Ullscarf

N

S

Morecambe Bay

wind shelter - a summer slum... a winter resort!

Bowland Fells

KENDAL

Wansfell Pike

Heron Pike

E

1 Harter Fell 2 Red Screes 3 Ill Bell 4 Yoke
5 Garburn Pass 6 Sallows 7 Sour Howes
8 Whernside 9 Ingleborough 10 Wetherlam 11 Harrison Stickle

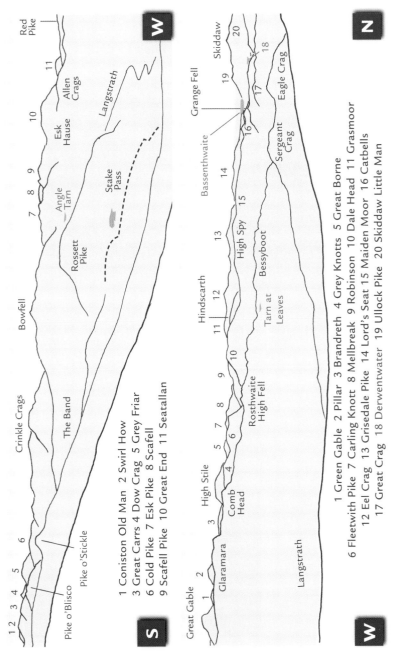

13 HIGH RIGG *(355m, 1165ft)*

With this being a low ridge, ways up are well defined. There are two northern lines direct to the summit, an approach which can be further enhanced and extended by including Tewet Tarn and Low Rigg as an aperitif and one pure ridge walk from the south (this has a westerly variation en route). Running along the fell base to east and west are footpaths that enable walkers to sample the two beautiful adjacent dales and so compose lovely fell and dale circular walks. While contrasting in their scenic qualities, both valleys do at least have the commonality of draining into the Greta.

The grandest circuit would introduce Castlerigg Stone Circle into the equation across Naddle Beck, and approaching the stones in this way provides the greatest visual impact. Bus stops on the A591 at Thirlmere Dam Road End (shelter) and Shoulthwaite lay-by underpin these as the best starting points for circular footpath tours. The Shoulthwaite route is given added charm by beginning upon the newly sur-faced forest track skirt-ing Shoulthwaite Moss, then passing old Smaithwaite to reach Bridge End (working farm and camp site).

Across the Naddle valley from Dodd Crag

ASCENT FROM TEWET TARN VERGE (11)

Direct 213m/700ft 2.5km/1½ miles

There is verge parking at GR306238 (avoid blocking field-gate access). **1** A footpath
is signed from a gate up a small field to a gateway. Continue on, guided by a wooden
waymark post by a curious rift feature, presumably laboriously cut for piping linked
to the tarn. Aim left of the sheet of water and cross the wall-stile left of the fenced
gateway. Quite naturally many visitors circle the tiny tarn, admire the backdrop of
Blencathra and watch the coots weaving among the weed. It is a place of quiet
repose and fun. Here
children may laugh
and play, and

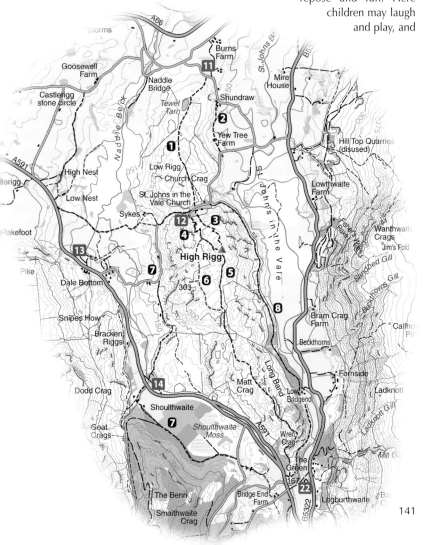

141

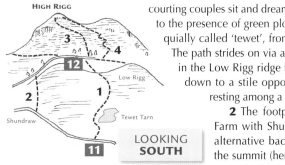

HIGH RIGG

LOOKING SOUTH

courting couples sit and dream. The tarn-name refers to the presence of green plover or lapwing, colloquially called 'tewet', from their distinctive call. The path strides on via a fence-stile, over a dip in the Low Rigg ridge to a wall-stile, and on down to a stile opposite St John's Church, resting among a shroud of trees.

2 The footpath linking Yew Tree Farm with Shundraw is useful as an alternative back-tracking route from the summit (hence is described south to north). From the church follow the approach road down, via the gate by the tiny Yew Tree Cottage, and at the road bend bear off left through the double gates signed to Row End. The track leads between the house and barn to the gate with a 'footpath' plate. Head straight across the ensuing rushy field, skipping over the open ditch mid-course, to a stepped wall-gate. Keep the wall close right until you reach a short gated lane beside the huge bank-barn at Shundraw, very like the barn back at Yew Tree Farm.

ASCENT FROM ST JOHN'S CHURCH (12)

3 Car parking – give preference to church centre visitors. Here you have a choice. You can embark upon the path rounding the west end of the main centre building, which leads up to a kissing-gate and continues as a steady uphill trod. The bracken has been suppressed by the regular pounding. In its later stages the path swings round the left-hand side of the final summit knoll, thereby approaching the cairn from the south. **4** Alternatively, go further along the hause road to the kissing-gate, where the road deteriorates to a track 'unsuitable for motor vehicles'. Now bear left

Eastern aspect of High Rigg (summer early afternoon)

St John's Church, a romantic setting for a wedding

by the seat, rising above the enclosure copse and water tank on a zig-zagging path which straightens onto a semblance of a ridge and reaches the top with alacrity and no little elation.

ASCENT FROM LEGBURTHWAITE (22)

Via the spine of the ridge   230m/750ft   3km/1¾ miles

On this route you see the very best of High Rigg, and the journey is given impetus by the magnificent surroundings, with eyes inevitably drawn to the most handsome fell of all, Blencathra. This is the epitome of Lakeland grandeur, with the fell providing the backdrop to views down the green strath of St John's in the Vale, and drawing the eye all the way to Tewet Tarn. The walk leaves the A591 at a ladder-stile/hand-gate at GR315196, 100m north of the bus shelter; to reach this spot from the Legburthwaite United Utilities car park follow the old road Cycle Way lane.

Wren Crags from Legburthwaite

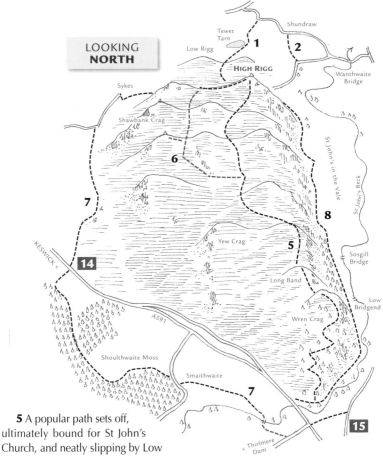

LOOKING **NORTH**

5 A popular path sets off, ultimately bound for St John's Church, and neatly slipping by Low Bridge Farm (tea garden), but within 50m the ridge path branches left, for the time being putting appetizing thoughts onto the back-burner. Early on, relish a delightful rising ridge garnished with Scots pines and giving superb views of Castle Rock of Triermain. Above the pines, the first knoll provides a stunning panorama. In view are Helvellyn and its mighty supplicants overbearing to the south-east, and the conifer-draped Thirlmere fells to the south-west beyond Great How, with Raven Crag an imposing feature above the dam. To the north the Skiddaw massif, Great Calva and Blencathra, beyond St John's in the Vale, are beautiful compositions – stirring stuff.

The path, showing signs of erosion, slips through a dip in the ridge, via a wall-gap, and clambers onto an attractive rocky step in the ridge. Passing a cairn perched on a splintered rock, the path strides along a lovely narrowing of the ridge above Long Band. At a wooden post the path is ushered left to a fence-stile. The regular path

Castlerigg Stone Circle backed by High Rigg and Helvellyn

sweeps to the left of the next knoll, while one may stroll up with the fence to the right onto a cairned top above a pool, following its outflow to rejoin the main path that leads down to a ladder-stile at a wall junction. Note the fine construction of the enclosure walling in this vicinity. Once over the stile there are two options. The ridge path heads up with the wall to the right. At the marshy hollow skirt left to cross the narrow outflow stones under Moss Crag, then either curve right, resuming beside the wall, or climb straight up the fell to the ridge top bearing right to rejoin the main path beyond the wall end. The summit beckons ahead.

6 From the ladder-stile branch left across the bracken slope on a sheep trod. Once level with the ash tree, curve right under the outcrop and gain a shallow rigg rising to the saddle. Briefly bear left to a viewpoint cairn with adjacent pool. Continue from the saddle with the slightly more apparent sheep path, and at the next saddle spur left again to the cairn at the top of Shawbank Crag. Both cairns enjoy lovely views across the Naddle valley to the shapely prow of Dodd Crag, foremost limb of Bleaberry Fell. The path, even more sure, advances across the broad hollow to link up with the popular path at the last lower saddle. This is the path rising from the St John's Church hause, via the water tank.

Castle Rock of Triermain from Wren Crag

Two valley variations – useful for creating a circular tour

7 The **western trail** (3 miles/5km) leads off from the church centre via Piper House, Rough How Bridge, Shoulthwaite Moss and Smaithwaite to Bridgend Farm. The route turns down the road to the left from St John's hause (from the gate the road is unsuitable for wheeled traffic). At the foot of the zig-zags follow the tarmac road left. Pass Piper House, a quintessential Lakeland cottage with a superb backdrop of Bleaberry Fell (cameras out!). Where the road turns right ignore this. Keep the wall to the right as you follow the byway past Shaw Bank, overlooked by Shawbank Crag, and Brownbeck.

Soon afterwards the road ends and forks into two bridle paths. The left-hand path rises invitingly to a ladder-stile, but there is little merit in the succeeding trail across a bracken hollow, though a footpath veering right along the back of the rigg may come to your rescue if by error you chose the wrong option at the fork. Better take the right fork via a stile, and a rocky path dips to a smooth green track and a gate, where the footpath reunites from over the brow on the left. The track leads through open woodland. Spot the old arched Rough How Bridge spanning Shoulthwaite Gill at the point where it becomes Naddle Beck. This is the original crossing point, truncated, and even its successor road has been sidelined by the wide A591. Here traffic speeds along with no sense of the former orientation of travel, as the path just followed was the old 'main road' to Keswick.

Cross the road and follow the lane to Shoulthwaite Farm, passing through by the camp site to enter Thirlmere Forest at a hand-gate. A path leads on, merging with a track from the right. This is now a well-graded track leading past Shoulthwaite Moss onto a minor road. Go right and first left with the signposted footpath, which leads via gates through the part-restored Smaithwaite farmyard. The path leads down by a fence to a footbridge over St John's Beck, and rises to meet the road at Bridge End Farm (camping site opposite).

Bridge End tea-room and camping barn

Lonscale Fell   Great Calva   Blencathra

Tewet Tarn   Threlkeld

Blencathra from High Rigg summit

8 The **eastern trail** (4.5km/2¾ miles) is part bridle path, part footpath, and while sheltered and shady it does have two notably appealing pluses – its fine view of Wanthwaite and Bram Crags, invariably bathed in afternoon sunlight, and the Low Bridgend tea-garden! The green track starts down immediately east of the church via a gate/stile. From there, navigation is an unnecessary fussiness – the paths just flow naturally as you walk upstream.

THE SUMMIT
A solitary cairn rests among the outcrop on a modest top, sufficient in area to give a party plenty of room to sit and consider the visual feast all round them! A large, shapely rock no doubt will take centre stage for photographic compositions.

SAFE DESCENTS
The main caution is that serious crags bound the fell to east and west. The palpable paths leading smartly down north-north-east to St John's Church and Youth Centre are without question the best options if in doubt or deteriorating weather. While the ridge path south has little to cause trepidation, it is nicer in foul conditions to trace the fell-foot trails. A particular incentive on the eastern trail is Low Bridgend tea-garden.

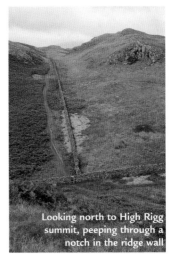

Looking north to High Rigg summit, peeping through a notch in the ridge wall

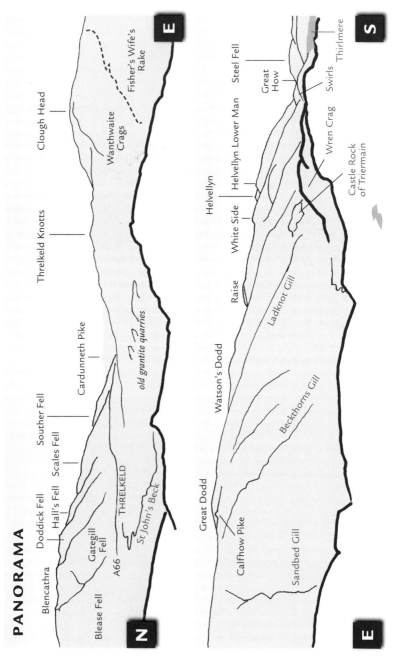

PANORAMA

N

Blencathra
Blease Fell
Doddick Fell
Hall's Fell
Gategill Fell
A66
THRELKELD
Scales Fell
Souther Fell
Cardunneth Pike
old granite quarries
St John's Beck
Threlkeld Knotts
Clough Head
Wanthwaite Crags
Fisher's Wife's Rake

E

E

Great Dodd
Calfhow Pike
Watson's Dodd
Sandbed Gill
Beckthorns Gill
Ladknot Gill
Raise
White Side
Helvellyn
Helvellyn Lower Man
Steel Fell
Great How
Swirls
Wren Crag
Castle Rock of Triermain
Thirlmere

S

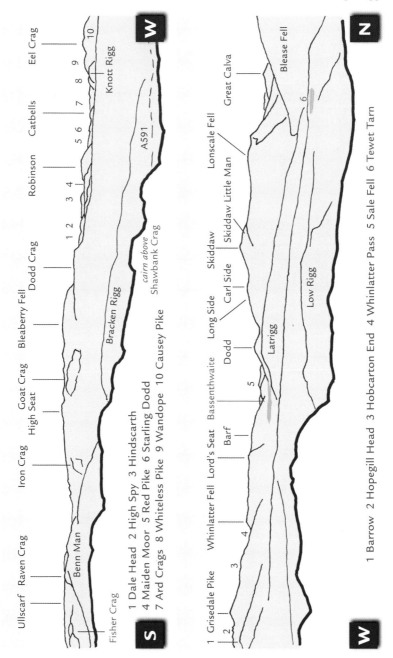

W

Eel Crag — Knott Rigg — 10 9 8 7 6 5 — Catbells — Robinson — 4 3 — 2 1 — Dodd Crag — Bleaberry Fell — Goat Crag — High Seat — Iron Crag — Raven Crag — Ullscarf — Benn Man — Fisher Crag

A591

cairn above Shawbank Crag

Bracken Rigg

S

1 Dale Head 2 High Spy 3 Hindscarth
4 Maiden Moor 5 Red Pike 6 Starling Dodd
7 Ard Crags 8 Whiteless Pike 9 Wandope 10 Causey Pike

N

Blease Fell — Great Calva — 6 — Lonscale Fell — Skiddaw Little Man — Skiddaw — Carl Side — Long Side — Dodd — 5 — Bassenthwaite — Barf — Lord's Seat — Whinlatter Fell — 4 — 3 — 2 — 1 Grisedale Pike

Low Rigg

Latrigg

W

1 Barrow 2 Hopegill Head 3 Hobcarton End 4 Whinlatter Pass 5 Sale Fell 6 Tewet Tarn

14 HIGH SEAT *(608m, 1995ft)*

The spine of the Central Fells dips from Ullscarf, switching north-east on Bell Crags, and runs its way due north, raising its head upon three summits – the middle one, the subject of this section, being the highest.

From a distance the fell-top does indeed look like a bench, so the 'seat' analogy is appropriate, a definite knoll perched above a general undulating marshiness. To the east of the ridge fence a cairned knoll bears the name 'Man', harking back to pre-Viking days, before the term 'Raise' was applied to significant cairns. While numerous summits are called 'high', that meant quite simply 'top pasture'. With impudence and distain, the eastern slopes drain into the Naddle valley via Shoulthwaite Gill, giving Thirlmere short shrift. The contrast between east and west could hardly be greater. The western slopes spread along the road all the way from Ashness Bridge to the hamlet of Watendlath, with Gowder and Reecastle Crags the main sporting outcrops. The lovely native woodland about

Ashness Bridge

Surprise View and Hogs Earth softens Watendlath Beck's break for freedom through the Lodore gorge.

Of all the ascents, that from Reecastle Crag is the most direct and least prone to wet ground. The more commonly followed ascent climbs from Ashness Bridge, the best of this journey being to the edge at Dodd, as the moor beyond is peaty indeed. The back route from Shoulthwaite is peaceful and an ideal out-of-the-way experience. Middlesteads Gill provides a novel quiet line too, with all the excitement confined to the gill and its minor arete, as the slopes thereafter are plain.

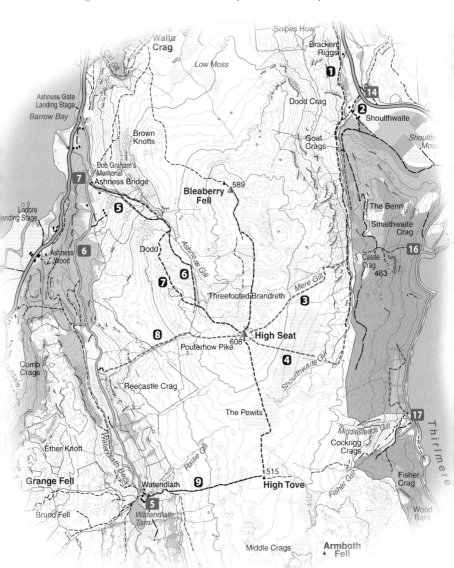

ASCENT FROM CAUSEWAY FOOT (13) OR ROUGH HOW BRIDGE (14)

Via Shoulthwaite Gill   457m/1500ft   3.5km/2¼ miles

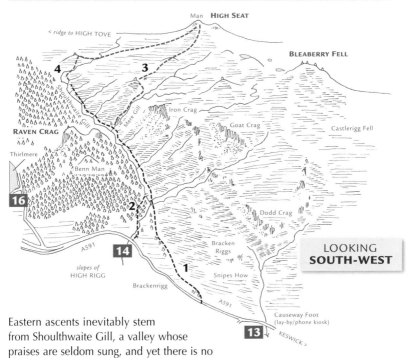

Man **HIGH SEAT**

< *ridge to* HIGH TOVE

BLEABERRY FELL

4   **3**

Iron Crag

Goat Crag

Castlerigg Fell

RAVEN CRAG

Thirlmere

Benn Man

16

2

Dodd Crag

A591   **14**

Bracken
Riggs

LOOKING
SOUTH-WEST

slopes of
HIGH RIGG

1

Snipes How

Brackenrigg

A591

Causeway Foot
(lay-by/phone kiosk)

13   KESWICK >

Eastern ascents inevitably stem from Shoulthwaite Gill, a valley whose praises are seldom sung, and yet there is no doubting its beauty, hemmed in between sheer cliffs and dense forest. The gill shakes off an unprepossessing start in life upon austere moorland at a peaty waste called The Pewits, and generates a special visual energy during this impressive passage towards the Naddle vale.

1 Follow the footpath from the ladder-stile off the main road south of Dale Bottom. This runs above Brackenrigg to a gate beside the footbridge and old weir. **2** This point can more efficiently be reached by starting from the Rough How Bridge lay-by and passing up the lane by Shoulthwaite Farm and on through the farmyard to a kissing-gate entering Thirlmere Forest.

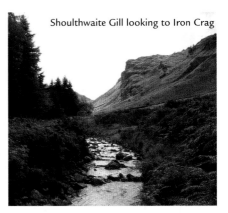

Shoulthwaite Gill looking to Iron Crag

Litt Memorial stones

Branch immediately half-right from the lower path, rising with a deer fence on the right to a forest track. Go right to where the track forks and bear right, exiting the forestry via the tall kissing-gate to cross the bridge. It is not unreasonable to consider following the forest track up to the Raven Crag and Castle Crag viewpoints, and either beating a way down from the duck-boarding to a ladder-stile directly beneath Castle Crag, or continuing to exit the forestry off the track near the head of the gorge. The preferred route keeps with the footpath running up the west side of the gill itself. The cliffs above are striking – note particularly the fall spilling from a high crag, then the bold profile of Iron Crag. Pass an old sheepfold close to where the route of Castle Crag is met, and soon afterwards encounter Mere Gill.

3 Ford and follow this impressive little ravine, climbing quite steeply west, with the minimum of inconvenience. As the gill opens, bear left to a cairned knoll, below which are located two slate slabs, like fairy gateposts. This is the Litt Memorial, a person of no known significance. One stone carries a fanciful poem telling of the gathering of the stone in Mere Gill, while the other has a brass disc inscribed 'In memory of J.Litt who died March 9, 1880'. There is nothing but a sheep trod pursuing the shallow ridge and, as far as possible, avoiding damp ground on the rise south-westward to the outcrop called Man.

4 Alternatively, continue with the gill-side path, which falters as it moves away from the proximity of the forest. This is just as well, as the upper reaches of Shoulthwaite Gill promise no more than peat and mire. So make a random right-hand move heading due east for the skyline fence and the summit.

ASCENT FROM ASHNESS BRIDGE (7)

Via Ashness Gill   442m/1450ft   3.2km/2 miles

Two routes depart from the Watendlath road – one the common way, the other far less so. Both benefit from good early stages, but the second gains commendation for having the driest line. The transition of Ashness Gill from its shy birth amid boggy heather moor is quite tumultuous, as it tumbles down a rocky defile, now as Barrow Beck, in full public gaze to slip under Ashness Bridge.

5 From Ashness Bridge (car park) a footpath climbs direct beside the wall via an early stile. As the wall gives way to a fence you can continue ahead, climbing to a kissing-gate in the intake wall and climbing on by a solitary roan to come level with the brink of an impressive waterfall.

Ashness Gill

LOOKING **EAST**

Alternatively, bear half-left to accompany Barrow Beck up to a hand-gate. The path rises through the bracken along the edge, overlooking the formidable dale head, to unite with the

Three-footed Brandreth boundary stone

Derwentwater from the head of Barrow Beck

main path. The more intrepid may fancy keeping even closer to the beck's bouldered course, though near the top the going gets tricky. The waterfall makes a worthy spot to pause and admire the broader scene, both gloriously back over Derwentwater and near at hand, peering down the upper cleft and across the cascading slab (see left) above. From this point the headwaters are called Ashness Gill and are tightly fenced to the north, conclusively denying access to Bleaberry Fell from this side.

6 The old path, less obvious and therefore less commonly trod, keeps strict company with the beck a little further, before drawing out onto the heather moor to pass to the left of a knoll crowned by a cairn. Continue, again quite near the gill, until an old wall is met. Keep close to the wall's foundations, which is useful where it traverses bog, to reach the point where the popular path crosses near the ridge top.

7 Alternatively, this place may be gained by climbing the newly pitched path leaving the environs of the waterfall, the path easing as it approaches the prominent cairn on the brink of the fell. (As is evidenced by a path some walkers, not aware of the craggy edge below, appear to have tried to descend directly – they must have rued their presumption!) The path is forced to meander by encounters with marsh as it follows on up the ridge to the wall crossing. Note the two cairned tops are bypassed to reach this point. The fell summit is clearly in view, but more marsh has to be rounded before the final rise to the old stone-built trig point.

High Seat from the path to Great Crag

LOOKING **EAST**

ASCENT FROM SURPRISE VIEW (6)

Via Reecastle Crag   350m/1150ft   3.5km/2¼ miles

8 Quite the most direct route to the summit is to be found taking a surreptitious line out of the Watendlath valley from the foot of the imposing Reecastle Crag ridge. Park either at Watendlath or Surprise View car parks. The popular road climbing into the hanging valley from Derwentwater, via Ashness Bridge, twists and turns through gorgeous woodland to emerge at a cattle grid. Ahead a succession of meadows grazed by cattle, sheep and ponies is flanked by rough fellsides. Those to the west are a tangle of trees and crags falling from Grange Fell, while to the east lies bracken-clad

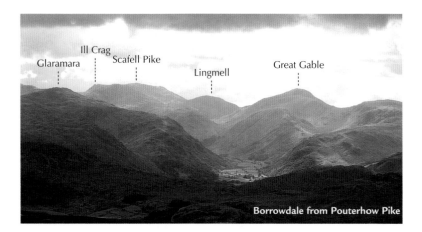

Borrowdale from Pouterhow Pike

From Dodd

Thwaite Bank. The road is unenclosed on this side. After passing
the Thwaite House (barn – useful
shelter in a downpour) the road
crosses Thwaitehouse Beck.
Rounding the next bend, short of
the cattle grid, find a short pull-
off where lazy rock climbers slot
their cars. You'll not need me to
point out that cars are like litter
in this setting, and anyone with
an ounce of sense will prefer to

Reecastle Crag backed by Heather Knott

park a mile distant at either of the two car parks hitherto mentioned.

The climbers' approach is the key to this ascent, and entails following a path that
rises with a gill to the marsh beneath Reecastle Crag. The crag forms a broad buttress
wall alternating damp and dry lines for the exclusive delight of the accomplished
rock gymnast. However, this is of no matter, for the route keeps left. Aim for the skyline dip between two outcrops. There is no path, but keep to the rough line of thorns,
en route passing a large fractured boulder.

At the top ignore the hand-gate in the enclosure wall. Bear left along the edge,
enjoying handsome views back over Reecastle Crag to Grange Fell. Pass an old
sheepfold and ford Thwaitehouse Gill to reach a ladder-stile in the intake wall. Go
half-right and ascend beside the gill and broken wall. Near the skyline, as the wall
curves left, slant right to crest the prominent outcrop. This is Pouterhow Pike, an

The summit from Man

excellent viewpoint (see below left). The summit is in view to the east-north-east, and the intervening ridge has but one small marsh and the occasional sheep path.

ASCENT FROM WATENDLATH (5)

Via High Tove   366m/1200ft   4km/2½ miles

9 From Watendlath, High Seat is within range, if not exactly within means. Follow the Armboth path onto High Tove, then follow the ridge fence north. It's easier said than done – bring back the pewits please, as a distraction from the mire!

THE SUMMIT

This was formerly open grazing, but unfortunately is now crossed by a fence, albeit periodically graced by stiles. One may consider the fence a blessing in mist to act as a guide, but in the main it would be deemed an eyesore, for all its practical stock-proofing intent. It partitions off the summit from the eastern knoll, called Man, the older British name (High Seat's earliest written record being 1569), which simply meant 'the stones'. The boss of rock that forms the summit is marked with a stone-built Ordnance Survey pillar. The science of surveying may have rendered it redundant, with triangulation a thing of the past, yet this well-made pillar lends a touch of order to the scene. And what a scene it is too, an unusually good all-round panorama sufficient to cause one to idle many minutes mentally ticking off the tops... while your mates plough on up through the bogs!

SAFE DESCENTS

All lines of ascent work in reverse, the quickest route to a useful road being Route 8 – going due W via Pouterhow Pike and slipping below Reecastle Crag.

RIDGE ROUTES

BLEABERRY FELL   ↓30m/100ft   ↑50m/160ft   2km/1¼ miles

In years gone by the normal practice was to follow the general line of the fence, but it has to be admitted that this is now less satisfactory, except in mist, as it encounters the worst of the marsh. A better option is to avoid crossing the fence, and instead dip off the north-west edge of the summit on a path that admittedly splodges through some pretty appalling peat to a stile at the head of Ashness Gill and below Threefooted Brandreth. Thereafter it winds north with varying degrees of peatiness, keeping left of a large pool to duly rise onto the dry summit ridge.

HIGH TOVE   ↓100m/330ft   ↑8m/25ft   1.6km/1 mile

Head S and cross the fence stile at the fence junction. Keeping to the E side of the fence all the way, though the path through The Pewits is a trial not a trail. Deep squidgy peat, invariably with the consistency of muck, turns the outing into an outrageous quest for a moment's firm footing. Where the fence turns some over-eager folk short-cut through yet more peat, the advantage is paltry, if not fowl! The heave-hove to High Tove ends on dry ground... what blessed relief.

High Seat summit pillar

PANORAMA

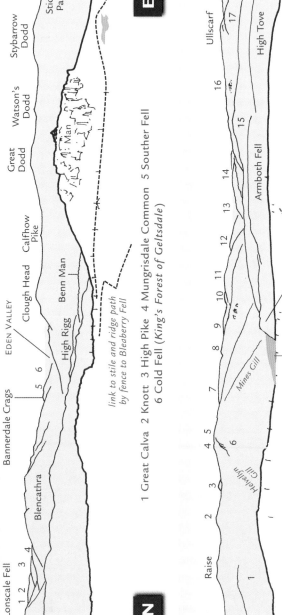

E

N

Lonscale Fell

1 2 3 4

Blencathra

Bannerdale Crags

EDEN VALLEY

Clough Head

Calfhow Pike

Great Dodd

Watson's Dodd

Stybarrow Dodd

Sticks Pass

High Rigg

Benn Man

:Man

5 6

link to stile and ridge path
by fence to Bleaberry Fell

1 Great Calva 2 Knott 3 High Pike 4 Mungrisdale Common 5 Souther Fell
6 Cold Fell (*King's Forest of Geltsdale*)

S

E

Raise

1

2

3

4 5

6

Helvellyn Gill

Mines Gill

7

8

9

10

11

12

13

14

15

16

17

Ullscarf

High Tove

Armboth Fell

Thirlmere

Fisher Crag

path to stile and ridge path to High Tove

1 Brown Crag 2 White Side 3 Catstycam 4 Helvellyn Lower Man 5 Helvellyn 6 Browncove Crags
7 Nethermost Pike 8 Dollywaggon Pike 9 Fairfield 10 Great Rigg 11 Seat Sandal 12 Heron Pike
13 Ward's Stone (*Bowland Fells*) 14 Steel Fell 15 Bell Crags 16 Standing Crag 17 Low Saddle

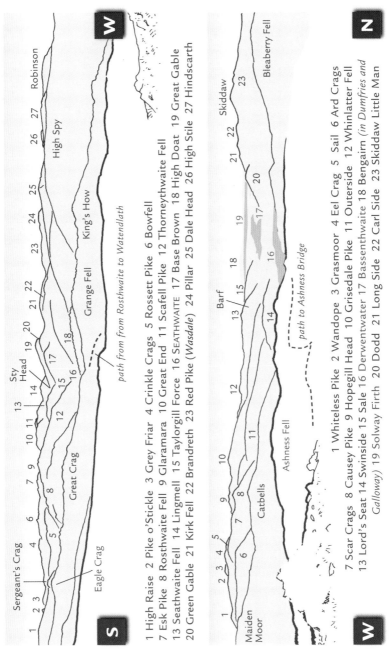

1 High Raise 2 Pike o'Stickle 3 Grey Friar 4 Crinkle Crags 5 Rossett Pike 6 Bowfell
7 Esk Pike 8 Rosthwaite Fell 9 Glaramara 10 Great End 11 Scafell Pike 12 Thorneythwaite Fell
13 Seathwaite Fell 14 Lingmell 15 Taylorgill Force 16 SEATHWAITE 17 Base Brown 18 High Doat 19 Great Gable
20 Green Gable 21 Kirk Fell 22 Brandreth 23 Red Pike (*Wasdale*) 24 Pillar 25 Dale Head 26 High Stile 27 Hindscarth

1 Whiteless Pike 2 Wandope 3 Grasmoor 4 Eel Crag 5 Sail 6 Ard Crags
7 Scar Crags 8 Causey Pike 9 Hopegill Head 10 Grisedale Pike 11 Outerside 12 Whinlatter Fell
13 Lord's Seat 14 Swinside 15 Sale 16 Derwentwater 17 Bassenthwaite 18 Bengairn (*in Dumfries and*
Galloway) 19 Solway Firth 20 Dodd 21 Long Side 22 Carl Side 23 Skiddaw Little Man

15 HIGH TOVE (515m, 1690ft)

The age-old cross-ridge footpath that linked Armboth Hall, beside Leathes Water (now lost under the lapping waters of Thirlmere), and the hamlet of Watendlath contradicted convention. Instead of seeking a low point in the ridge, it slipped precisely over the summit of High Tove. The reasoning, eminently sane on this otherwise soggy trail, is that it is high and dry. There are moments when webbed feet would be a distinct advantage – the Watendlath ducks would be in their element! The tough tussocks of heather and rush must always have been taxing to the stride – hence the fell-name Tove, a variant of 'tuft', descriptive of those very clumps of rushes.

To north and south the ridge's easy gradients should give cause for a little questioning. Journeys to either Bell Crags or High Seat look nothing on the map, but there is dismay awaiting the ill prepared. Good gaiters are a basic necessity, particularly at the worse of 'the sponge', encountered at the hollow called The Pewits, at the source of Shoulthwaite and Raise Gills, which is more than a match for any Pennine peat bog! A period of drought or intense frost is a distinct advantage for any degree of comfort. A 'pewit' is another name for the green plover or lapwing, one of the most enchanting of native British birds, and the name mimics the bird's distinctive 'peewit' call. Water from the fell initially flows without due haste, then smartly spills into both Thirlmere and into the exquisitely shy, but far from secret, Watendlath Tarn... everyone's quintessential idea of a Lakeland tarn.

ASCENT FROM ARMBOTH (17)

Direct   350m/1150ft   1.5km/1 mile

The creation of the reservoir and, in particular, the planting of forestry inevitably affected the early course of this old path. Evidence of its route survives where it rises as a forest track, beginning a short distance south of the entrance to the Armboth car park. It effectively climbs on the north side of Fisher Gill, though the higher section now runs through a young plantation, and for all that high ladder-stiles have been inserted, this is most definitely not a recommended line of approach.

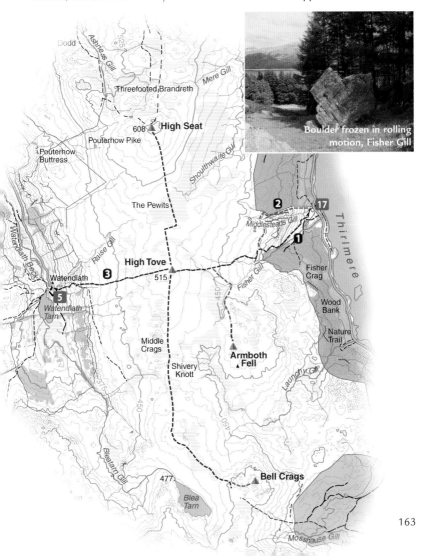

Boulder frozen in rolling motion, Fisher Gill

1 Leave the car park and turn right to the hand-gate, with footpath sign 'Watendlath', at the first bend in the road. There are two lines of ascent from this point. The made-way passes over the little bridge spanning Middlesteads Gill and continues to a hand-gate, then rises through the hurdle sheepfold on a green trail. As the forestry wall comes near, pass a distinctive group of large boulders, after which the wall is replaced by a fence partitioning the path from Fisher Gill. As the slope

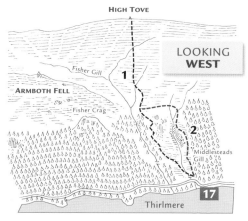

steepens below Cockrigg Crags, the name a reference to 'the courtship ground of black cock', the path makes exaggerated zig-zags and passes under a sycamore tree with some juniper evident, and rises to a wall-gap at the top of the forestry.

Via Middlesteads Gill   2km/1¼ miles

2 This point can be reached with more interest – and effort – from the hand-gate off the road by ascending by the right-hand forest fence, which is steep and has no path. As the slope scoops, angle half-left onto the arete overlooking the impressively deep Middlesteads Gill ravine, with natural tree growth enhancing the view to Fisher Crag

High Tove from Green Comb, Great Crag

Middle Crags on the ridge path to Bell Crags

Looking down on Watendlath from the bridle path

(see this view in the ARMBOTH FELL chapter, page 22) and across Thirlmere to Helvellyn. Keep to the rim of the gill, and eventually angle right to slip round the right-hand end of the fell-bounding wall where it all but abuts the forest fence. Go left, keeping this wall to the left, to reach the gap mentioned earlier. Now follow the well-defined path leading west. Avoid fording the tributary gill as bracken is entered, and keep uphill to ford a little higher. The path becomes far less certain and contrives to deliver damp ground underfoot as it nears the top, even in dry weather, though it offers nothing to match the bogginess of The Pewits. The summit cairn is your skyline target.

ASCENT FROM WATENDLATH (5)

Direct   265m/870ft   1.5km/1 mile

3 Start from the National Trust car park, crossing the ladder-stile, or go right from the point of entry and by either means reach a gate. The way-marked footpath fords Raise Beck, and soon commences the zig-zag ascent of the steep bank, grooved by centuries-old sled trails used to convey peat from High Tove for domestic heating. The path is in a well-repaired state and rises onto the pasture beyond the wall corner. Where the old bridle path meets the brow, the Harrop Tarn path departs right. Continue up the easier ground due east. The occasional cairn reflects the idle boredom of pedestrians, rather than navigational need, though in mist the lack of landmarks lends them a certain credibility. There are worn sections higher up – watch

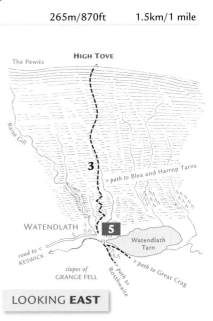

for sly holes, as the author managed to 'lose' a leg down one, thus providing a moment of surprise and jocularity on an otherwise dead-beat journey to the hand-gate in the ridge fence.

THE SUMMIT

A solitary cairn (see opposite) rests on the eastern edge of the summit as a skyline marker and a sure guide for wayfarers traversing the ridge east to west. The hand-gate in the fence some 50m further west rests on slightly higher ground. The view is remarkably good for all the modesty of the setting – westward the array of tops will keep you amused for several minutes, though the stronger horizon is east from Blencathra through Helvellyn to Heron Pike. Catstycam makes a cheeky appearance

High Tove summit cairn

over the saddle south of White Side, in much the same way as Raven Crag and Castle Rock of Triermain raise their respective heads further north above the thoroughly hidden Thirlmere. In fact, the only named water in view is the Solway Firth, which sneaks into shot over the left shoulder of High Seat.

SAFE DESCENTS
Compass bearings due east for the Armboth road and, better, due west for habitation at Watendlath are the only sane options. All else is ankle-twisting, bewildering misery in mist.

RIDGE ROUTES

ARMBOTH FELL	↓75m/250ft	↑45m/150ft	1.3km/1¾ mile

Dismiss all thoughts of a bee-line. The heather is cruelly rank, and the hollow at the source of Fisher and Launchy Gills is on a par with that at The Pewits, which IS saying something! Follow the eastward course of the traversing footpath, bearing southeast after the first hint of a gill to meet, ford and follow upstream Fisher Gill, then bearing half-left to the prominent summit outcrop.

BELL CRAGS	↓10m/30ft	↑50m/160ft	3.2km/2 miles

The ridge fence south provides the guide, but there are too many marshy moments to call this a joyous escapade.

HIGH SEAT	↓8m/25ft	↑100m/330ft	1.6km/1 mile

Again the fence does the navigation for you, but a religious faith in an ultimate salvation would provide useful personal strength through The Pewits!

PANORAMA

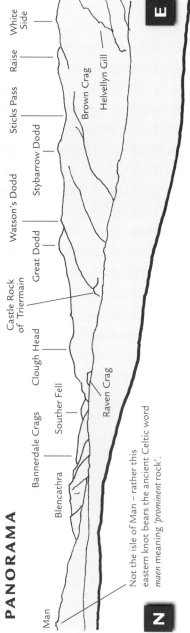

White Side
Raise
Sticks Pass
Watson's Dodd
Great Dodd
Castle Rock of Triermain
Clough Head
Bannerdale Crags
Souther Fell
Blencathra
Man

Brown Crag
Helvellyn Gill
Stybarrow Dodd
Raven Crag

E

N

Not the isle of Man – rather this eastern knot bears the ancient Celtic word *maen* meaning *'prominent rock'*.

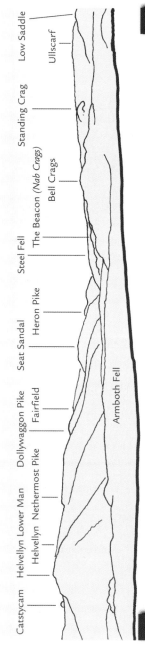

Low Saddle
Ullscarf
Standing Crag
Steel Fell
The Beacon (*Nab Crags*)
Bell Crags
Seat Sandal
Heron Pike
Dollywaggon Pike
Fairfield
Helvellyn Lower Man
Helvellyn Nethermost Pike
Catstycam
Armboth Fell

S

E

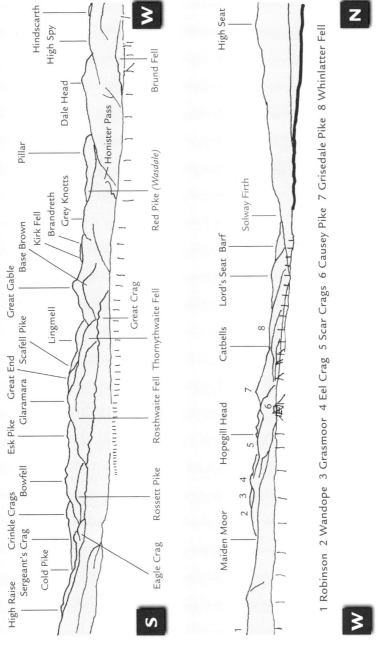

Hindscarth
High Spy
Dale Head
Brund Fell
Honister Pass
Pillar
Kirk Fell
Base Brown
Brandreth
Grey Knotts
Red Pike (*Wasdale*)
Great Gable
Lingmell
Great Crag
Scafell Pike
Great End
Esk Pike
Glaramara
Rosthwaite Fell
Thornythwaite Fell
Crinkle Crags
Bowfell
Sergeant's Crag
Cold Pike
High Raise
Rossett Pike
Eagle Crag

S

W

High Seat
Solway Firth
Lord's Seat
Barf
Catbells
Hopegill Head
Maiden Moor

8
7
6
5
2 3 4
1

N

W

1 Robinson 2 Wandope 3 Grasmoor 4 Eel Crag 5 Scar Crags 6 Causey Pike 7 Grisedale Pike 8 Whinlatter Fell

16 LOFT CRAG *(692m, 2270ft) (estimated height)*

To rock climbers this is the ultimate point of Gimmer Crag, a loft in the attic of a famous and much revered cliff. To fellwalkers it is the central component of the trinity of peaks, along with Harrison Stickle and Pike o'Stickle, collectively known as the Langdale Pikes. Its underling top, Thorn Crag, cramping the top ravine of Dungeon Ghyll, cannot properly be called a pike, though many find it difficult to exclude Pavey Ark from any expression of the ensemble.

A long facade of crags and scree forms an impressive wall above Mickleden between Dungeon Ghyll and Troughton Beck, supremely judged during an ascent of The Band. However, in isolation the best view of the fell is from Pike o'Stickle. From this location tiers of rock spill impressively down its southern flank towards Mickleden, backed by Lingmoor Fell and the distant Windermere.

One cannot know the fell by allegiance to the ridge-top alone, so a spot of exploration is called for. Follow the climbers' traverse off the Mark Gate path to admire Gimmer Crag from below. Then, with a modicum of effort, clamber up beside the easternmost gully and venture onto the tiny col where Junipal (the most striking feature in the view above) and South-eastern Gullies converge. It will come as no surprise to learn that this is the most thrilling spot to admire Pike o'Stickle. The fell has a short northern slope, craggy at first, then descending to the marshy hollow of Harrison Combe.

ASCENT FROM GREAT LANGDALE (32–33)

Via Mark Gate 600m/1970ft 2.5km/1½ miles

Routes spring from either of the two Dungeon Ghyll Hotels. The most secure path, known as Mark Gate, has received a tremendous amount of sturdy structuring – sufficient pitching and paving to lead one to believe one is climbing a castle rampart rather than a wild fell.

Middlefell Buttress Raven Crag
Old Dungeon Ghyll Hotel

1 Start from either of the pay and display car parks and walk up behind the New Dungeon Ghyll Hotel. Keep left in rising to a hand-gate, go right past the seat and clamber over the stile. Turn left, dipping to ford Dungeon Ghyll. Now that you are properly upon Mark Gate, respect those sections shut off to nurture turf recovery. As the path veers from the wall one may slip into the ravine to squint into the dark recesses of Dungeon Ghyll Force – there is no way through at this point. Backtrack and follow the path winding uphill. At the next relaxation in the ravine, directly upstream of the 'dungeon' section, one may either keep with Mark Gate or take the opportunity to enter the ravine proper. Mark Gate is the unambiguous high way to the top, winding steeply above the lower tier of buttresses and pell-mell of outcrops

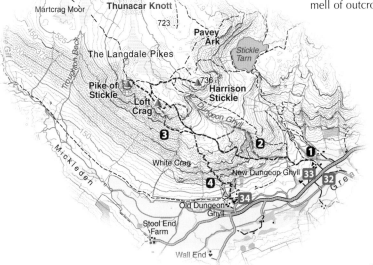

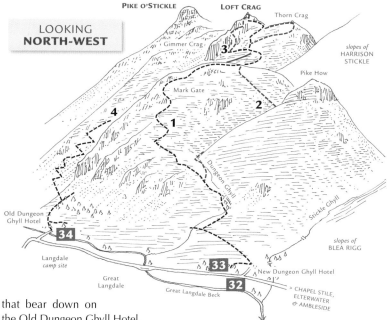

that bear down on
the Old Dungeon Ghyll Hotel.

2 The middle section of Dungeon Ghyll runs so
deep into the breast of the Pikes that one feels one is venturing beyond the limits of
reason to end in some hidden kingdom of doom – so do not enter unless you are
confident in such surroundings. Cautiously enter, and beware of the tree roots as you

Gimmer Crag from Mickleden

Loft Crag from Thunacar Knott

do. Scramble over the mid-gill rocks to follow the right bank up to the first mare's-tail waterfall. Scramble dexterously up the right-hand outcrop. The scenery is superb. Keep to the right bank until forced onto the left side, then climb up through the large boulders to reach the baulking upper fall. A thunderous scene awaits: water crashing into a pool before finally spilling to the gill floor. The exit is the unlikely looking gully to the left, and a sinister but safe scramble leads onto the open fell pasture to join Mark Gate – and so is vanquished the kingdom of doom!

Mark Gate duly arrives on this moor and advances west-north-west to a sheepfold and cairn, where outcrops resume. This is a significant point. From this point on the slope steepens once more, bringing further paving either leading directly onto the saddle overlooking Harrison Combe or, rounding the first outcrop, bearing up right onto Thorn Crag. On a faint path, pass the cairn with its fine view of Harrison Crag across the gulf of the upper gorge of Dungeon Ghyll. The paths reunite, and you contour, then bear up left, on a loose, stony-bedded path to access the summit.

3 From the cairn the climbers' traverse to the famous buttresses of Gimmer Crag may be pursued. While confident climbers may tackle the South-eastern Gully, those less adept

Chockstone exit of the east gully

173

Pike o'Stickle from the top of Junipal Gully

Looking down the South-east Gully

should divert earlier off the path and aim up to the much shorter easternmost gully. Even this has a 3m chockstone 'bad step', side-stepped up easily handled rocks on the right-hand side. Once above one may simply follow the grassy ledge above the North-western Gully to join the ridge west of the summit, or take the opportunity to visit the thrilling col at the top of Gimmer Crag. (The crag-name derives from the term for a 'ewe-lamb between its first and second shearing'.) Look for, then follow, the short, tilted rock-and-grass rake to the left, switching precisely at its top. Zig-zag through the early outcrop and contour along a ledge on the right to arrive at the tiny col immediately above the plummeting Junipal Gully. From here Pike o'Stickle seems to soar! Looking back up the fellside, a solid mass of banded rock suggests you are crag-bound, and you would be... but for the knowledge of your approach! Before you retreat, gaze behind you down South-eastern Gully.

ASCENT FROM OLD DUNGEON GHYLL (34)

Direct   2.5km/1½ miles

4 From the Old Dungeon Ghyll car park follow the path up behind the hotel, via a gate. Cross directly over the bridle way to the ladder-stile. Winding up the light plantation,

Top of Dungeon Ghyll

Western aspect of Loft Crag

Harrison Stickle from the summit cairn

bear left just as the flight of steps begins – these are for the express use of rock climbers accessing Middlefell Buttress and Raven Crag. Ford the tiny gill to reach a stile in the fence at the top of the wall. The path, never in doubt, tackles the scree slope, and progressively firmer footing is found through the mild outcrops and light bracken as it climbs to an obvious fork. The climbers' path, rather oddly, chooses to follow the initially inviting ledge path on the left. The path falls foul of steep ground as a gill re-entrant is neared, causing it to climb steeply before slanting left beneath the upper fall, angling up towards Gimmer. The immeasurably better route is straight up, being an easy grassy slope directly to the cairn, where the climbers' traverse leaves Mark Gate.

THE SUMMIT
The ideal summit in many respects – quite small, yet with ample room for a party to sit and drool over the view. Great Langdale is especially prominent, with Mickleden far below, and Bowfell forming the dark majestic backdrop. Ahh, the stuff of fellwalking dreams… don't you just love it?

SAFE DESCENTS
For all the ferocity of tiered crags directly beneath one's feet the walker has a sure recourse in Mark Gate. Leave the summit on the path heading south-east. Bear left down the stony trail, and note that at the foot of this short ramp the stones at their loosest. Join the contouring path below the northern slope of the summit. Go right, and the evident cairned path soon begins its newly paved descent – destination the New Dungeon Ghyll.

RIDGE ROUTES

HARRISON STICKLE	↓60m/200ft	↑105m/345ft	0.4km/¼ mile

To split hairs, this is not strictly a ridge route – rather these are two summits with a natural harmony. You climb one… you want to climb the other! Go north-west off the summit ridge to join the worn trail from Pike o'Stickle, then go right to cross the large boulders in the peaty hollow of Harrison Combe, and two paths lead to the summit. The direct route encounters an easy rock step, whilst the left-hand route sweeps up and round to approach from the north-west over easy ground every step of the way.

PIKE O'STICKLE ↓25m/80ft ↑60m/200ft 0.4km/¼ mile

Leave the summit to the north-west, following the undulating ridge to the top of South Scree. From here there are at least four lines of scrambly ascent up the massive summit cone – how many can you discover?

Wetherlam

Blake Rigg

The west face of Gimmer Crag

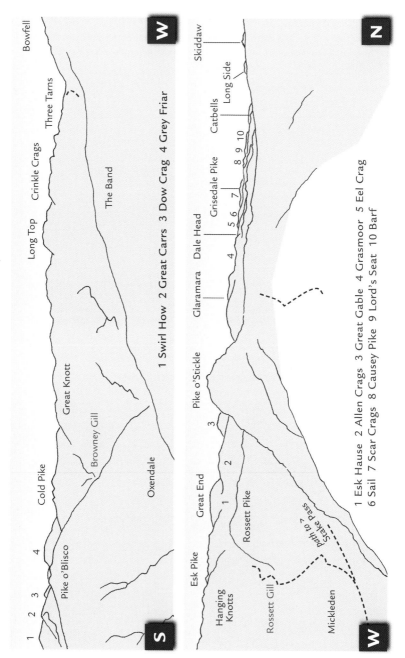

Top panel (W/S):

Bowfell

Three Tarns

Crinkle Crags

Long Top

The Band

Cold Pike

Great Knott

Browney Gill

Oxendale

Pike o'Blisco

1 Swirl How 2 Great Carrs 3 Dow Crag 4 Grey Friar

1 2 3 4

Bottom panel (N/W):

Skiddaw

Long Side

Catbells

8 9 10

Grisedale Pike

5 6 7

Dale Head

4

Glaramara

Pike o'Stickle

3

Great End

2

1

Rossett Pike

Esk Pike

Hanging Knotts

Rossett Gill

Path to Stake Pass

Mickleden

1 Esk Hause 2 Allen Crags 3 Great Gable 4 Grasmoor 5 Eel Crag 6 Sail 7 Scar Crags 8 Causey Pike 9 Lord's Seat 10 Barf

PANORAMA

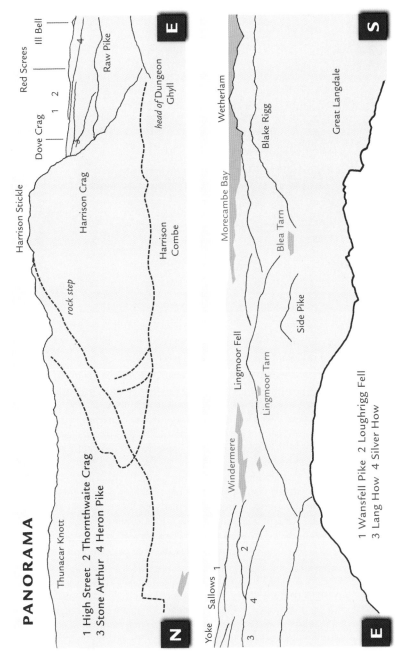

N

Thunacar Knott

Harrison Stickle

rock step

Harrison Crag

Dove Crag

Red Screes

Ill Bell

Raw Pike

head of Dungeon Ghyll

Harrison Combe

E

1 High Street 2 Thornthwaite Crag
3 Stone Arthur 4 Heron Pike

S

Wetherlam

Morecambe Bay

Blake Rigg

Blea Tarn

Great Langdale

Lingmoor Fell

Side Pike

Windermere

Lingmoor Tarn

Yoke

Sallows

E

1 Wansfell Pike 2 Loughrigg Fell
3 Lang How 4 Silver How

17 LOUGHRIGG FELL *(335m, 1099ft)*

At the point where the rivers Rothay and Brathay meet to flow into Windermere, the Central Fells are born in the irregular form of Loughrigg Fell. The fell climbs above Clappersgate and the site of Galava Roman fort and rises onto Todd Crag, a lowly but strategic viewpoint for the great lake. It trends north-westward, a gently undulating mass of bracken-clad fell and pasture, including the former site of Ambleside golf course, then a further ridge rises from the vicinity of Rydal village and runs south-westward over Lanty Scar. The two ridges converge at a damp amphitheatre beset with bracken before mounting more confidently over Ivy Crag to the triple-top summit.

The fell-name means 'ridge above the lake', and the lake in question, Loughrigg Tarn, is sweetly cradled in a bowl of trees and green pastures on the southern flank. (Curiosity is aroused by the term 'lough', absent elsewhere in Lakeland – might it betray an ancient Irish cultural connection?) From the vicinity of the tarn the fell appears compact and characterful, but other aspects are less convincing, apart from the neat backdrop profile in views across Grasmere.

Well endowed with paths at every level the fell is a parade for all manner of walks and walkers. By Rydal Water and Grasmere the fell provides a near perfect expression of the picturesque in the promenade of Loughrigg Terrace. The higher portions of the fell have wilder ground, harbouring pools and undulations, where, were it not for the bracken, one might wander at will enjoying the exceptionally

Rydal Water

lovely outlooks. The fell also has one great work of audacious quarrying, Loughrigg Cavern (sometimes called Rydal Cave) above Rydal Water. For anyone nervous of caves and dark places, here is a dank, eerie hollow you can stroll into with the minimum of claustrophobia and sense of chill, though a recent rock-fall has resulted in cautionary notices being posted.

As the map shows and the diagrams endeavour to simplify, there is a cobweb of paths deviating hither and thither all over the fell. In the service of this guide I have traced them all, and they offer the explorer the chance to lose themselves on the fell for an hour or two!

ASCENT FROM AMBLESIDE (28) OR CLAPPERSGATE

Direct	270m/890ft	3.2km/2 miles
Via Todd Crag	277m/910ft	3.7km/2¼ miles

Ambleside, for all the congregation of casual visitors, has got rich pickings beyond the shops, cafés and sundry innocent diversions of the pocket and flesh. Fells rise in such a way that the fellwalker may quickly escape to loftier thoughts and scenes. Loughrigg is pronounced 'luff-rigg', and it is also usual to drop the 'Fell' in conversation. By comparison with many a neighbour, such as Red Screes or Wansfell Pike even, this may be a lowly fell, but it has so many paths that encounters with fellow walkers are relatively infrequent. From the town, Todd Crag is the first fell-top port of call – certainly a high point in terms of its superb position at the head of Windermere.

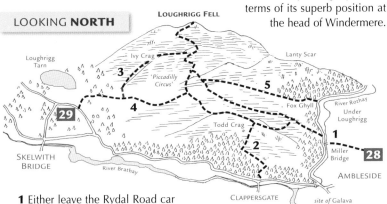

1 Either leave the Rydal Road car park to the left, following the footway and turn left into Stoney Lane (cul-de-sac), which leads onto a path direct to Miller Bridge; or (to get to this point from Zeffirelli's pizzeria and cinema) follow Vicarage Road, signed 'Rothay Park, Loughrigg', which leads between the spired parish church of St Mary's and the primary school to a gate into the park, where you continue via the open metalled path. Cross Miller Bridge and turn right, then take the metalled lane rising left signed to 'Browhead and Pinerigg'. One may follow the road and subsequent track via gates above Pinerigg through the old golf course, as the direct route for the fell proper. However, Todd Crag should not be lightly dismissed. A footpath is signed 'Clappersgate' at the first bend above Browhead up the wall steps. Follow this, and pass through a wood to a squeeze-stile, then ascend, keeping left to pass a

Miller Bridge

Windermere from Todd Crag

large cairn – a viewpoint for Ambleside. Advance to a ladder-stile and then onto the prominent top; the second top is the main Todd Crag viewpoint.

2 This top can also be reached from Clappersgate. A footpath signed from the main road leads up a narrow walled path to a gate then winds up by the 'Sid Cross Memorial Seat', dedicated to the former landlord of the Old Dungeon Ghyll and much-loved doyen of Langdale climbing society who died in 1998 at the age of 85. The plaque reads 'A true Westmerian who loved his Langdale' – how ironic that the seat predominantly overlooks the soft wooded hills of old Lancashire's Furness!

The ridge walk by Lily Tarn is a very pleasing stroll that leads via a hand-gate in the cross-ridge fence where the enclosure walls bottleneck. Either cross the next knoll or skirt to the left to reach a 'Piccadilly Circus' of pathways. Cross the bridle path from Pinerigg to Tarn Foot en route to the main body of the fell. Climb from the bracken-beset hollow, appropriately known as Black Mire, onto the ridge, and a left-hand spur leads to the Ivy Crag viewpoint.

Black Mire

ASCENT FROM TARN FOOT (29)

Via Ivy Crag   235m/770ft   2.2km/1½ miles

A popular route onto the fell begins from the vicinity of the Tarn Foot camp site, close to Loughrigg Tarn. A small car park at GR345039 provides a useful start point up the lane under Little Loughrigg from Skelwith Bridge. **3** Follow the bridle lane from Tarn Foot Cottage via two gates leading east. After the second gate with slate sign 'Ambleside' go just 100m, and with a walled-up gate visible on the right branch

Great Langdale from below Ivy Crag

up left through the bracken. Soon you are climbing steeply, with a wall to the left and the Ivy Crag ridge above on the right, up the ridge path. Turn left to reach the summit, via a lateral trough hollow. **4** Or, more simply, keep along the track to the 'Piccadilly Circus' of paths and streams. Bear left onto the ridge, as with the route off Todd Crag. **5** From the Under Loughrigg road a footpath is signposted south-west, behind Fox Ghyll (house), and runs up beside the gill itself to reach the aforementioned path interchange.

Loughrigg Tarn from Ivy Crag

ASCENT FROM PELTER BRIDGE, RYDAL (27)

Via Fox Ghyll, Lanty Scar or Loughrigg Cavern   275m/900ft   3.2km/2 miles

Quite the majority of casual walkers stroll from White Moss GR350065, where lovely paths lead to Loughrigg Terrace, Loughrigg Cavern and the gentle wood-fringed delights of both Rydal Water and Grasmere. It is a mercy that the tree canopy dulls the traffic noise. Redbank Road offers access to Grasmere lake shore, woods and direct climbs to the summit. However, the more complete and intimate approaches

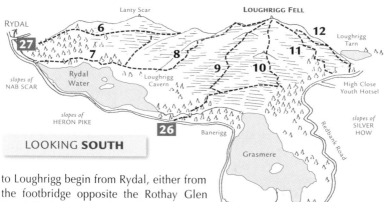

LOOKING **SOUTH**

to Loughrigg begin from Rydal, either from the footbridge opposite the Rothay Glen Hotel (Badger Bar), or from the small Pelter Bridge car park at GR366059. The back road going west from the car park leads by Steps End into a bridle lane, the quarry extraction track for Loughrigg Cavern, and paths lead on beyond the Cavern to Loughrigg Terrace or down by the shore of Rydal Water.

6 Take the footpath signposted left after the entrance to Cote How and before the pair of cottages. Ascend the bank to a gate, now with a wall on the right and handsome views to Nab Scar and the Rydal Beck valley. In high summer the bracken is commensurately high too, but a path exists that runs on by a hand-gate and, when the wall ends, traverses the damp slope to join a path now heading south. A spur path on the left gains the cairn on top of Lanty Scar (Lanty being a pet-name derived from 'Lancelot'). Continue south over a saddle to reach the 'Piccadilly Circus' path interchange, and go right, climbing above Black Mire onto the ridge proper bound for the summit.

Cairn on Lanty Scar

7 Take the lane beyond Steps End and, short of the cavern, ascend the valley to link up with Route 6 where it traverses from the wall end, before the Lanty Scar spur. **8** On reaching Loughrigg Cavern, admire the gaping mouth; a recent rock-fall has sadly brought a discouraging notice cautioning entry via the stepping stones. Now head up the bank from the left-hand (east) side of the cave entrance. A path winds up the edge of the ridge

Loughrigg Cavern

to become less that certain as damp hollows are encountered. Either keep south to eventually join up with the main path from Black Mire, or be intrepid and find your own way westward, through the confusion of irregular and fragmented paths that will take you to the top.

ASCENT FROM WHITE MOSS (26)

Via Loughrigg Terrace   274m/900ft   2km/1¼ miles

9 From White Moss car park follow the compacted path to the footbridge. Paths on either side lead upstream to Grasmere lake shore and ultimately to Redbank Road. Cross the bridge and head up into the wood ahead, reaching a hand-gate. Go right and embark upon Loughrigg's most treasured possession, the Terrace – not a row of

Nab Scar from the ridge above Loughrigg Cavern

Grasmere from the Grasmere cairn

industrial housing, but a wonderful path traversing the fellside. Seats en route allow for a prolonged admiration of a stunning composition, with Grasmere seen as a great lake in a bowl of fine fells.

10 Short of the gate into woodland, join the staircase path on the left; much effort has been employed to give durability to this popular climb. Mount to a ragged cairn, often called the 'Grasmere cairn' for its the prime viewpoint qualities, and continue to the summit knoll set back from the brink. This route can be reached from the Redbank Road. Unavoidably, approaches from the village of Grasmere are obliged to follow this narrow, windy road, and cars become the hazard for walkers in summer months. A permissive path dips off the road to the left from a hand-gate and steps just beyond Lea Cottage. This leads down to the lake shore then wends delightfully through to open woodland. One may switch back right, up to the lodge, and there switch again to the left in front of the lodge on the cobbled track (avoiding the road altogether). Still within the wood, rise to a gate into a lane, go the few paces left to the gate, and from directly onto Loughrigg Terrace and the flight of steps to the top. There are two further lines of ascent, paths less travelled but equally efficacious.

ASCENT FROM HIGH CLOSE (31)

Via the west ridge or Intake Wood   174m/570ft   0.8km/½ mile

11 South of the road fork, at the top of Redbank Road, opposite the High Close Arboretum at GR341053, a path leaves the road (no sign) and winds up an open section of slope to a hand-gate. Continue up, eventually with the wall to the right, then

Boathouse at the foot of Rydal Water

go onto the open fell-side, climbing to join the main north-west path to the top. **12** Further south down the minor road, a footpath is signed at a stile beside a cottage. This contours through coniferous woodland via stiles to a cairn short of a gate. Bear immediately left climbing with a gill, and continue direct to the top.

CIRCULAR TOUR (27)

from Pelter Bridge, Rydal   8km/5 miles

As a special treat, walkers may forget the summit altogether and entertain a circular tour, a useful option when the fell-top is enveloped in cloud. Starting from the Pelter Bridge car park, walk south along the Under Loughrigg road and branch off right, following the path via hand-gates and entering Fox Ghyll. Join the bridle path from Ambleside crossing under Ivy Crag, with Great Langdale displayed ahead. Descend to Tarn Foot Cottage and go right, through the gate, onto the fenced drive above Loughrigg Tarn. Either follow the path off right after the The How or continue directly to the road. Rise to Redbank top road junction, taking the path in an avenue, signed right, leading down to Loughrigg Terrace. Keep right to visit either Loughrigg Cavern, or the Rydal Water shore en route to Pelter Bridge. This is a grand tour with remarkably little ascent.

THE SUMMIT
A fine stone-built Ordnance Survey column takes pride of place on a rock plinth. Two other contesting tops to the north-east and south fail to claim summit status by a matter of a few feet. The view makes this a place of special attraction, and the panorama in this guide will help you identify the surrounding fells.

SAFE DESCENTS

There is craggy ground due south from the summit and much muddled cropping out elsewhere. The advice is to stick to the worn paths; they are reliable. The nearest road is due west. For Grasmere, White Moss and Rydal follow the north-western path down to the west end of Loughrigg Terrace. For Ambleside the journey is

Loughrigg summit pillar looking north

that much longer – heading south-east along the ridge, the path dips beyond Ivy Crag to join the bridleway east, via Pinerigg.

RIDGE ROUTE

SILVER HOW	↓230m/750ft	↑290m/950ft	4km/2½ miles

Follow the north-west path down to the east end of Loughrigg Terrace. Go left through the gate, keep right at the first fork and soon join the Redbank Road. Go right, and first left at the footpath sign, but go up the three immediate steps onto a footpath that curves left into the Huntingstile Gap, via a hand-gate. Join the ridge path proper climbing onto Dow Bank. Follow the switch-back course over Spedding Crag until a more significant step in the ridge occurs. Take the rising line by a large cairn, angling right for the scarp-top summit.

Fairfield Horseshoe from Todd Crag

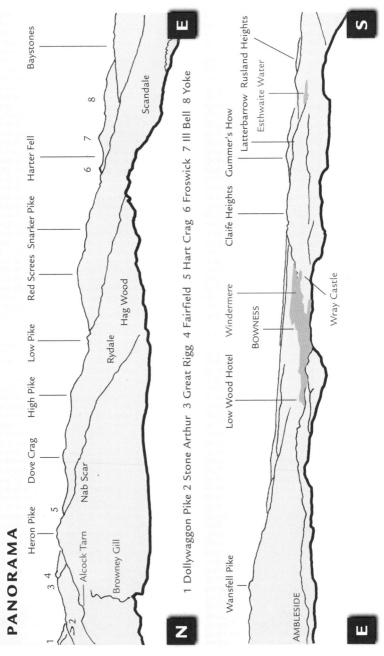

PANORAMA

Baystones

Scandale

8

Harter Fell

7

6

Snarker Pike

Red Screws

Hag Wood

Low Pike

Rydale

High Pike

Dove Crag

Nab Scar

Heron Pike

5

Alcock Tarn

Browney Gill

3 4

2

1

E

N

1 Dollywaggon Pike 2 Stone Arthur 3 Great Rigg 4 Fairfield 5 Hart Crag 6 Froswick 7 Ill Bell 8 Yoke

Rusland Heights

Latterbarrow

Esthwaite Water

Gummer's How

Claife Heights

Windermere

BOWNESS

Wray Castle

Low Wood Hotel

Wansfell Pike

AMBLESIDE

S

E

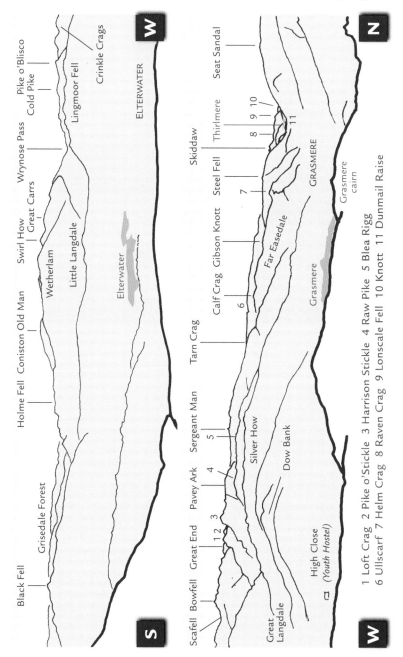

W

N

S

W

Crinkle Crags

Pike o'Blisco
Cold Pike

Wrynose Pass

Swirl How
Great Carrs

Coniston Old Man

Holme Fell

Black Fell

Lingmoor Fell

ELTERWATER

Little Langdale

Wetherlam

Elterwater

Grisedale Forest

Seat Sandal

Skiddaw

Thirlmere

9 10

Steel Fell

8

11

7

GRASMERE

Calf Crag Gibson Knott

Tarn Crag

Far Easedale

6

Grasmere cairn

Grasmere

Sergeant Man

Pavey Ark

5

4

3

Silver How

Dow Bank

1 2

Great End

Bowfell

Scafell

High Close
(Youth Hostel)

Great Langdale

1 Loft Crag 2 Pike o'Stickle 3 Harrison Stickle 4 Raw Pike 5 Blea Rigg
6 Ullscarf 7 Helm Crag 8 Raven Crag 9 Lonscale Fell 10 Knott 11 Dunmail Raise

18 PAVEY ARK *(697m, 2287ft)*

From the New Dungeon Ghyll Hotel the dark, brooding brow of Pavey Ark can just be seen peering over the corrie lip at the top of Stickle Ghyll (the view from the Langdale Webcam). In summer endless processions of people wend up the much-strengthened path to behold, awestruck, the mighty walls across the steely waters of the tarn. Many visitors are content just to look at the fearful buttresses. Others, with measured confidence, orbit the tarn and ascend the scree to tackle the rock-ladder of Jack's Rake. On this route hands and feet are in action all the way, on the firmest of rock, with remarkably few moments of real exposure to daunt the spirit. It is a uniquely wonderful opportunity for the average fellwalker to experience the thrill of a classic Lakeland cliff. But it becomes increasingly serious with wind and rain, and in winter conditions reverts to the sole preserve of mountaineers, equipped with ropes.

Easy Gully, which rises at a tangent to the right, is not quite as simple as the name would imply. Loose scree leads to a chaos of large chock-stones at the top that require delicate manoeuvres not in the arsenal of every walker (admission: the author was pulled up by a passing rock climber – phew!). The North Rake provides the one direct ascent for the fellwalker, climbing from Bright Beck. Path erosion is advanced so careful footing is required. The term 'Ark' suggests a place of refuge or shelter, while 'Pavia' was a personal name.

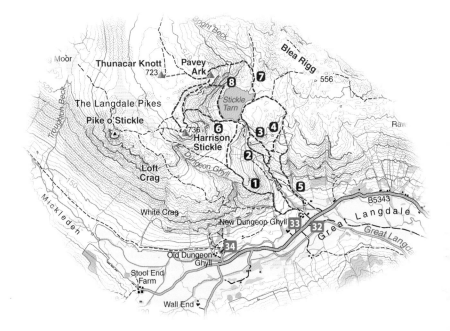

Jack's Rake

Easy Gully

The great cliff of Pavey Ark

Stickle Tarn and Pavey Ark

PAVEY ARK

slopes of
SERGEANT MAN

slopes of
HARRISON
STICKLE

Stickle Tarn

Tarn Crags

Stickle Ghyll

slopes of
BLEA RIGG

slopes of
LOFT CRAG

LOOKING
NORTH

Dungeon Ghyll

Great Langdale

New Dungeon Ghyll Hotel
and Sticklebarn Tavern

Langdale
National Trust
camp site

Great Langdale Beck

ASCENT FROM NEW DUNGEON GHYLL (32–33)

Via Pike How   610m/2000ft   2.5km/1½ miles

Either go directly up the bridle path from the hotel or ascend from Stickle Ghyll car park information shelter. The paths meet up by the fenced gap. **1** The Pike How route leads off left from the fence gap and rises to a hand-gate where you turn right, passing a seat to a stile. Keep the wall to the right, and do not ford Dungeon Ghyll. The well-marked path bears left, mounting the steep slope in steady stages. Much of the path has been re-engineered to cope with the inevitable heavy foot traffic. Many walkers use this as their return leg after the ascent via Stickle Ghyll, though they would be better resorting to the Mark Gate path off Loft Crag, as it has the best base. Climbing up to the saddle behind Pike How, make a move to the right to stand on top; it is a splendid viewpoint for Great Langdale. While the main path angles west-north-west a useful lesser path leads along the rim of the slope on a right-hand curve to reach the Stickle Tarn dam. This route gives a fine perspective view across the gulf of Stickle Ghyll to Tarn Crag.

Pavey Ark from Sergeant Man, backed by the Coniston Fells

Via Stickle Ghyll   588m/1930ft   2.5km/1½ miles

2 Go straight up the paved rock path beside the tree-shaded section of Stickle Ghyll. Cross the footbridge and rise to a stile. Keep to the right-hand side of the valley – the paths to the west are in a poor state, so give them a miss. Stepping through a fold,

Stickle Ghyll

wind up the rigg between small fenced conifer plantings to reach a fine four-part waterfall. At this point there are three options (see also Routes 3 and 4). The first is to continue up the gill, negotiating a rock-step and rising to a ford, and then to complete the climb directly upon Stickle Tarn dam. Alternatively, **3** ascend the well-made stone stair which zig-zags to a higher level before angling left onto a shelf beneath Tarn Crag. **4** A turf trail continuation goes further up the fell, from where the stone stair effectively ends. Keep to the right of the Tarn Crag outcrops, with a roofless shelter on the left and an isolated walled enclosure to the right. Cross over the shoulder to reach Stickle Tarn at its eastern end.

5 A far more pleasant and less well-known alternative line begins directly after

An evening profile, on the approach from Harrison Stickle

leaving the New Dungeon Ghyll. Cross the footbridge located half-right after the initial gate. The path runs up behind Millbeck Farm and enters a lane via a hand-gate, and then rises from the wall onto the bracken ridge. Avoid outcrops by slanting left. Either contour onto the main zig-zagging path or climb, with tenuous initial evidence of a path in the bracken. On finding the green path skirt the right-hand shoulder of a knoll above a steep gill. Subsequently traverse the walled enclosure diagonally to a narrow wall-gap and join up with the upper section of the old shepherds' path. This passes walled boulders and slips over a saddle depression to meet the path running along the eastern shore of the tarn from the outflow.

Ahead, the massive eastern face of Pavey Ark in all its glory smiles down upon the cool, dark waters of the tarn.

There are three popular lines of ascent for the fell-walker from the dam – left (Route 6), right (Route 7) and centre (Route 8). **6** Go left on the obvious path, which has received some restorative paving, although more is needed. Work up the loose slope to the right of the buttresses of Harrison Stickle. Go right on meeting the higher contouring path, venture onto the distinctively coarse-rocked ridge and clamber through the crag-shielding wall onto the summit.

7 Via the North Rake: Go right from the dam along the shore path to follow, then ford, Bright Beck and mount the prominent gully or rake up the east ridge. This is North Rake. All too often used as a line of descent, it has inevitably become badly eroded, and the day will not be far off when the sterling energies of path-makers will be directed at stabilising this trail too. Gaining the ridge top, the path swings round by the broken wall and passes a pooled hollow to gain the summit, as from the north-west.

JACK'S RAKE, PAVEY ARK

Looking down the first section

Looking up to the ash tree

Upper terrace

The gun rock squeeze

Outlook from the ash tree

Stickle Tarn from the top of Jack's Rake

8 Jack's Rake, along with the tiny climb onto Helm Crag summit outcrop, marks the zenith of fell-walking technical difficulty and endeavour in the Central Fells. Paths approach from either side of the tarn. That by the west shore is the old-time favourite, climbing the scree slope from the north-west edge of the tarn via a prominent memorial cairn inscribed 'S.W.S. 1900'. The eastern approach crosses possibly the looser scree, but by keeping up to the right, early on, and by a deft slight of foot, one may avoid almost all of the scree! The two approaches converge at the very centre of the cliff base.

Stickle Tarn from the less-than-easy Easy Gully

EASY GULLY V. JACK'S RAKE – A WORD OF ADVICE

While Easy Gully angles seductively up to the right, at its foot is an awkward rock-lip, from which scree shoots, and this is indicative of a greater challenge at the top. For, while in the main part the gully is straightforward and provides stunning views back over the tarn to the Coniston Fells, the gully concludes in a manner ill suited to the faint-hearted. The author fortuitously met up with descending rock climbers who took pity on him, lifted his day-sack and watchfully guided him up the few delicate steps that clinch the climb. So don't go this way unless you are happy on rock. Jack's Rake, on the other hand, for all it requires a confident approach, is hands-on walking. If you can climb a step-ladder then you have the basic technique for this climb, for all it appears to take the cliff 'by the scruff of its neck'. In the preparation of this guide the author made two ascents of Jack's Rake, then wished he had the time to do it again (and again).

Easy Gully

Memorial cairn during
the climb to the foot
of Jack's Rake

There are five distinct stages to the climb. It would be an over-elaboration to call them 'pitches', as the groove takes several lateral 'breathers', via an ash tree and a patch of thistles. It features a squeeze behind a fallen splinter of rock, The Gun, and concludes above Great Gully, dipping momentarily, then scrambling up rock slabs to the wall end above a projecting rock. The instinct to climb, so well developed by now, means that one naturally finds a scrambly way to the top, brushing aside all notion of linking to the ridge path.

THE SUMMIT

All trace of a cairn has been lost, and to be frank the bare rock top requires no such monument to idle industry. The rocks themselves are fascinating igneous exposures, displaying intricately confused patterns. There is one large perched erratic boulder just to the south, and a few pools on the north and west enhance the rock-garden effect. The view is not 'the best a man can get' in these parts, but the imminence of an immense cliff under one's feet brings its own sense of tingling drama.

SAFE DESCENTS

North Rake, whilst loose in parts, is a secure line of retreat. Head slightly west of north from the top, passing through the wall, and the well-defined path curves to the right into the Rake, bound for Stickle Tarn's east shore. Though don't 'bound', as a steady stride will be kinder on the trail!

Rock wall on Pavey Ark summit

RIDGE ROUTES

HARRISON STICKLE	↓12m/40ft	↑60m/200ft	0.8km/½ mile

This peak is view from the outset. The consistent path runs just under the edge, avoids the ridge-top rock tors, links with the path climbing from the south shore of Stickle Tarn, and rises with two paths mounting either from the east or north. There is scope for good sport in following the ridge-top all the way. Though there is no continuous path, the final grassy rise to the summit is quite trouble free.

THUNACAR KNOTT	↓10m/30ft	↑30m/100ft	0.5km/¼ mile

A clear path leads off west, curving north-west and aiming for the depression at the head of Bright Beck. Take an early deviation to the left, with no trace of a path, and attain the summit cairn short of the pool.

PANORAMA

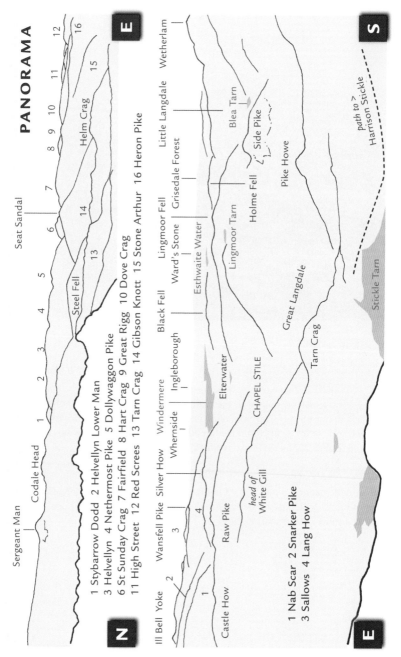

Sergeant Man

Codale Head

Seat Sandal

Steel Fell

Helm Crag

E

1 2 3 4 5 6 7 8 9 10 11 12

13 14 15 16

1 Stybarrow Dodd 2 Helvellyn Lower Man
3 Helvellyn 4 Nethermost Pike 5 Dollywaggon Pike
6 St Sunday Crag 7 Fairfield 8 Hart Crag 9 Great Rigg 10 Dove Crag
11 High Street 12 Red Screes 13 Tarn Crag 14 Gibson Knott 15 Stone Arthur 16 Heron Pike

N

Ill Bell Yoke

Wansfell Pike Silver How

Whernside Windermere

Ingleborough

Black Fell

Lingmoor Fell

Little Langdale

Wetherlam

Castle How

Raw Pike

head of
White Gill

Elterwater

Esthwaite Water

Ward's Stone

Grisedale Forest

Blea Tarn

Side Pike

CHAPEL STILE

Lingmoor Tarn

Holme Fell

Pike Howe

Tarn Crag

Great Langdale

Stickle Tarn

path to >
Harrison Stickle

S

1 Nab Scar 2 Snarker Pike
3 Sallows 4 Lang How

E

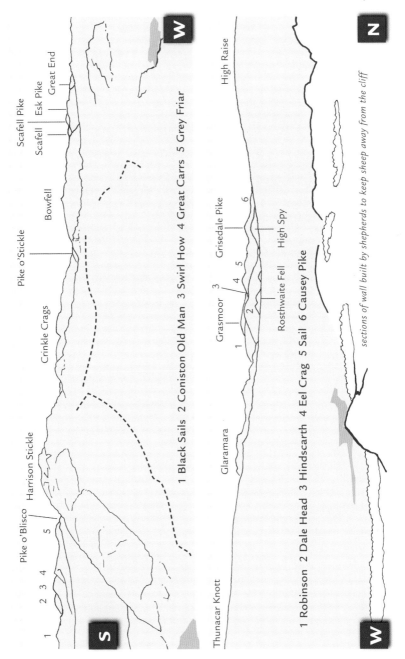

W

Great End
Esk Pike
Scafell Pike
Scafell
Bowfell
Pike o'Stickle
Crinkle Crags
Harrison Stickle
Pike o'Blisco

1 Black Sails 2 Coniston Old Man 3 Swirl How 4 Great Carrs 5 Grey Friar

S

1 2 3 4 5

N

High Raise
Griesdale Pike
High Spy
Grasmoor
Rosthwaite Fell
Glaramara
Thunacar Knott

1 Robinson 2 Dale Head 3 Hindscarth 4 Eel Crag 5 Sail 6 Causey Pike

1 2 3 4 5 6

W

sections of wall built by shepherds to keep sheep away from the cliff

19 PIKE O'STICKLE *(708m, 2323ft)*

The fell-name is a contraction from 'the Pike of Harrison Stickle', where pike is 'peak' and stickle is 'steep'. The fell's stack-like structure is indicative of an particularly hard igneous rock, a quality that drew the attention of early industrialists – tool-makers in stone. These Neolithic tool-makers operated some 4000–6000 years ago, from what is now known as South Scree. They fashioned axes, about the length of a spread hand, which were roughed on site, wrapped in leather, slung over the shoulder and carried to nearby polishing shops (the polished finish gave the tool its working edge and durability). The valley track they followed featured a wayside shrine where stylised blessings (rock-art) were pecked out by hammering, probably with poorer specimen axes themselves. The fashioning of such a high-status, culturally important stone harvest brought wealth and esteem to the locality. The axes were traded throughout the British Isles, and over 2000 have been found, all in pristine condition, confirming their high worth.

The etchings, on the large erratic boulders below Copt How, remained obscure until 1999, when they were identified during intensive searching by rock-art specialists Barbara and Paul Brown. Fortuitously the constant wear of hands and feet of bouldering rock climbers has not affected them. However, the South Scree is no longer a place to venture – it has in the past been torn and worn by countless scree-runners – and the tiny alcove where the prized axes were quarried should be considered from the top of the gully and not visited. The shrine, rock-art and South Screes feature on page 212.

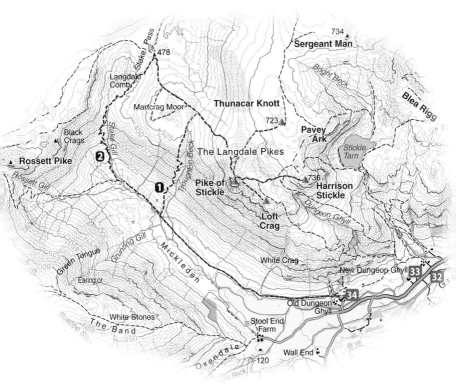

The Pike both backs the familiar view of the Langdale Pikes from Great Langdale and cheekily pokes up to tease on an otherwise quite feature-free skyline in views from the north, on the Borrowdale flank of the range. As the object of a climb it is often taken at the tail-end of a tour of the Pikes, though it can worthily be ascended in its own right.

Pike o'Stickle from Thunacar Knott, backed by Crinkle Crags

ASCENT FROM MICKLEDEN (34)

Via Troughton Beck   655m/2150ft   5.2km/3¼ miles

1 Start from the Old Dungeon Ghyll, pass up behind the hotel to the kissing-gate and follow the valley track, via a further kissing-gate, where the broad lane opens into Mickleden. Stride along the floor of this grand mountain arena with Gimmer Crag and Pike o'Stickle eye-catching features up to the right, while Pike o'Blisco, The Band, Bowfell and Rossett Pike rise to the left and ahead. The well-graded track helps mountain rescue vehicles to approach the foot of Rossett Gill. Pass under Pike o'Stickle, glancing up at the ribbon of unstable scree spilling from the south gully. Neither ascent nor descent by this line should be considered; it is a strait in a dire state.

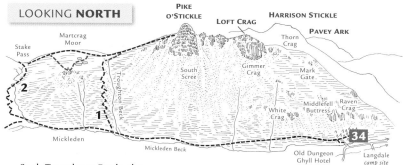

LOOKING **NORTH**

PIKE O'STICKLE

LOFT CRAG

HARRISON STICKLE

PAVEY ARK

Martcrag Moor

Stake Pass

Thorn Crag

Troughton Beck

South Scree

Gimmer Crag

Mark Gate

2

1

White Crag

Middlefell Buttress

Raven Crag

Mickleden

Mickleden Beck

Old Dungeon Ghyll Hotel

Langdale *camp site*

34

Seek Troughton Beck, the tumbling, stony watercourse (frequently dry in summer) issuing from the open ravine high up the fell, spanned by stone flags. Ascend on the west side, skirting the flood boulders, and a well-used and -maintained path soon comes into view. Wind up the bracken slope. Climbing well above the gill it provides suitably handsome views, all the excuse a walker needs for the occasional breather on the steady ascent. Once the moor brink is attained, follow the beck on a less distinct path, until a natural fording point enables one to sweep half-left to a cairn to join the popular path from the Stake Pass. Go right, and the path duly curving right avails itself of the boulders to cross a particularly peaty patch, then climbs easily to the brow to be confronted by the final rocky stage

Mickleden from Stake Gill

Pike o'Stickle from Troughton Beck

Looking down the South Scree into Mickleden

of Pike o'Stickle. The ultimate point is not gained without the hands being brought into action. Several scrambly paths lead to the top.

Via Stake Pass   670m/2200ft   7km/4¼ miles

Stake Pass

Stepping-stones over exposed peat crossed en route from Stake Pass

2 A few paces on from Troughton Beck notice the poignant plaque to Jim Dearden, installed by his 'best mate' – one feels an immediate empathy with fellow fell-folk. Continue to the simple footbridge crossing Stake Beck, and a stone indicates left to Rossett Gill and right for Stake Pass. Bear right, and from the sheepfold the old pass winds up the slope away from the beck, then comes closer to it again higher up, from where Pike o'Stickle looks strikingly solitary. The view down Mickleden is memorable, while across the dale head admire the high buttresses of Bowfell. Fording the beck the path winds along the moraine on

South Scree from Mickleden

the eastern side of Langdale Combe, the former site of a tarn. Some 50m short of the cairn marking the top of the pass, reach a junction with a path leading left bound for Rossett Pike.

Pike o'Stickle from a pool on Martcrag Moor

Go right, mounting the often wet slope on a strong path that skirts several marshes en route to the cairn on the main slope, encountered from the Troughton Beck ascent. An attractive loop can be entertained by wandering south to the rocky summit of Martcrag Moor – no finer place exists to study the craggy face of Bowfell. A crude shelter has been created by walkers in need of a wild country bivouac among the large boulders, while several pools adorn the plateau, giving scope for camera-play towards Pike o'Stickle. The name Martcrag derives from 'the lair of pine marten', a shy species that still finds a tenuous haven in Cumbria.

Natural 'howff' stone shelter on Martcrag Moor

Copt How erratic spiral pattern rock art, the axe-makers' wayside shrine?

Pike o'Stickle summit looking to Harrison Stickle

THE SUMMIT

A cairn rests aloft the airy location, with plenty of space for a small party to sit at ease. This is one of the treasured places in the Central Fells, living up to the great expectations. The gulf of Mickleden gives scale to Bowfell and Pike o'Blisco. But the most exciting subject is near neighbour Loft Crag, buttressed by Gimmer Crag.

SAFE DESCENTS

Your first move must be north to the foot of the stack, and you will have judged, during your scrambling ascent, that this cannot be undertaken speedily. For Langdale follow the prominent path east down into Harrison Combe; and for Borrowdale take the clear path north-west leading down to the top of the Stake Pass, then go right with the bridle path descending beside Stake Beck into Langstrath.

RIDGE ROUTES

LOFT CRAG	↓60m/200ft	↑25m/80ft	0.4km/¼ mile

Descend north off the stack, then follow the obvious ridge to the south-east, not the clear path which drifts down into Harrison Combe.

THUNACAR KNOTT	↓55m/180ft	↑70m/230ft	0.8km/½ mile

From the foot of the stack head north (no path), off the line of the path to Stake Pass. Traverse the spongy depression to link up with the narrow path, running up the slope west to east, bound for the summit.

PANORAMA

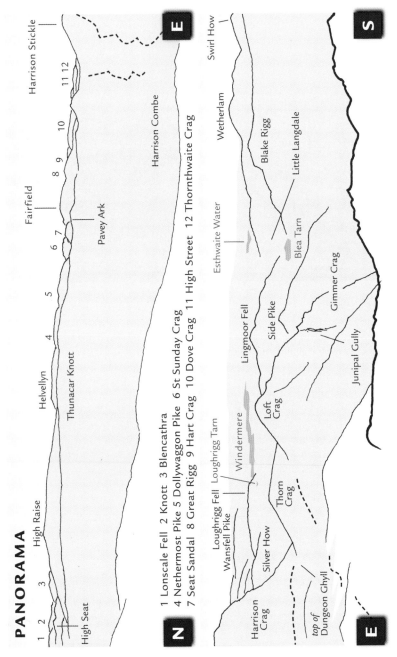

1 Lonscale Fell 2 Knott 3 Blencathra
4 Nethermost Pike 5 Dollywaggon Pike 6 St Sunday Crag
7 Seat Sandal 8 Great Rigg 9 Hart Crag 10 Dove Crag 11 High Street 12 Thornthwaite Crag

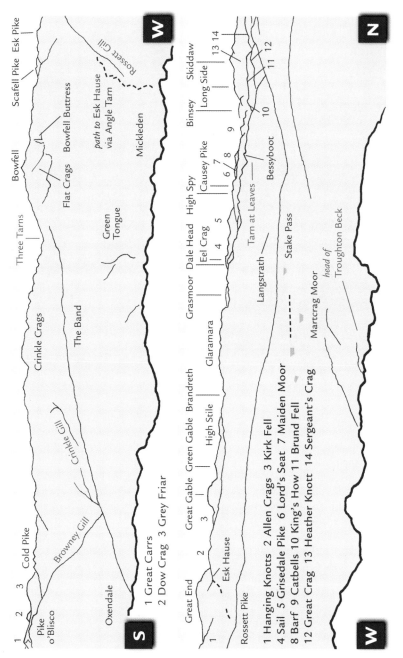

S panel (top-left):

W

Rossett Gill

path to Esk Hause
via Angle Tarn

Scafell Pike   Esk Pike

Bowfell

Bowfell Buttress

Flat Crags

Three Tarns

Green Tongue

Mickleden

Crinkle Crags

The Band

Cold Pike

Crinkle Gill

Browney Gill

Oxendale

Pike o'Blisco

1 2 3

1 Great Carrs
2 Dow Crag 3 Grey Friar

N / W panel:

N

Skiddaw

13 14

11 12

Long Side

Binsey

10

9

Causey Pike

7 8

6

High Spy

Bessyboot

Dale Head

5

Grasmoor

Eel Crag

4

Tarn at Leaves

Stake Pass

Langstrath

Martcrag Moor

head of
Troughton Beck

Brandreth

Green Gable   Great Gable

High Stile

Glaramara

Great End

Esk Hause

2 3

Rossett Pike

1

W

1 Hanging Knotts 2 Allen Crags 3 Kirk Fell
4 Sail 5 Grisedale Pike 6 Lord's Seat 7 Maiden Moor
8 Barf 9 Catbells 10 King's How 11 Brund Fell
12 Great Crag 13 Heather Knott 14 Sergeant's Crag

20 RAVEN CRAG *(463m, 1519ft)*

Above all else mountains beget water, and inevitably engineers will seek to draw from this resource for a swelling population. Those that care for the wilderness must always fight with ardour to stifle dams at birth – John Muir set the first precedent in Yosemite. In the 19th century the two sections of Leathes Water, linked by a midriff bridge, lay in broadened Wythburn Dale amid green pastures and beechwood – one has but faded black-and-white images to hint at a lost beauty. It fell prey to the needs of Manchester, and a great dam was constructed and foreign conifers swept up the surrounding fell-sides.

Some 100 years on, seeking redeeming qualities, one may admit a certain charm in peeping towards the Helvellyn range from the Armboth road, but progress towards the introduction of a greater diversity of deciduous trees along the lakeside margins must continue to be a priority. Travellers crossing the dam road between lapping depths and fringing trees will have their attention firmly arrested by Raven Crag at the lake's end – the great buttressed bluff, for all its smothering of trees, commands avid attention. This bulwark ridge denied water engineers the considerable drainage of High Seat and Bleaberry Fell by hemming in Shoulthwaite Gill.

The summit of Raven Crag is not a viewpoint, being consumed by trees, but the brink of the cliff most certainly is. Tucked under its eastern slope is a rocky hillock, Castle Crag, complete with Iron Age ramparts and, due north, a bare-topped crest called Benn Man. Although not often visited, it is a fine viewpoint for the forbidding crags across Shoulthwaite Gill and Raven Crag itself (see left). The coniferous slope between Middlesteads Gill and Shoulthwaite Farm comes within the domain of Raven Crag, and offers a mixture of ascents and gradients. These woods are famous for the indigenous population of red squirrels, but recent sightings of grey squirrels, which carry para-pox (a virulent virus that kills the reds), have brought about a community watch campaign for these unwelcome intruders.

Raven Crag from Benn Man

Raven Crag from below

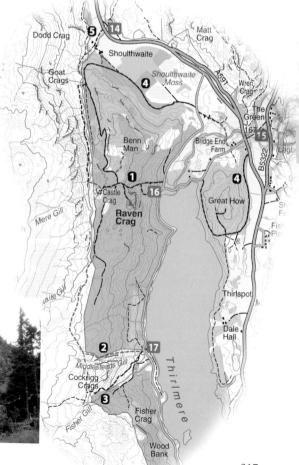

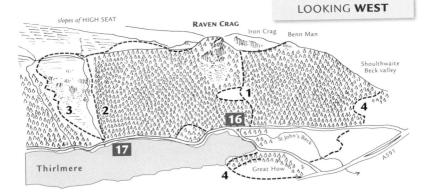

slopes of HIGH SEAT   **RAVEN CRAG**   Iron Crag   Benn Man

Shoulthwaite Beck valley

1

3   2   16   4

17   St John's Beck

Thirlmere   Great How   4   A591

ASCENT FROM THIRLMERE DAM (16)

| *Direct* | 305m/1000ft | 0.8km/½ mile |

1 This is the hot route to the top. The steepest, shortest and most popular path leads off from the small car park at the road junction west of the dam. Go right, then after some 100m go left at the hand-gate into the mature plantation. The path rises to a forest track. Either cross it, via the tall kissing-gate, or go left, sweeping round the fenced enclosure and thus getting a close-up view of Raven Crag from below – this route is often followed during the descent on a there-and-back outing. The direct route winds up through the young plantation in the deer-excluding enclosure to the top kissing-gate. Crossing the forest track once more, continue resolutely to the top of the plantation, and emerge onto a broad forestry track at the key point for unlocking Raven Crag. Waymarking directs left, on a made-path winding up through the conifers and over the crown of the bluff to steps onto the heathery crag brink.

ASCENT FROM ARMBOTH (17)

| *Via Middlesteads Gill* | 320m/1050ft | 3.2km/2 miles |

2 Middlesteads Gill is a sneaky, distant, side-door approach, ideal for creating a bigger circular outing exclusive to the Raven Crag ridge. Leave the Armboth lakeside car park and follow the road north (right), going through the kissing-gate at the first bend at the beginning of the Watendlath path. Ignore the inviting path over the 'sma' brig', and while one may ascend the footpath rising above Fisher Gill and follow the wall right at the top (**3**), the more inviting line climbs directly from the road beside the right-hand forest fence. It is steep going, and you hug the fence to help avoid the bracken. As the slope scoops, angle half-left onto the arete overlooking the impressive Middlesteads Gill ravine, enhanced by natural tree growth.

Keep to the rim of the gill, and eventually angle right to slip round the right-hand end of the fell-bounding wall where it almost abuts the forest fence. Bear up right by the gill and fence, and at the next corner angle up the slope to top the length of ascending wall, and thus gain the low ridge. Advance beyond a cairn, on a descending line, to the gate entering into the forestry. Follow the main track left, with continued fine views down the Shoulthwaite Gill valley towards the Glenderaterra Gap. Arriving at the broad turning area, you can go left to follow the made-path to Castle Crag or, right, to take the similarly prepared trail to Raven Crag. If you continue, also consider branching half-right, just before the track begins to descend, to join a narrow path leading through the pines to the top of Benn Man (see summit details).

4 All three viewpoints, Castle Crag, Raven Crag and Benn Man, can be included in a grand tour of 7¼ miles that would continue north with the forest track and sweep round in the valley by Shoulthwaite Moss, Smaithwaite and orbit Great How (and this can include the summit, though the view is blanked out by trees!) to the dam – all on firm paths (see map).

ASCENT FROM ROUGH HOW BRIDGE (14)

Direct   335m/1100ft   2km/1¼ miles

If, having perhaps viewed the fearsome crag during the crossing of Thirlmere dam, you are disinclined to follow the direct climb, then take heart – it d̶̶̶̶̶̶̶̶̶̶̶̶̶ to be a slog; there is another way. For all we may find conifers a mixed bl̶̶̶̶̶̶̶ sion of access tracks brings collateral benefits, and the track rising from Shoulthwaite to the north is as sweet a route to the top as could be devised.

5 From the lay-by cross the busy A591 into the lane leading to, and through, Shoulthwaite Farm, entering Thirlmere Forest at a kissing-gate. Either follow the level bridle path ahead to the track and turn acutely right, or branch off immediately

Raven Crag from Fisher Crag

following the impromptu path. The tall deer fence, close right, leads directly up to the track, which you follow to the right. Ignore the option to exit the woodland via the tall kissing-gate and bridge. Although it must be said that the Shoulthwaite Gill valley path has its own unique quality as a line of ascent, back-tracking, literally, from the gate entry to the forestry at GR299181, there are two earlier ladder-stiles that give access. The first climbs pathless among the tangle of trees beside a gill from beneath Castle Crag, and the second links directly onto the track a little further south. The main forest track is signposted 'Raven Crag, Fort and Viewpoint' and leads, via a sweeping zig-zag under Sipping Crag and a later bend, to the turning area on the saddle.

THE SUMMIT

The United Utilities signboards are correct, the brink of Raven Crag IS a viewpoint. The whole of Thirlmere reservoir can be seen, backed by the high rolling skyline of the Helvellyn range, with tantalising glimpses south over Dunmail Raise, and north to Skiddaw and Blencathra. To complete the view-spotting one needs to move around to evade the trees, an activity hampered by deep heather and the knowledge that the cliff is all too imminent. This is not the summit of the bluff – there is a cairn to be found among the ragged trees behind the ~~viewpoint. A cairn does mark the viewpoint itself. Close b~~ ~~from the days when they~~ ~~risking their necks~~ grazing too close to the edge. This is the ideal picnic place, nicely distanced from the car-wedded tourists consuming ice cream at Station Coppice. Thirlmere meant 'lake of the giant' and Dollywaggon Pike meant 'peak of the elevated giant', so was there a time when monsters were thought to inhabit these wild hills.

There are two other special viewpoints in the vicinity, well meriting a visit. Castle Crag, replicating Legburthwaite's more famous Iron Age site, is waymarked from the

Castle Crag from the southern rampart

track at the saddle. A made-path, with duck-boarding, leads to a low rampart embracing a rocky knoll, with a narrow path via the rampart circling clockwise over the bluff (rock step). Re-trace the approach to continue. Benn Man (or The Benn), the second high point on the ridge to the north, is reached from the track just before it shapes to descend. Bear

Raven Crag viewpoint cairn directly above the cliff

right on a narrow path through the pines and larches, and climb the heather and bilberry hillock for a superb summit prospect back to Raven Crag (see page 217) and westward to the crags lining Shoulthwaite Gill, most notably Iron Crag, again.

SAFE DESCENTS
All routes of ascent can comfortably be reversed.

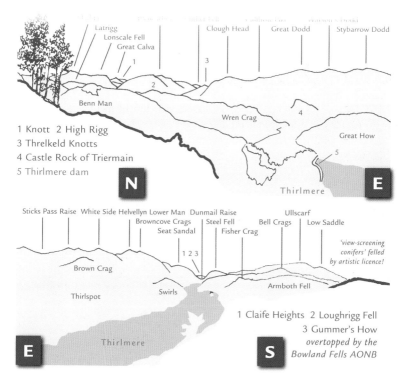

Latrigg
Lonscale Fell
Great Calva
Clough Head
Great Dodd
Stybarrow Dodd
1
3
2
Benn Man
Wren Crag
4
Great How
5

1 Knott 2 High Rigg
3 Threlkeld Knotts
4 Castle Rock of Triermain
5 Thirlmere dam

N

E

Thirlmere

Sticks Pass Raise White Side Helvellyn Lower Man Dunmail Raise
Browncove Crags Seat Sandal
Steel Fell
Fisher Crag
Ullscarf
Bell Crags Low Saddle
'view-screening conifers' felled by artistic licence!
1 2 3
Brown Crag
Armboth Fell
Thirlspot
Swirls

E

Thirlmere

S

1 Claife Heights 2 Loughrigg Fell
3 Gummer's How
overtopped by the Bowland Fells AONB

21 SERGEANT MAN *(736m, 2414ft)*

Just as Pavey Ark is the most startling component of Thunacar Knott, so the unusual stack-like summit of Sergeant Man belongs to the basic plateau structure of High Raise. It marks the umbilical ridge connection with Easedale, from where it makes a superb objective for a fellwalk, the knobbly top of Codale Head appearing to be the summit for much of the journey. Its waters drain into Wythburn, Easedale and Great Langdale.

Among the delightful lexicon of fell-names, this one has an enigmatic ring. But the prosaic truth is that, like Sergeant's Crag, it contains a 17th-century land owner's name tagged onto the older Celtic term 'Man', meaning 'a landmark cairn'.

For all its distance from a main valley base, one may climb the fell exclusively via Stickle Ghyll and Bright Beck or, having indulged in the drama of Whitegill Crag, from Great Langdale. From Grasmere one may climb onto

Sergeant Man from above Bright Beck

the ridge via Silver How and Blea Rigg, or trek up Easedale via Belles Knott or even Far Easedale, approaching from the top of Codale Head. No route is dull. How could they be with such marvellous surroundings?

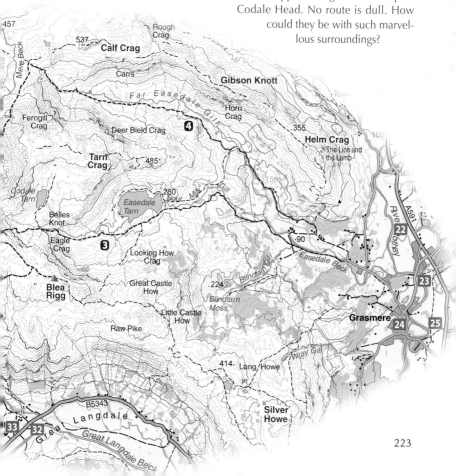

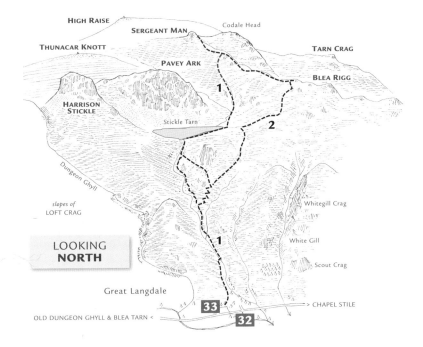

HIGH RAISE
SERGEANT MAN
Codale Head
THUNACAR KNOTT
TARN CRAG
PAVEY ARK
BLEA RIGG
1
HARRISON STICKLE
Stickle Tarn
2
slopes of
LOFT CRAG
Whitegill Crag
LOOKING **NORTH**
White Gill
1
Scout Crag
Great Langdale
33
OLD DUNGEON GHYLL & BLEA TARN <
32
> CHAPEL STILE

ASCENT FROM NEW DUNGEON GHYLL (32–33)

Via Stickle Ghyll   655m/2150ft   4km/2½ miles

A cluster of routes inevitably present themselves from this hugely popular walking base in Great Langdale. The diagram shows the primary lines, though only one can be considered exclusive to this one destination (Route 1). **1** The direct route climbs Stickle Ghyll to the Stickle Tarn dam and follows the east shore path. (**2** There is a fork as the first feeder-gill enters the tarn. The right-hand path, well cairned, curves round a marsh and rises easily north-eastward onto the Blea Rigg ridge; this is the steadier line of approach.) The direct route (Route 1), however, accompanies Bright Beck, which you do not ford, with Sergeant Man clearly in view ahead (see page 223). Coming level with the steeply rising east ridge of Pavey Ark, a tangible path trends up a narrow defile due north beside a tributary gill, though the path becomes less convincing higher up as the route naturally merges with the ridge ris-

Sergeant Man from the south

Pavey Ark during the ascent from Bright Beck

ing to the summit. As the ridge is gained a lower path may be spotted, traversing below the fell-top from the great slab to the head of Bright Beck. One presumes it came into being as a hasty short-cut to avoid Sergeant Man.

The main routes to Thunacar Knott, up the slopes of Harrison Stickle, give a counter-slant, but are more likely to be used in descent on a circular tour.

Harrison Stickle and Pavey Ark from the path below the summit

225

Central Fells

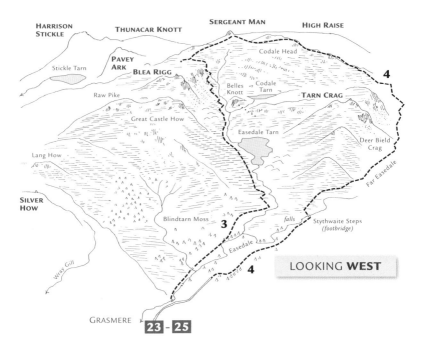

HARRISON STICKLE · THUNACAR KNOTT · SERGEANT MAN · HIGH RAISE
PAVEY ARK · BLEA RIGG · Stickle Tarn · Raw Pike · Codale Head · Belles Knott · Codale Tarn · TARN CRAG · Great Castle How · Easedale Tarn · Deer Bield Crag · Lang How · Far Easedale · SILVER HOW · Blindtarn Moss · 3 · falls · Stythwaite Steps (footbridge) · Easedale · 4 · Wray Gill · 4

LOOKING **WEST**

GRASMERE 23 - 25

ASCENT FROM GRASMERE (23–25)

Via Easedale Tarn 686m/2250ft 5.5km/3½ miles

Natural routes lead up the ridges of Blea Rigg and Tarn Crag (see the respective fell chapters), though the two dale approaches are excellent alternatives. **3** The popular path to Easedale Tarn leaves the Easedale Road via the footbridge opposite Oak How (teas), traversing meadows via gates. Much of the way is paved. The path winds up beside Sour Milk Gill, the excited waters churning down frenzied falls. The approach to the tarn is currently receiving the finishing touches to complete the paved parade, as this walk has long attracted visitors, for all the drabness of its immediate surroundings. Conical drumlins on either side of Easedale Tarn emphasise

Belles Knott and pitched path

226

Belles Knott

the glacial origins of this bleak amphitheatre. The conical top of Tarn Crag looms close right, while Blea Crag forms the southern sidewall.

The old path continues along the southern side of the tarn and its main feeder-gill, and has several essentially stepped sections beside steep cascades. Up to the right the arresting Belles Knott flatters as a peak to climb (scramblers only), but once you get above the falls the Knott soon shows itself to be a sham. A side-path bears right, fording the gill, to visit the hanging waters of Codale Tarn, with its tiny outflow and picturesque isle set beneath the great slope of Codale Head. Any ascent from here is best accomplished by keeping north beyond a ruined sheepfold to join the Tarn Crag ridge path, going west, and continuing to the rising ridge en route for Codale Head. Otherwise, keep with the main path which zig-zags up to a ridge-top path interchange west of Blea Rigg. Turn right and mount the rocky ridge to the north-west for the very first glimpse of the fell-top. Two early path options reunite at the giant slab, and a solitary path continues to ford the outflow of a marsh and then climbs the distinctive summit knoll beyond.

Codale Tarn

Via Far Easedale   686m/2250ft   6km/3¾ miles

4 The old pony path up Far Easedale provides an enjoyable alternative, and is sign-posted 'Greenup Edge' from the Easedale road-end. Proceed via the Stythwaite Steps footbridge to the saddle at the very top of the dale. Follow the metal stakes of the old county boundary fence left over Broadstone Head and on to Codale Head. Only now does the summit come into view.

THE SUMMIT

Not quite the bold stack of Pike o'Stickle, rather a kid-brother of similarly resilient rock. Fellwalkers instinctively love this high place, for all that the bare outcrop has but a bedraggled cairn as monument to the many thousands of appreciative visita-tions. Note the old Ordnance Survey bench-mark on the very top, dating from the survey of 1860, almost obscured by wear.

SAFE DESCENTS

Being the lynch-pin off High Raise for Great Langdale and Grasmere, the clear path leading south-east down the ridge is a reliable guide in doubtful conditions.

RIDGE ROUTES

BLEA RIGG   ↓205m/670ft   ↑15m/50ft   2km/1¼ miles

The ridge path descending south-east is well marked and supported with cairns. The slope eases at a meeting of paths, which marks the transition to the broader ridge of

Sergeant Man summit cairn

Codale Head from the summit

Blea Rigg. Weave by a rock pool and skirt three distinct rock knolls to reach the summit, distinguished by its tiny cairn perched on a chunky rock.

HIGH RAISE	↓8m/25ft	↑30m/100ft	0.8km/½ mile

Head north-west, passing pools in crossing the open plateau. Miss the old fence corner by even larger pools to reach the jumble of rocks, wind-shelter and Ordnance Survey pillar at the summit.

THUNACAR KNOTT	↓60m/200ft	↑45m/150ft	1.6km/1 mile

Head west, the going is easy underfoot, a clear path on the ground leads to a wide shallow depression at the head of Bright Beck. Here join the prominent ridge path from High Raise heading south. As the first rocks are encountered on the easy rise, bear off right from the main trail to reach the summit cairn.

PANORAMA

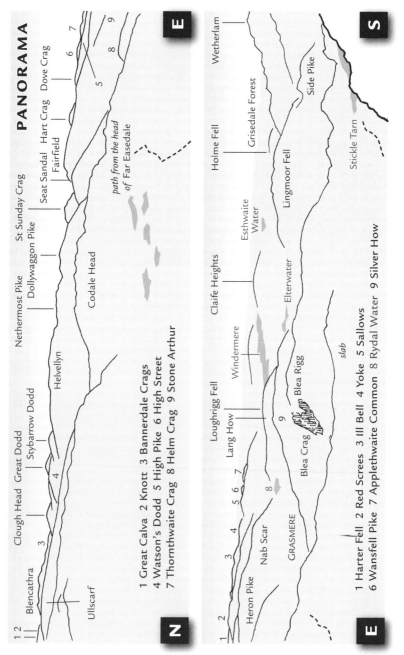

E

Dove Crag
Hart Crag
Seat Sandal
Fairfield
St Sunday Crag
Dollywaggon Pike
Nethermost Pike

6 7
8
9
5

path from the head
of Far Easedale

Codale Head

N

Blencathra
Ullscarf
Clough Head Great Dodd
Stybarrow Dodd
Helvellyn

1 2
3
4

1 Great Calva 2 Knott 3 Bannerdale Crags
4 Watson's Dodd 5 High Pike 6 High Street
7 Thornthwaite Crag 8 Helm Crag 9 Stone Arthur

S

Wetherlam
Holme Fell
Grisedale Forest
Lingmoor Fell
Side Pike
Stickle Tarn

Claife Heights
Esthwaite
Water
Elterwater

E

Windermere
Loughrigg Fell
Lang How
Blea Crag Blea Rigg
slab

Heron Pike
Nab Scar
GRASMERE

1 2
3
4
5 6 7
8
9

1 Harter Fell 2 Red Screes 3 Ill Bell 4 Yoke 5 Sallows
6 Wansfell Pike 7 Applethwaite Common 8 Rydal Water 9 Silver How

230

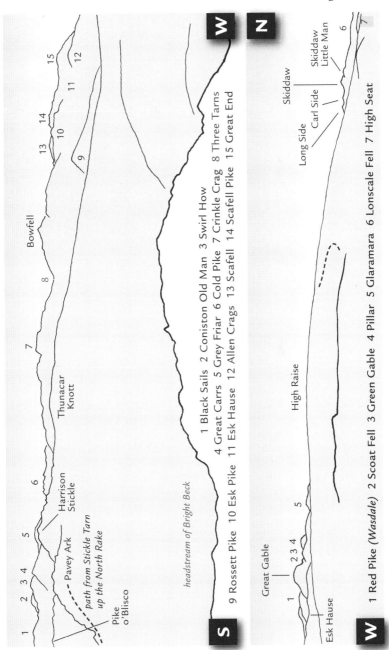

S — **W**

1 Black Sails 2 Coniston Old Man 3 Swirl How
4 Great Carrs 5 Grey Friar 6 Cold Pike 7 Crinkle Crag 8 Three Tarns
9 Rossett Pike 10 Esk Pike 11 Esk Hause 12 Allen Crags 13 Scafell 14 Scafell Pike 15 Great End

Bowfell

Harrison Stickle

Thunacar Knott

Pavey Ark

path from Stickle Tarn up the North Rake

Pike o'Blisco

headstream of Bright Beck

N — **W**

Skiddaw

Long Side   Carl Side   Skiddaw Little Man

Great Gable

High Raise

Esk Hause

1 Red Pike (*Wasdale*) 2 Scoat Fell 3 Green Gable 4 Pillar 5 Glaramara 6 Lonscale Fell 7 High Seat

22 SERGEANT'S CRAG (574m, 1883ft)

The natural, relaxed, comparatively uneventful northern fall of the fell from High Raise, the crest of the range, tapers to an eye-catching halt on Sergeant's Crag. Flanked by considerable crags overlooking Langstrath, the crag has one great pleat gully and several bold slabby pockets. It has a neighbour, Eagle Crag, from which, and to which, it can be compared and admired. There is no hint of twinning, the character of each is distinct.

Sergeant's Crag may now be the focus of climbers' attention, notably the slabs part-way up the broken face, but in recent centuries it has been mined and quarried, though the untrained eye would find it difficult to detect the residual spoil of such activity. Conventionally walkers approach the fell-top by following the ridge wall, having first tackled Eagle Crag. An alternative line, bereft of bracken and crags, can be found climbing from the footbridge at the foot of Stake Beck. Its one and only merit is the majestic view back across Langstrath to Rosthwaite Cam and Glaramara.

With the company of mountains on every hand, Langstrath looks like a Scottish glen, which might explain the corruption of the earlier form of the name 'Langstrode' (the long marsh) to Langstrath ('strath' meaning 'valley'). That most walkers know the valley in haste from walking the Cumbria Way does it less than justice. It is a place to amble as well as stride, relished best on the circuit of the dale-floor paths from Stonethwaite. Switch on the Tray Dub footbridge below Stake Beck, and take time to inspect each cascade, dub and pot.

It would appear that the fell-name derives from a William Sargyante, referred to in 1602; he probably gave his name to Sergeant Man too.

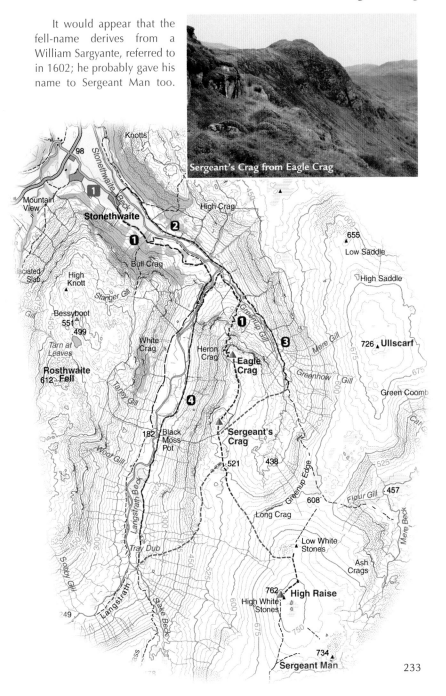

Sergeant's Crag from Eagle Crag

Sergeant's Crag from the head of Willygrass Gill,
with Eagle Crag left – itself overtopped by High Raise

ASCENT FROM STONETHWAITE (1)

Via Eagle Crag	480m/1580ft	3.6km /2¼ miles
Via Greenup Gill	480m/1580ft	4km/2½ miles

Use roadside lay-by parking, which is preferable to cluttering up the hamlet. **1** Follow the direct ascent of EAGLE CRAG (page 67) and the subsequent ridge. Amazingly the state of the path suggests only a comparatively few undertake this initially steep, later intricate, but utterly exhilarating route. **2** To avoid encounters with campers and their vehicles, cross Stonethwaite Bridge, as with the former route, then cross the footbridge at the confluence of Greenup Gill with Langstrath Beck to embark on the bridle path up Langstrath turning quickly left at the fence stile joining the Eagle Crag direct ascent. **3** Alternatively, the eastern back door approach contin-

ues with the popular bridleway ascending the Greenup Gill valley, in harmony with the Coast to Coast walk. As the eastern slopes of Eagle Crag turn to grass, break off the trail, ford the gill and make a pathless ascent of the steep slope to reach the ladder-stile in the ridge wall, following the clear path north to the summit.

Sergeant's Crag southern aspect

Via Langstrath   5.5km/3½ miles

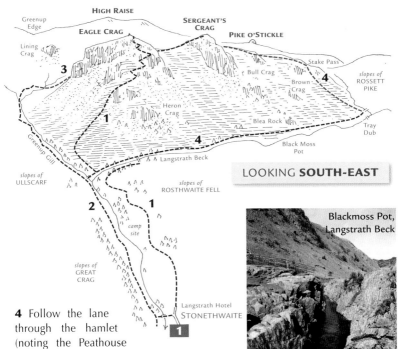

LOOKING **SOUTH-EAST**

Blackmoss Pot, Langstrath Beck

4 Follow the lane through the hamlet (noting the Peathouse tea-room and Langstrath Hotel for end-of-walk refreshment). The gated track passes above the popular camping meadow, latterly passing Alisongrass Hoghouse (camping barn). As the beck comes closer listen to the roar of Galleny Force down in the tree cover left. The track bends right, via a gate to accompany the clear cascading waters of Langstrath Beck, through a gate to a footbridge. Cross the footbridge to follow the bridle path to the gate at Black Moss Pot, by so doing coming under the slopes of Heron and Sergeant's Crags, and close to the striking Gash Rock sporting a plume of heather, otherwise known as Blea Rock.

Black Moss Pot is a tight water rock channel, deserving a moment's appreciative look, for the next mile of bridle path pursued to the footbridge at the foot of Stake Beck is quite uneventful, although there is no denying the magical feel of this deep mountain valley. Alternatively, follow the west-side footpath that climbs over the ladder-stile at Blackmoss, and at this point look up to the left to possibly spot climbers scaling Sergeant's Crag Slabs. Below and above Black Moss Pot the beck takes a wide, shingled, meandering course, with the craggy slopes of Rosthwaite Fell and

View from the top of Sergeant's Crag Gully

Glaramara high to the right. Swan and Tray Dubs offer fine moments to draw close to the lively beck. 'Dub' suggests that these were sheep-washing pools, as the term derives from the British *dubh*, meaning 'dark, or shadowed place', which is frequently applied to areas used for this purpose. Cross Tray Dub footbridge and ascend directly.

THE SUMMIT

The imposition of a wall, effectively isolating the upper dome of the fell, has served to restrict grazing and support a better flora than occurs in the poor acidic grassland beyond. A small cairn rests upon a modest outcrop, with little hint of the impending precipice to the west to deflect attention from the fine view across and to the head of

Sergeant's Crag summit cairn

Langstrath. With a little time one may investigate down the slope to the north then west, where a grass ramp leads to the top of Sergeant's Crag Gully. One may also peer down the steep, broken face towards the climbers' slabs and Blea Rock – impressive rock and valley scenery for the eagle-eyed.

SAFE DESCENTS

In dubious weather, by far the best option is to cross the stile in the wall immediately south of the summit, and head north-east to join the bridle path below Lining Crag that leads down Greenup Gill for Stonethwaite.

RIDGE ROUTES

EAGLE CRAG	↓60m/200ft	↑10m/30ft	0.8km/½ mile

Navigation just could not be simpler. Head north-north-east from the summit on the one path with the ridge wall coming close right, then cross the step-up stile at the wall corner that gives access to the neighbouring top.

HIGH RAISE	↓10m/30ft	↑195m/640ft	2.4km/1½ miles

Go south crossing the wall-stile, and a narrow path weaves through a long marshy saddle. Rising onto drier ground, with less evidence of a path, at the same time losing all sense of a ridge. Keep right of Long Crag to reach the skyline at Low White Stones, and go south to the summit.

Glaramara and Rosthwaite High Fell

PANORAMA

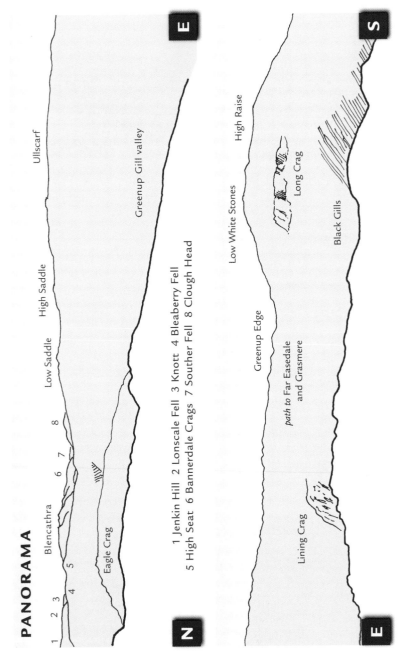

Ullscarf

High Saddle

Low Saddle

Blencathra

Greenup Gill valley

Eagle Crag

E

N

1 Jenkin Hill 2 Lonscale Fell 3 Knott 4 Bleaberry Fell
5 High Seat 6 Bannerdale Crags 7 Souther Fell 8 Clough Head

High Raise

Low White Stones

Long Crag

Greenup Edge

Black Gills

path to Far Easedale
and Grasmere

Lining Crag

S

E

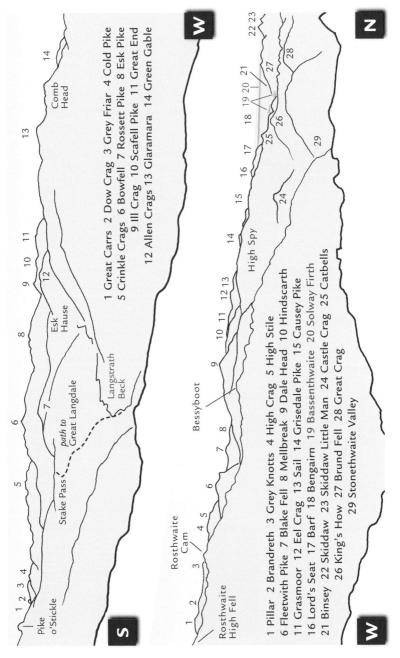

W

N

1 Great Carrs 2 Dow Crag 3 Grey Friar 4 Cold Pike
5 Crinkle Crags 6 Bowfell 7 Rossett Pike 8 Esk Pike
9 Ill Crag 10 Scafell Pike 11 Great End
12 Allen Crags 13 Glaramara 14 Green Gable

Comb Head

Esk Hause

Langstrath Beck

path to Great Langdale

Stake Pass

Pike o'Stickle

S

Bessyboot

Rosthwaite Cam

Rosthwaite High Fell

1 Pillar 2 Brandreth 3 Grey Knotts 4 High Crag 5 High Stile
6 Fleetwith Pike 7 Blake Fell 8 Mellbreak 9 Dale Head 10 Hindscarth
11 Grasmoor 12 Eel Crag 13 Sail 14 Grisedale Pike 15 Causey Pike
16 Lord's Seat 17 Barf 18 Bengairn 19 Bassenthwaite 20 Solway Firth
21 Binsey 22 Skiddaw 23 Skiddaw Little Man 24 Castle Crag 25 Catbells
26 King's How 27 Brund Fell 28 Great Crag
29 Stonethwaite Valley

High Spy

W

239

23 SILVER HOW *(395m, 1296ft)*

It is said that, in certain lights, the screes of Silver How give off an argent hue, which may explain its name. Whether or not this is so, it certainly has an elegant profile that melds into the Grasmere scene so sweetly that many walkers, quite wisely, assume it a peak they must climb really to know the famous literary vale. Whilst it forms a backdrop to sylvan views across the lake (see above), appearance is deceptive here, for the fell is nothing more than the scarp-end of a broad ridge; it subsequently gathers up height over two further knolls to Swinescar Hause, from which

point the terrain becomes altogether rougher. From the top of the Redbank Road, by High Close, a rolling ridge advances in a north-westerly direction over Dow Bank and Spedding Crag to where Meg's Gill slices into the fell. The ridge smartly rises and extends its girth, with the top of the fell lying at the northern tip

From the Rothay vale to the north-east

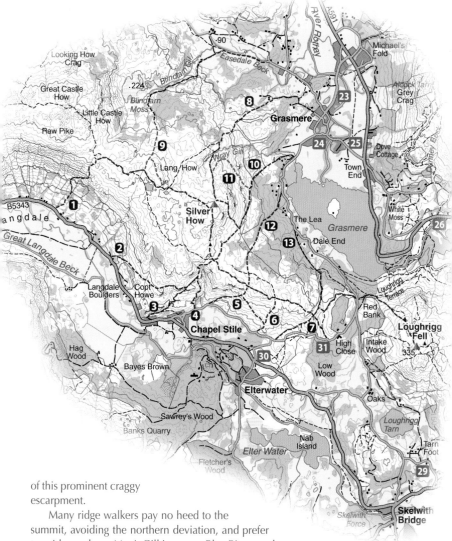

of this prominent craggy
escarpment.

Many ridge walkers pay no heed to the
summit, avoiding the northern deviation, and prefer
to stride on above Meg's Gill intent on Blea Rigg, yet the summit merits a deliberative visit. The ridge to Castle How is a grand scenic parade with numerous undulations to intrigue the wanderer, though many of the
paths are little better than sheep trods. Routes to the top are plentiful, and all are worthy – made the more so by the scenic virtues of the ultimate point. There are four
prime routes from Grasmere and three out of Great Langdale, so much mixing and
matching can be achieved to vary a circular tour.

ASCENT FROM GREAT LANGDALE

Via Pye How   305m/1000ft   2km/1¼ miles

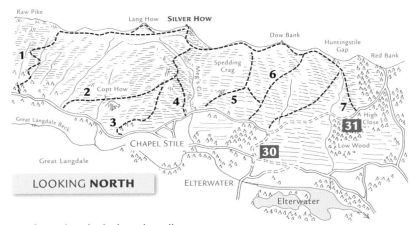

Raw Pike
Lang How **SILVER HOW**
Dow Bank
Huntingstile Gap
Red Bank
1
Spedding Crag
6
Meg's Gill
Copt How
2
4
5
7
High Close
3
Great Langdale Beck
31
Low Wood
CHAPEL STILE
30
Great Langdale
LOOKING **NORTH**
ELTERWATER
Elterwater

1 A footpath embarks from the valley
road midway between Pye How and
the Long House, GR306066, though
the lack of immediate car parking
tends to ensure the path is used more
in descent. It is nonetheless an excellent approach to the Silver How
ridge, especially if time is taken for
frequent pauses to look back upon
the stunning surround of majestic
fells.

A kissing-gate gives entry into a
pasture, where you initially keep the
wall to the left. Ascend with half-a-
dozen waymark posts as aids and
cross broken intermediate walls;
much mature scrub colonises the
enclosures. A ladder-stile crosses the
intake wall at the top, and the path, at
first stony, becomes a pleasant turf
trail, beyond the solitary, gill-shading
holly. Wind steadily to the ridge-top
at Swinescar Hause, joining the ridge
path heading right (south-east).

Youdell Tarn

Before Youdell Tarn take the opportunity to include Lang How (some 19m, 62ft, higher than Silver How) – scant trace of a path leads up onto its grassy ridge, and a cairn gives reason to pause before the path winds down the southern slope to rejoin the ridge path, traverse the headstream of Wray Gill direct to the summit.

Lang How

Via Copt How 2km/1¼ miles

Meg's Gill

Chapel Stile has no public parking facility (please respect residents' parking). Rock climbers honing their skills on the Copt How buttress make opportunist use of the brief widening of the road at Thrang Close at GR315057 to park; this is the one place available for parking in the village, but only takes the odd car! Walkers should either employ the 'Langdale Rambler' bus or use the National Trust Walthwaite Bottom car park and stroll into the community via the minor road or beside Great Langdale Beck from Elterwater Bridge. In Meg's Gill, a stunning re-entrant ravine, the village has an irresistible climb, aided by various paths conveniently converging in its upper section. There are six points from which one may leave the road to climb onto the Silver How ridge between Meg's Gill and Huntingstile Gap. The first four routes focus on Meg's Gill itself.

2 A matter of 100m east of Harry Place Farm, opposite a roadside barn, a footpath is discreetly signposted. The path climbs the bank to a stile in a wall-linking fence. Ascend with the wall to the right and join a green track going right. Cross the saddle behind Copt How, which meant 'the look-out hillock'; it was indeed a look-out point, and is not an easy top to get onto for a watching brief! The path traverses the rough slopes, taking one notable rocky step up during its approach to Meg's Gill. This top path can be joined from three other paths ascending from the village.

3 One path begins from the aforementioned verge parking space, where a footpath is signed from a gate that leads to a stile and an awkward descent through the old Thrang Quarry. Just before entering a lane – another access point from the village street west of Holy Trinity Church – bear up left between the retaining walls in the quarry to mount the ridge with a gill to the left. The path forks, and both ways meet the Copt How path; however the right-hand path is the better option.

Via Meg's Gill   1.5km/1 mile

4 A further path leaves the road east of the church before Walthwaite Lodge. Climb the bank, with the wall to the right, on a narrow path through the bracken. Rounding the wall on the brow, ascend on the upper west side of the Meg's Gill ravine, rising to meet the top path. Now continue up the gill to a high ford, and contour with a fine view down and across to a waterfall below the ford. Finally rise onto the ridge, precisely where the Silver How escarpment imposes itself on the lesser ridge from High Close.

Via Dow Bank   300m/990ft   2km/1¼ mile

5 Other paths from the road include the route onto Spedding Crag / Dow Bank saddle beginning east of Speddy Cottage; here pass through a hand-gate and ascend with a wall on the right. Up to the left see Raven Crag, a popular evening haunt for climbers. Rise to a turning point where the path switches left and leads straight up to the saddle. **6** From GR328054, on the minor road running east from the village, a turf path bears off half-left for 150m, then turns directly uphill through the bracken. A strong sheep path may be followed to the left, contouring to the turning point on the path up from Speddy Cottage, or one may simply keep going up to the cairn on Dow Crag. **7** From the open common above the Walthwaite Bottom car park several paths leave the road for the Huntingstile Gap. The first is the primary route, and departs some few metres right of the steep road junction at GR332052. An early branch left climbs onto the Dow Bank ridge, while the main thrust of the path takes a steady line, passing an electricity compound to reach the deep gap. Ostensibly this is a route over to Grasmere, which later descends as a cobbled lane to the Redbank Road at Lea Cottage.

ASCENT FROM GRASMERE (23–25)

Via Wray Gill   332m/1090ft   1.5km/1 mile

Choose from three popular paths, plus a rough invention and a surreptitious approach (Route 9). **8** From the middle of Grasmere village, at the junction of Broadgate with Langdale Road, take the no-through road leading north-west. Enter the parkland environs of Allan Bank. Keep right on the approach drive to reach the cottages and enter a narrow gated lane. (This point can be reached from Easedale Road, via Goody Bridge Cottages, where a footpath leads over stepping-stones, via hand-gates, and up a pasture to cross a drive that rises to a fence-stile into the lane above the cottages.) The lane duly emerges at a kissing-gate onto the open fell. The path climbs initially with a wall close left and rises through juniper. Watch for the path forking left to a ford of Wray Gill. This is the direct line to the fell summit, while the right path wanders onto the ridge under Lang How.

Via Blindtarn Moss   332m/1190ft   2.5km/1½ miles

The name Blindtarn probably derives from the hidden nature of the combe's draining watercourse. **9** Follow Easedale Road and cross Easedale Beck via the footbridge at

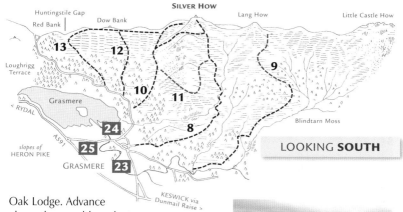

SILVER HOW

Huntingstile Gap · Red Bank · Dow Bank · Lang How · Little Castle How

13 **12** **9**

Loughrigg Terrace

10 **11**

Grasmere

< RYDAL

24 **8**

slopes of HERON PIKE **25**

GRASMERE **23**

Blindtarn Moss

LOOKING **SOUTH**

KESWICK via Dunmail Raise >

Oak Lodge. Advance along the roughly cob-bled path, which soon runs with a wall to the left and beck to the right. After the restored New Bridge watch for the yellow waymark on the gate to the left. The path guides, via a meadow, to a metal gate and through light woodland to join, at another a gate, the track leading to a pair of holiday cot-tages. Pass on by the white railings to a wooden gate in the field corner. Continue with

Crinkle Crags and Great Langdale Swinescar Hause

the wall on the left, the route jostling with the gill as it ascends to a waymark post directing right, below a gate with private notice affixed. Dense bracken is replaced by juniper at the open hollow of Blindtarn Moss. The path forks – take the more minor left-hand path. After a small ford the indistinct path continues up the wet slope through juniper and rushes. The fell eases and a sheep path materialises, drawing up onto skyline and the ridge path. Turn left and pass three pools beneath Lang How, known as Youdell Tarn. The largest pool, encroached by reed, has the least open water, but it makes a fine viewpoint for the Langdale Pikes' Youdell Tarn. The other two pools have tiny isles and are host to bogbean. At the third tarn take the right-hand-fork path bound for Silver How, now clearly in view ahead.

Via Kelbarrow 305m/1000ft 2.5km/1½ miles

For many months in the year the Redbank Road, a back way over the hill between Grasmere and Elterwater, seems to be colonised by a walkers and cars in almost equal proportion, to the annoyance of both! **10** From the entrance to Redbank Road car park follow this road left. At the drive entrance to Kelbarrow, opposite the Faeryland boat hire/tearoom, go right, up the walled lane. Ascend via two kissing-gates, now under the rough slope of the fell, and the path keeps the intake wall close left. (**11** Should you relish a spot of rough-stuff walking, you may consider branching

North from the path above Kelbarrow

right as the path first levels. A sheep path contours across the scree and bracken slope, becoming less definite as you come high above the open-pasture section of the approach. Climb to the skyline well before the craggy ravine of Wray Gill and follow the scarp top (there is no path). The views of the lake and over the village to Great Rigg and Fairfield are exceptional. Otherwise continue to the wall corner and either ascend the eroded gully direct to the summit or continue, via two fords, to the ridge-top path interchange. Turn right, mounting via a large cairn, and keep right along the scarp brow to the summit.

Via Dow Bank   320m/1050ft   3.2km/2 miles

12 For a more sylvan option, though with hampered views, continue with Redbank Road to turn right into the drive leading to The Wyke. The fenced drive passes between stately oaks. At a gill crossing, with the house in view, turn right, slipping over the higher bridge. Go via the remains of a metal kissing-gate, and embark upon a path which rises as a stony trail through light birch wood to reach a wall-stile and hand-gate onto the fell. Either continue through the scrub and bracken onto Dow Bank, or go right, with the wall to the right, via marshy patches, to the curving wall corner and ascend the gully direct. **13** Another path leaves the Redbank Road further up opposite Lea Cottage. Initially rising as a drive to Huntingstile House, this becomes a cobbled lane to a hand-gate then rises to the Huntingstile Gap. A metal gate, immediately left of the hand-gate, provides access to a lovely woodland parade, and rejoins Redbank Road opposite the path to Loughrigg Terrace. At this point a path steps off the road and goes up three immediate steps to curve round, via a hand-gate, into the Gap. To complete the suite, impromptu paths leave the open road west of High Close Youth Hostel, again gathering in the Gap in readiness to mount the Dow Bank ridge.

THE SUMMIT

A tumbled wreck of a cairn sits on the bare top surveying the luxuriant Grasmere vale. The all-round view is most rewarding. Visitors can train their eyes both at the detail within the vale, of village, meadow, woods and lake, and to the lovely surround of higher fells. So whilst it is not the highest point upon the near mass of fell, Lang How having that status, it is the natural viewpoint. This is a place to gaze at ease and compose worthy words to eloquently express the enchanting scene, thus following in the footsteps of the esteemed local wordsmith William Wordsworth. Be sure he too sat here too!

SAFE DESCENTS

The eastern slope of the fell is lined with crags, so all descents need to begin from the depression some 100m west-south-west from the cairn. The path leading north, fording Wray Gill and bound for Allan Bank, is the best in poor visibility. To the south find assurance in the ridge path leading south-east that reaches the unenclosed Elterwater to High Close road off Dow Bank.

RIDGE ROUTES

BLEA RIGG	↓45m/150ft	↑205m/670ft	3.2km/2 miles

The path leads off north-west, passing below Lang How, superior to Silver How by 19m (62ft). Pass two pools hosting bogbean and continue over the brow to a much larger tarn, where reed encroachment is so advanced that it has the least open water of the three. Many a camera must have been directed at this view of the Langdale Pikes. The path weaves easily along the ridge until the marshy hollow of Swinescar Hause, and the line of least resistance trends diagonally across the slope by a curious low shelter to traverse Castle How. Fellwanderers may choose to head up from the sheepfold (pathless) to reach to top of Raw Pike (no cairn) and the southern top of Great Castle How, with its fine view of Blea Rigg ahead. These routes reunite at the quartz stones and pass pools en route to the summit.

LOUGHRIGG FELL	↓290m/950ft	↑230m/750ft	4km/2½ miles

Leave the scarp-top summit, angling left to a large cairn, from where the ridge path pitches purposefully downhill. From the foot of this initial bank a sequence of switchback tops is crossed via Spedding Crag and Dow Bank. Reaching Huntingstile Gap bear left via a hand-gate in a fence, and the path curves right via steps onto the Redbank Road – watch for traffic. Turn right and first left, descending through a gate onto the east end of Loughrigg Terrace. Climb the prominent path southeast via the Grasmere cairn to reach the summit.

PANORAMA

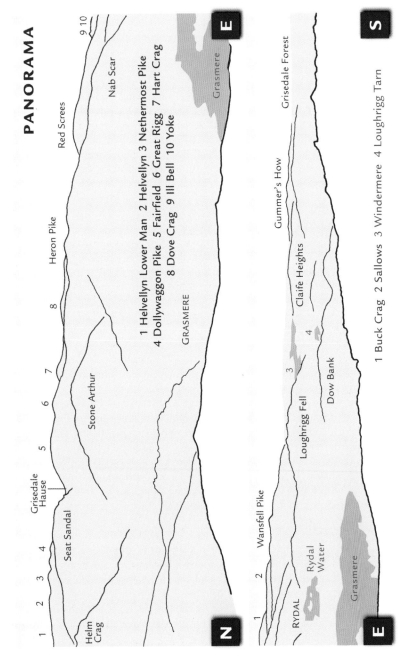

Red Screes   Heron Pike   Stone Arthur   Griesdale Hause   Seat Sandal   Helm Crag

Nab Scar   9 10   8   7 6 5   4 3 2 1

1 Helvellyn Lower Man   2 Helvellyn   3 Nethermost Pike
4 Dollywaggon Pike   5 Fairfield   6 Great Rigg   7 Hart Crag
8 Dove Crag   9 Ill Bell   10 Yoke

GRASMERE

Grasmere

E   **N**

Griesdale Forest   Gummer's How   Claife Heights   Wansfell Pike   RYDAL

Loughrigg Fell   Dow Bank   Rydal Water   Grasmere   3   4

1 Buck Crag   2 Sallows   3 Windermere   4 Loughrigg Tarn

2   1

S   **E**

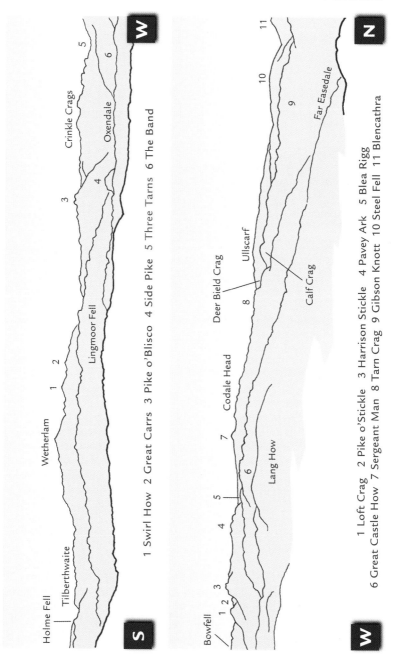

Holme Fell — Tilberthwaite — Wetherlam — Lingmoor Fell — Crinkle Crags — Oxendale — The Band

1 Swirl How 2 Great Carrs 3 Pike o'Blisco 4 Side Pike 5 Three Tarns 6 The Band

Bowfell — Lang How — Codale Head — Deer Bield Crag — Ullscarf — Calf Crag — Far Easedale

1 Loft Crag 2 Pike o'Stickle 3 Harrison Stickle 4 Pavey Ark 5 Blea Rigg
6 Great Castle How 7 Sergeant Man 8 Tarn Crag 9 Gibson Knott 10 Steel Fell 11 Blencathra

24 STEEL FELL (553m, 1814ft)

This is a triangle of sturdy fell defined by Greenburn, Wythburn and Dunmail Raise. It is infrequently considered as a direct objective from Grasmere yet, when undertaken from Town End, as the first part of a Greenburn horseshoe, it really shows its metal. This is a lovely little fell to climb, and the proximity to the A591 makes it easily accessible. The fell name does not relate in any way to either ore or any allied alloy, but is actually a variant of *shieling*, meaning 'fell of the summer steading'. Overlooking Dunmail Raise and set upon the Lakeland watershed, its situation lends it quite some distinction as a viewpoint, and from here the massive bulk of Helvellyn can be fully appreciated. Being so distantly connected to Calf Crag lends the fell a certain stand-alone quality, which may cause it to be considered a single afternoon's objective. However, circular tours can easily be contrived, based upon either Wythburn Dale or Dunmail Raise.

ASCENT FROM MILL BRIDGE (21)

Direct   475m/1560ft   2.5km/1½ miles

1 There is lay-by parking at Mill Bridge (bus stop above Town Head). Follow the road down to Low Mill Bridge, crossing the Rothay, then turn right, and directly after Ghyll Foot bear left up the 'private driveway' via a pair of cattle grids to pass the tree-screened Helmside. Go through the gate beyond Turn Howe and keep right, rising to

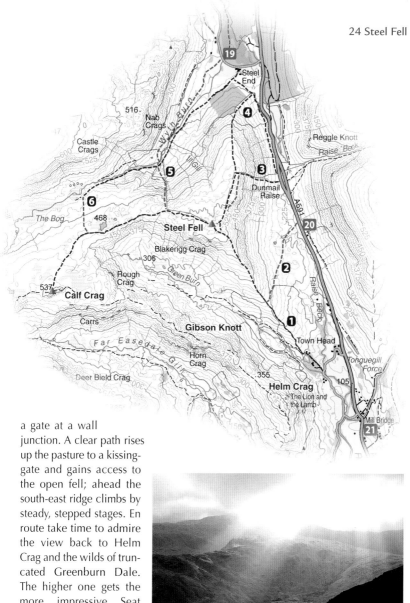

a gate at a wall junction. A clear path rises up the pasture to a kissing-gate and gains access to the open fell; ahead the south-east ridge climbs by steady, stepped stages. En route take time to admire the view back to Helm Crag and the wilds of truncated Greenburn Dale. The higher one gets the more impressive Seat Sandal looks, very reminiscent of Beinn Dorain (a landmark mountain overlooking the West Highland Way) and quite unlike the

Sun bursting into Greenburn Dale from Blakerigg Crag

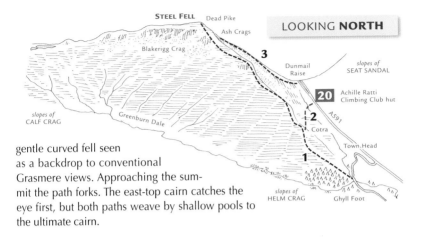

LOOKING **NORTH**

STEEL FELL   Dead Pike
Ash Crags
Blakerigg Crag
3
Dunmail
Raise
slopes of
SEAT SANDAL

20 Achille Ratti
Climbing Club hut

slopes of
CALF CRAG
Greenburn Dale

2
Cotra

Town Head

1

slopes of
HELM CRAG
Ghyll Foot

gentle curved fell seen
as a backdrop to conventional
Grasmere views. Approaching the sum-
mit the path forks. The east-top cairn catches the
eye first, but both paths weave by shallow pools to
the ultimate cairn.

ASCENT FROM DUNMAIL RAISE (20)

Via Cotra   320m/1050ft   2.7km/1¾ miles

2 A useful optional route onto the south-east ridge begins from the ladder-stile opposite the Achille Ratti Hut lay-by. A pathless line is followed that fords the diminished
Raise Beck, severed from its upper section by the construction of the Thirlmere
Reservoir, which diverted the head-stream into the reservoir. Cross the Cotra moraine
keeping right, encountering bracken on the rise, and contour above the enclosure
wall to the skyline ridge.

Steel Fell from Helvellyn Screes

Direct   305m/1000ft   0.8km/½ mile

3 Gird your loins and steel yourself for this one, though there is actually nothing out of the ordinary about this quick climb. Either use the generous lay-by at GR329111, or draw off the highway on the north-bound dual-carriageway adjacent to the ladder-stile at GR327117. Then climb the pasture slope that drifts towards the gill and boundary fence. As a finger of scree reaches down, slip over the gill and, keeping the fence tight right, climb the steep final section to the top. Take a breather and gaze over the gulf of Dunmail Raise into the impressive ravine of Raise Beck, sliced into the Helvellyn massif as if struck by a massive lumberjack's axe. Either follow the sheep trod along the edge of Ash Crags or keep to the ridge path that runs closer to the fence (a sensible

Dunmail Raise from Ash Crags

precaution on those frequent gusty days) and leads to the summit at the fence corner.

ASCENT FROM STEEL END (19)

Direct   375m/1230ft   1.5km/1 mile

Before the Thirlmere valley was drowned, two farms – West Head and Steel End – overlooked the confluence of the Wythburn with Raise Beck. Each farm had 100 acres of valley pasture and when the holdings were necessarily amalgamated, West Head was pulled down. Fortunately the handsome traditional field-barn, Stenkin, survived the upheaval. Two, or at a pinch three, routes (Routes 4–6) can be contemplated from this northern base.

4 The principal route is the north ridge. Leave the Steel End car park and turn left. Follow the road to the entrance to West Head Farm. A sign directs to the right at the beginning of the old bridle path to Dunmail Raise. Pass up by the cottages and subsequent farmhouse and follow a short lane leading to a gate. Ignore the obvious gravel track to the right, and instead keep the wall close right along a green track. Pass through a gate, then leave the bridleway. Head up the bank and come above the plantation to reach a hand-gate where a wall straps the ridge. This is a good moment to look across the valley to Birkside Gill, draining Nethermost and Dollywaggon Pikes.

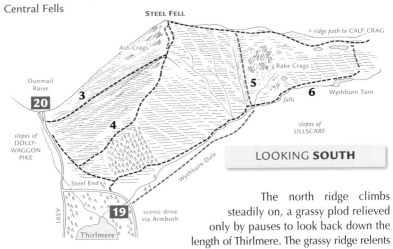

STEEL FELL

> ridge path to CALF CRAG

Ash Crags

Rake Crags

Dunmail Raise

20

3

5

6 Wythburn Tarn

falls

4

slopes of DOLLY-WAGGON PIKE

slopes of ULLSCARF

Wythburn Dale

Steel End

LOOKING SOUTH

A591

19 scenic drive via Armboth

Thirlmere

The north ridge climbs steadily on, a grassy plod relieved only by pauses to look back down the length of Thirlmere. The grassy ridge relents to a gentler gradient on the broadening upper ridge, and leads by a metal stake on a knoll to a stile in the right-angle of the boundary fence. From here the fence makes the awful drop directly to Dunmail Raise, making this edge is a fine spot to gaze down on the ancient cairn in the pass, as well as up the facing Raise Beck to Cofa Pike and Fairfield. Continue either along the brink of Ash Crags with the sheep track or stay closer to the fence for the easy final ¼ mile to the summit. The latter option is prudent when a strong wind funnels through the Dunmail gap.

Via Rake Crags 380m/1250ft 2km/1¼ miles

Two ascents (Routes 5 and 6) can be considered out of upper Wythburn Dale. From the Steel End car park go left the few metres to a kissing-gate or continue over the bridge a further few metres to a hand-gate and steps leading down into the meadow. The two paths advance in harmony either side of the fenced Wythburn Beck, via gates, ladder-stiles or stiles, and reunite at a wooden footbridge.

5 This first option will appeal to people a little less concerned about ease of travel and more intent on getting to the top. Ascend beside the wall and fence adjacent to the minor gill due south. As a means of gaining the ridge, it is practical and safe, but oh so steep!

Via Wythburn Dale 390m/1280ft 3.5km /2¼ miles

6 For a more serene option, continue on the dale path that climbs above the southern bank of Wythburn Beck. There are two fine waterslide cascades, which are all the more exciting when a strong wind surges spray back. Pass the twin portal moraines, anciently breached, that drain the former Wythburn Dale Tarn. Water nonetheless does tend to linger; it must love the place, as I suspect you will. Above, Castle Crag's overhanging buttress catches the eye. Pass the sinuous vestigal tarn and branch off the clear path, climbing pathless to the left onto the ridge. Skirt right, around the two large plateau-top tarns, to join the ridge path that leads unerringly east for 1 mile to the summit.

THE SUMMIT

Otherwise curiously known as Dead Pike, this is a cracking viewpoint, with its principal cairn resting on a small plinth of reddish rock beside the remains of the old metal county boundary fence. Some 100m due east, at a slightly lower elevation, a second cairn sits at the angle of the old metal fence. A more recent wooden fence switches upon the summit, taking a cleaner line north to the point, nearly a mile distant, where the pre-1974 Cumberland–Westmorland boundary fence plummets east to Dunmail Raise. The all-round view is inspiring. Grand is the huge whaleback western aspect of the Helvellyn range; and charming the long view up Thirlmere to Blencathra. Elsewhere see the Coniston Fells in a tight huddle and the massive bulk of fell at the core of the Central Fells rising to High Raise and, much nearer, the broad mass of Ullscarf, enhanced when shafts of sunlight play on the near buttresses of Nab and Castle Crags.

SAFE DESCENTS

The north and south ridges are benign enough.

RIDGE ROUTE

CALF CRAG	↓90m/300ft	↑70m/230ft	2.4km/1½ miles

Walk west beside the fence with the occasional marshy hollow to straddle. The path dips as the fence departs north, and several knolls are avoided en route to a large marsh containing two innominate tarns. After this point the path is less well defined. It loses company with the intermittent metal boundary stake as it sweeps south-east over damp ground at the head of Greenburn Dale to rise to the prominent knoll-top of Calf Crag.

Steel Fell summit cairn

PANORAMA

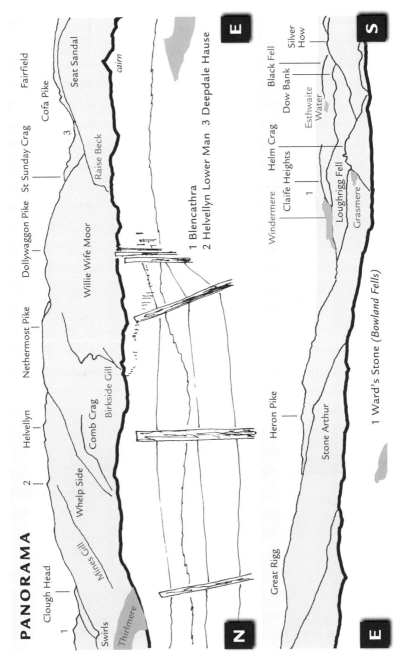

Clough Head
Swirls
Thirlmere
1
Mines Gill
Whelp Side
2
Helvellyn
Comb Crag
Birkside Gill
Nethermost Pike
Willie Wife Moor
Dollywaggon Pike
St Sunday Crag
Raise Beck
3
Cofa Pike
Fairfield
Seat Sandal
cairn

1 Blencathra
2 Helvellyn Lower Man 3 Deepdale Hause

Great Rigg
Stone Arthur
Heron Pike
Windermere
Claife Heights
1
Helm Crag
Loughrigg Fell
Grasmere
Black Fell
Dow Bank
Esthwaite Water
Silver How

1 Ward's Stone (Bowland Fells)

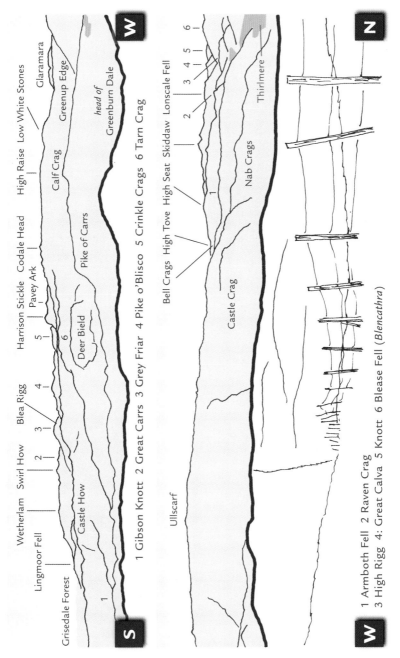

24 Steel Fell

Lingmoor Fell Wetherlam Swirl How Blea Rigg Harrison Stickle Codale Head High Raise Low White Stones Glaramara

Griesdale Forest Castle How Pavey Ark Deer Bield Pike of Carrs Calf Crag Greenup Edge

head of Greenburn Dale

1 Gibson Knott 2 Great Carrs 3 Grey Friar 4 Pike o'Blisco 5 Crinkle Crags 6 Tarn Crag

Bell Crags High Tove High Seat Skiddaw Lonscale Fell

Ullscarf Castle Crag Nab Crags Thirlmere

1 Armboth Fell 2 Raven Crag
3 High Rigg 4: Great Calva 5 Knott 6 Blease Fell (*Blencathra*)

257

25 TARN CRAG *(485m, 1591ft)*

Codale Head, the 'cold dalehead' of Easedale, throws down ridges to embrace two chill-watered corries, Codale and Easedale Tarns. With Blea Rigg casting shadows from its southern brink, Tarn Crag basks in the sun to the north, and in turn casts cool shade into Far Easedale. The tiny upper Codale Tarn has a certain charm, which to be frank is absent from the lower lake, for all that the earlier tourists made it a place of special resort. What is witnessed is a post-glacial landscape of moraine and barren slopes; bracken is everywhere, paler strips betraying the course of rills spilling from the stony fellsides. From the outflow, where Sour Milk Gill begins its eventful journey, the domed top gives the fell identity with Easdale tarn; hence its name.

Sour Milk Gill

The fell can be conveniently climbed via the spine of its east ridge, from either flank via Easedale Tarn or, more intriguingly, from directly under Deer Bield Crag. A more circuitous route via Codale Tarn gives prominence to the pencil-point of Belles Knott. For all the shadows the fell is best seen from high on Calf Crag, with Deer Bield and

Deer Bield Crag

Ferngill Crags adding a rugged grandeur to Far Easedale. There are no ascents worthy of normal discourse in these upper reaches, though one may climb from the saddle at the head of the dale and join the ridge from Broadstone Head.

ASCENT FROM GRASMERE (22–25)

Via Easedale Tarn 427m/1400ft 3.5km/2¼ miles

1 Follow Easedale Road via Goody Bridge to cross the footbridge opposite Oak Lodge. A path leads via a hand-gate across a meadow, coming close to Easedale Beck with a wall close to the left.
Ignore the inviting New
Bridge to the

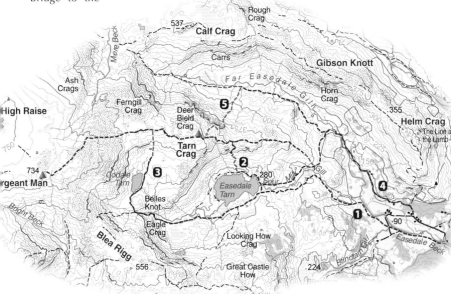

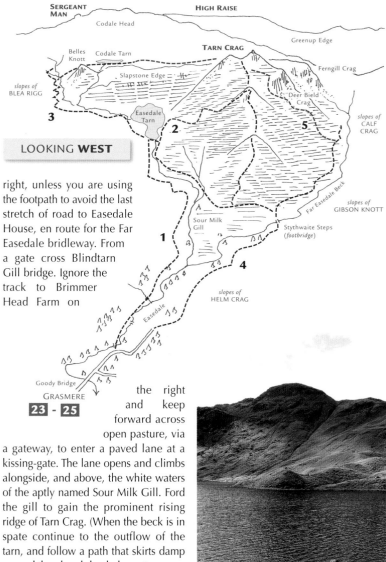

LOOKING **WEST**

right, unless you are using the footpath to avoid the last stretch of road to Easedale House, en route for the Far Easedale bridleway. From a gate cross Blindtarn Gill bridge. Ignore the track to Brimmer Head Farm on

23 - 25

the right and keep forward across open pasture, via a gateway, to enter a paved lane at a kissing-gate. The lane opens and climbs alongside, and above, the white waters of the aptly named Sour Milk Gill. Ford the gill to gain the prominent rising ridge of Tarn Crag. (When the beck is in spate continue to the outflow of the tarn, and follow a path that skirts damp ground then heads back downstream on the north side.) By either means take the first strike onto the rising ridge of Tarn Crag; bracken is the challenge, as not enough fellwalkers come this way to

Tarn Crag from the outflow of Easedale Tarn

Tarn Crag from Easedale Tarn

beat it back. Climb, faithful to the ridge-top, by a rock tor above Greathead Crag, aiming for the ultimate skyline notch, then turn right to reach the small summit cairn on the prominent and well-defended headland. **2** Another option is to fight through the bracken on the north side of the tarn, through the moraine from its outflow, and to climb an old shepherds' trod on an indistinct zig-zag onto the high ridge left of Greathead Crag.

Via Codale Tarn   442m/1450ft   4.5km/2¾ miles

3 Anyone seeking to develop a circular tour with the sole intent of visiting Tarn Crag would be wise to bring Codale Tarn into the equation. Continue with the main path from the outflow, running along the south side of the tarn to join the main feeder-gill below Blea Crag. The path has been greatly improved, and in parts forms a stone staircase rising with the cascades, a scene enhanced by the spire-like presence of Belles Knott. A minor path forks right above the cascades, fords the gill, and climbs over the west shoulder of Belles Knott to reach Codale Tarn, a place of quiet retreat. The quaint rocky isle may tempt a few to try their luck at reaching it without wetting their socks! Pass the tiny outflow and climb the damp northern slope by a ruined sheepfold to join the ridge path, and turn right to the summit.

Via Far Easedale   427m/1400ft   3.7km/2¼ miles

4 The fell can be approached with equal alacrity from Far Easedale, using the bridle path that was made all the more popular when it became part of Wainwright's Coast to Coast Walk. That route naturally takes advantage of the Helm Crag – Gibson Knott ridge as a choice variation to the wild, shadowy depths of the dale. From the road-end at Easedale House follow the public bridleway signs indicating 'Far Easedale,

Borrowdale'; this route advances to the Stythwaite Steps footbridge. The name Stythwaite indicates a former 'steep clearing', perhaps in some way reflected in the walled enclosures up to the right on the slopes of Gibson Knott.

'Dinosaur' rock, Deer Bield Crag

Cross the footbridge, and here you have a choice. The first option is to follow the path up by the wall, noting the massive boulder capped with a luxuriant heather growth to the left, onto the ridge-end, thus linking to the path to Easedale Tarn and Route 1.

5 Keep right right on the clear path running up Far Easedale. Pass on by the naturally drained site of a tarn overlooked by Pike of Carrs. Try branching from the path to search for the least bracken in the vicinity of a gill; an apparent grass strip gives the illusion of an easy way, but keep eyes focused on the towering cliff of Deer Bield. There is no path, but the going is basically trouble free, if tangly and wet. Near the base of the crag is a group of mighty boulders; the bottom one, a particularly fine specimen, has the demeanour of a dinosaur! Boulder hop – there is precious little scree – then either clamber straight onto the ridge or keep up to the right above the crag. Prolong contact with the eastern rim of the fell before you are finally forced to drift left to join the ridge path that rises up through the notch to the ultimate point.

Tarn Crag from Blea Crag

Tarn Crag summit cairn

THE SUMMIT
The craggy top-knot is a thoroughly delightful place to visit, and from the small cairn you can enjoy a lovely view back towards the green vale of Grasmere – the only thing lacking is Easedale Tarn itself. This deficiency is speedily remedied by going south, back across the ridge path in the notch, some 100m, to stand beside a significantly larger and strategically placed cairn that commands a bird's-eye view down upon the glistening waters. The summit ridge, running westwards, deserves to be relished for its own sake – the pools and rocks a wild garden to explore.

SAFE DESCENTS
Stick to the ridge due east, and at the foot go either left for the Stythwaite Steps footbridge or right to ford Sour Milk Gill.

RIDGE ROUTE

SERGEANT MAN	↓6m/20ft	↑255m/840ft	2km/1¼ miles

A narrow ridge path weaves west along the marshy top amid glaciated rock outcrops. As the slope steepens, be careful not to catch your feet in peat holes caused by surface wash-out. The path ascends beside a gill to reach a cigar-shaped pool adorned with bogbean, then links up with the ridge path ascending Broadstone Head from the saddle at the top of Far Easedale. Follow the old county boundary fence metal stakes on the left to Codale Head, rounding a marsh to the summit stake.

PANORAMA

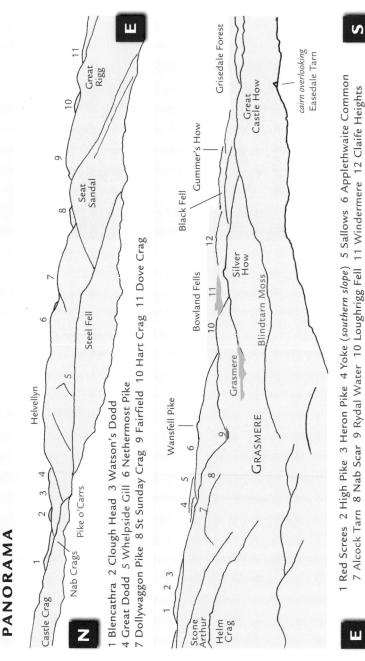

N

E

Castle Crag

Nab Crags

Pike o'Carrs

Helvellyn

Steel Fell

Seat Sandal

Great Rigg

1   2   3   4   5   6   7   8   9   10   11

1 Blencathra 2 Clough Head 3 Watson's Dodd
4 Great Dodd 5 Whelpside Gill 6 Nethermost Pike
7 Dollywaggon Pike 8 St Sunday Crag 9 Fairfield 10 Hart Crag 11 Dove Crag

E

S

Stone Arthur

Helm Crag

Wansfell Pike

GRASMERE

Grasmere

Blindtarn Moss

Silver How

Bowland Fells

Black Fell

Gummer's How

Great Castle How

Griesdale Forest

cairn overlooking Easedale Tarn

1   2   3   4   5   6   7   8   9   10   11   12

1 Red Screes 2 High Pike 3 Heron Pike 4 Yoke (*southern slope*) 5 Sallows 6 Applethwaite Common
7 Alcock Tarn 8 Nab Scar 9 Rydal Water 10 Loughrigg Fell 11 Windermere 12 Claife Heights

264

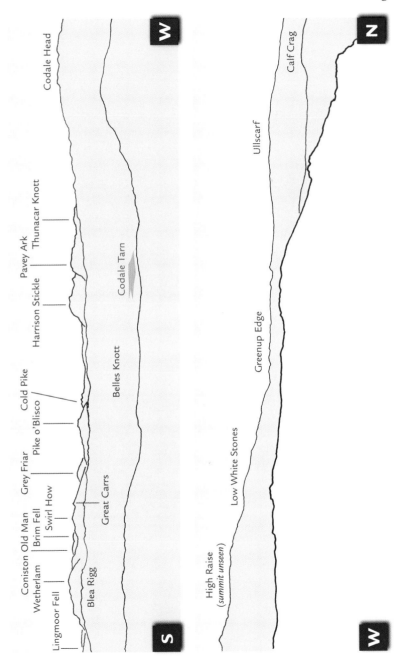

W

Codale Head

Thunacar Knott
Pavey Ark
Harrison Stickle

Codale Tarn

Cold Pike
Grey Friar
Pike o'Blisco

Belles Knott

Coniston Old Man
Wetherlam
Brim Fell
Swirl How

Great Carrs

Lingmoor Fell

Blea Rigg

S

N

Calf Crag

Ullscarf

Greenup Edge

Low White Stones

High Raise
(*summit unseen*)

W

26 THUNACAR KNOTT *(723m, 2372ft)*

The Old Norse terms *thunr* 'thin' and *karr* 'man' suggest that this fell derives its name from the nickname of some early Scandinavian shepherd who was a particularly lanky character. Above the handsome face of Pavey Ark the fell is the natural crown, highbrow and aloof. The summit is a gentle final

Looking east to Seat Sandal and Fairfield

swelling abraded with vertically fractured rock clitter and a shallow pool. Even the summit fails to be a convincing moment. Authoritive writers have frequently cited the 'lower' north top as the summit, such is the uncertainty. Most fellwalkers hasten on to High Raise, Sergeant Man or the Pikes, brushing over the eastern shoulder, little caring, nor even aware, that a separate fell is at hand. It has barely a watercourse to call its own, nor other feature to stand it apart. There is nothing but the great sky above, a panorama of fells that would be the envy of many a lesser compatriot height... and, yes, the raging fury of the elements.

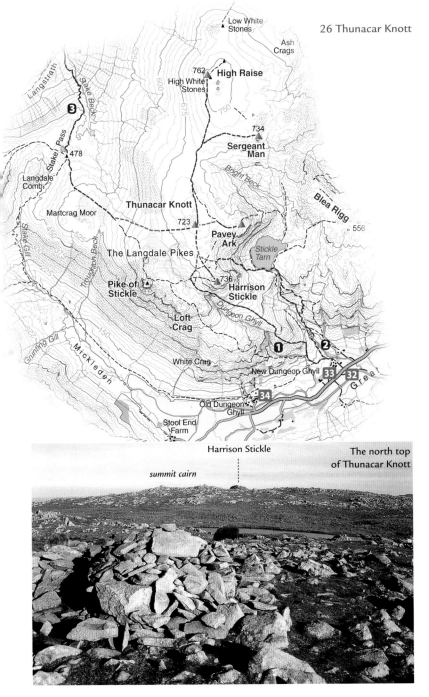

Low White
Stones

Ash
Crags

762
High Raise
High White
Stones

600

3

Langstrath

Stake Beck

675

750

478

Langdale
Comb

734
Sergeant
Man

Bright Beck

Thunacar Knott

Blea Rigg

556

Martcrag Moor

649

723

Stake Gill

450

525

Troughton Beck

Pavey
Ark

Stickle
Tarn

The Langdale Pikes

Pike of
Stickle

736
Harrison
Stickle

Grunting Gill

150

Loft
Crag

Dungeon Ghyll

1

2

Mickleden

White Crag

New Dungeon Ghyll

33

32

34

Great

Old Dungeon
Ghyll

Stool End
Farm

Harrison Stickle

summit cairn

The north top
of Thunacar Knott

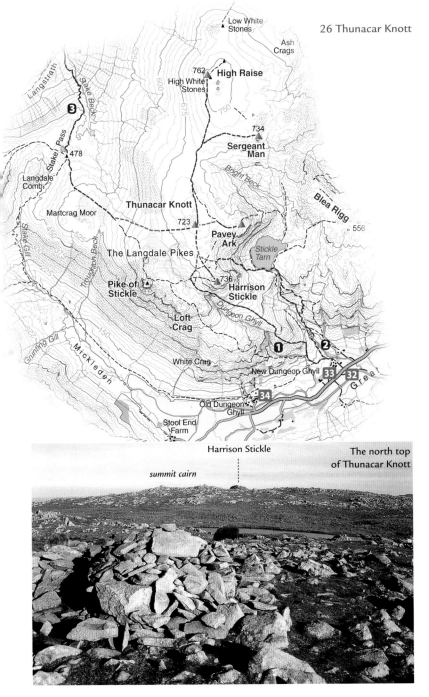

ASCENT FROM GREAT LANGDALE (32–33)

Via Pike How or Stickle Ghyll   652m/2140ft   2.5km/1½ miles

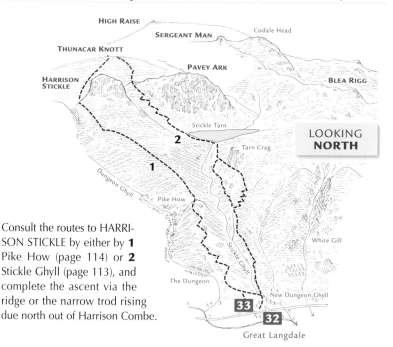

Consult the routes to HARRI-
SON STICKLE by either by **1**
Pike How (page 114) or **2**
Stickle Ghyll (page 113), and
complete the ascent via the
ridge or the narrow trod rising
due north out of Harrison Combe.

Vertically fissured plateau outcrop
on Thunacar Knott

Looking south to the Coniston Fells

ASCENT FROM STONETHWAITE (1)

Via Langstrath 640m/2100ft 8.7km/5½ miles

The long stride from Rosthwaite (4½ miles) or Stonethwaite up Langstrath via the Stake Pass is normally undertaken as an integral part of the Cumbria Way. Most walkers are content to slip over Langdale Combe into upper Mickleden, with fabulous scenery every step of the way. But 'red-blooded' sorts with energy to burn will think nothing of knocking off the Pikes, with Thunacar Knott taken en route to Harrison

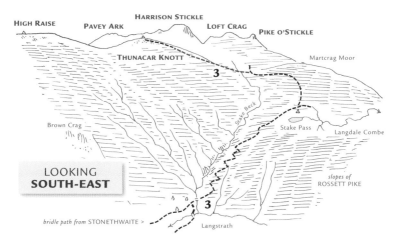

LOOKING
SOUTH-EAST

True summit of Thunacar Knott

Stickle. Alternatively, it may be considered as part of a great circular route with High Raise, returning via Greenup Edge.

3 For the early stages consult SERGEANT'S CRAG pages 235–236. From the cairn at the top of the pass a strong path branches south onto the peaty ridge of Martcrag Moor, traversing some pretty horrid ground before the slope steepens. Coming close to a gill, branch half-left (east-south-east) from the main path to Pike o'Stickle. Rising up the grassy fell, skirt the rocky rim to reach the summit cairn.

THE SUMMIT

There are two tops, each with a cairn, to the north and south of a shallow hollow filled with a pool. The southern cairn is 'the' summit, whatever the quirks of tradition may try to claim – in my book the top of a fell is the summit! The panorama is the meat and matter of this place – there is a lot to see, but qualitatively the view is at its best to the west.

SAFE DESCENTS

A narrow trod leads due south into Harrison Combe and joins the path directly below Harrison Crag above the upper Dungeon Ghyll gorge. It runs perilously along the rim of the ravine, so care is needed here. An alternative option would be to cross the large stepping-stones and make for the Thorn Crag col joining Mark Gate, a very well-secured path that leaves from Loft Crag. Both routes reach down to the New Dungeon Ghyll.

RIDGE ROUTES

HARRISON STICKLE ↓45m/150ft ↑60m/200ft 0.8km/½ mile

Head south largely over a grassy terrain and eventually swerve to the right of a rock tor.

HIGH RAISE ↓50m/160ft ↑85m/280ft 1.6km/1 mile

At last a chance to lengthen the stride – one might be walking the Wessex Downs, but for the scenery! Go north, drifting down to join the ridge path from Pavey Ark, and cross the depression at the head of Bright Beck. Beyond, the path has been re-aligned to reduce wear on fragile soil along the gentle rise to the summit.

SERGEANT MAN ↓45m/150ft ↑60m/200ft 1.6km/1 mile

Follow suit with the High Raise path, only take the second path angling half-right. As the ground begins to rise after the depression contour to the summit knot. The first path leads through an outcrop and traverses the slope well below Sergeant Man – a kind of speedy short-cut for anyone racing to Grasmere. Shame on them!

Looking to Sergeant Man

PANORAMA

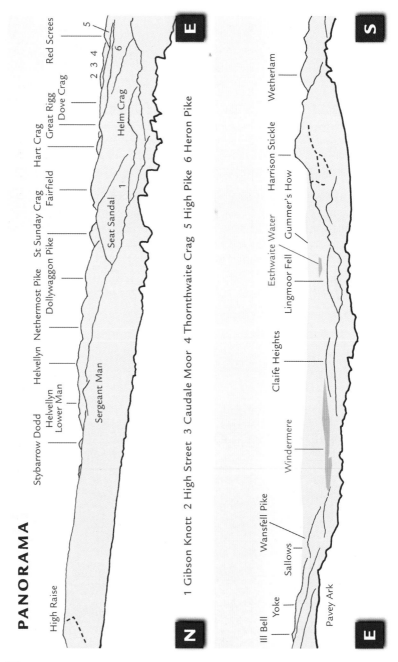

High Raise

Stybarrow Dodd

Helvellyn Lower Man

Helvellyn

Nethermost Pike

St Sunday Crag

Dollywaggon Pike

Fairfield

Hart Crag

Great Rigg

Dove Crag

Red Screens

2 3 4

5

6

Sergeant Man

Seat Sandal

Helm Crag

1

E

N

1 Gibson Knott 2 High Street 3 Caudale Moor 4 Thornthwaite Crag 5 High Pike 6 Heron Pike

Ill Bell

Yoke

Wansfell Pike

Sallows

Windermere

Claife Heights

Esthwaite Water

Lingmoor Fell

Gummer's How

Harrison Stickle

Wetherlam

Pavey Ark

S

E

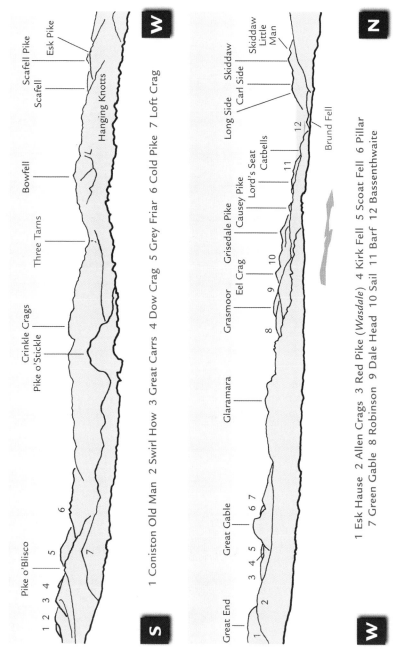

1 Coniston Old Man 2 Swirl How 3 Great Carrs 4 Dow Crag 5 Grey Friar 6 Cold Pike 7 Loft Crag

1 Esk Hause 2 Allen Crags 3 Red Pike (*Wasdale*) 4 Kirk Fell 5 Scoat Fell 6 Pillar
7 Green Gable 8 Robinson 9 Dale Head 10 Sail 11 Barf 12 Bassenthwaite

27 ULLSCARF *(726m, 2382ft)*

One seldom hears the praises of Ullscarf. For all the comparative tameness of the upper plateau, in harmony with High Raise, it really is a splendid place to stride. The summit, and several lateral points including Low Saddle, Standing, Tarn and Nab Crags, are all quite exceptional viewpoints in their own right. The higher ground fails to live up to its brave front of crags, and those that form a stern defence to Wythburn Dale, especially, give observers the illusion of a seriously craggy height.

A cursory knowledge of the drainage of the fell is crucial to knowing where you are, as a wrong turn can leave you a long way from your intended valley base. Ullscarf is not a fell to toy with in misty conditions, as the whole point of its pivotal situation is lost, as may the hapless wanderer

Ullscarf from Low White Stones

↑ Ullscarf from the top of the plantation above Harrop Tarn

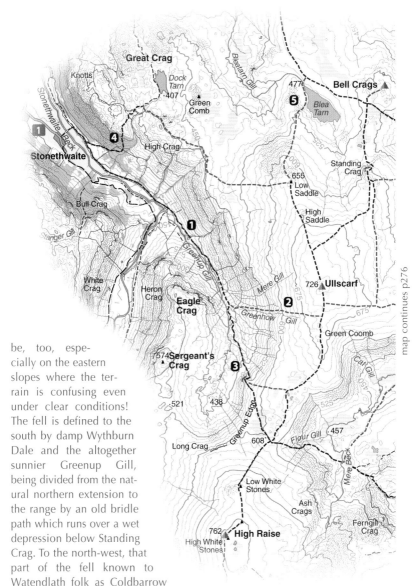

map continues p276

be, too, espe-
cially on the eastern
slopes where the ter-
rain is confusing even
under clear conditions!
The fell is defined to the
south by damp Wythburn
Dale and the altogether
sunnier Greenup Gill,
being divided from the natural northern extension to
the range by an old bridle
path which runs over a wet
depression below Standing
Crag. To the north-west, that
part of the fell known to
Watendlath folk as Coldbarrow
Fell descends in an uncluttered fashion
to Green Comb and Great Crag either side of Dock Tarn.

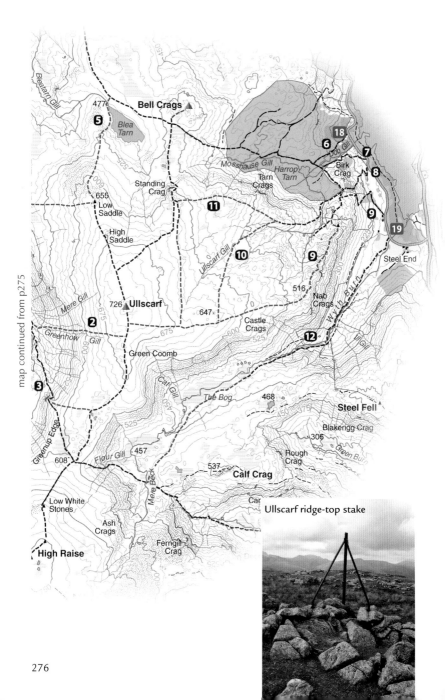

Ullscarf ridge-top stake

map continued from p275

ASCENT FROM STONETHWAITE (1)

Via Greenhow Gill   628m/2060ft   4.7km/3 miles

1 From the three-way signpost beside the telephone kiosk, leave the hamlet by the lane on the left to 'Greenup Edge'. Cross Stonethwaite Bridge, momentarily pausing to gaze into the turquoise waters of Stonethwaite Beck and lean on the pipe railings to look upstream to the shapely profile of Eagle Crag, which maintains a strong presence during this valley approach. After the gate meet the

The Beacon, Nab Crags

bridle path from Rosthwaite, turn right, and through the next gate enter a lane on a rough track that continues via several further gates. Across the beck upon the valley meadow the camping field is seldom empty, such is the perennial allure of the Stonethwaite valley as a base for fell adventurers. Proceed beyond the footbridge above the Langstrath Beck – Greenup Gill confluence. Keep ahead up the Greenup Gill valley. At the hand-gate notice the overhanging crag high on the left along the rim of the valley, where peregrine falcons have been known to nest. The path receives periodic remedial repair to cope with the heavy boot traffic.

2 Gird your loins for a simple, yet energetic pull up the steep fellside. After fording Greenhow Gill the path bears onto the right-hand side of the first tongue of moraine. Abandon the bridle path, bearing up onto this ridge to the left, and climb beside Greenhow Gill, keeping to the west side to ascend steeply onto the brow. The slope begins to ease, enabling one to enjoy the handsome views back to Pounsey Crag. Keep beside the dwindling gill and come up by a line of quartz outcrops. Cross peaty exposures to join the ridge path, then go left, with little remaining ascent to the summit.

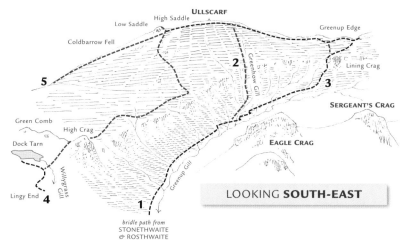

LOOKING **SOUTH-EAST**

bridle path from STONETHWAITE *& ROSTHWAITE*

Via Lining Crag   630m/2070ft   5.2km/3¼ miles

3 Normal people choose moderate routes, and without a second thought will continue with the pony path through the moraine, crossing the dry-tarn site, to ascend the gully to the left of Lining Crag. At the top, the way ahead is in sore need of a sabbatical, as the multitude of cross-ridge walkers have churned so much of the path down to bare peat. In order to help minimise the damage to Greenup Edge, divert due east onto the ridge. There is little or no evidence of a path, but the

Lining Crag

going is so much sweeter. The broad ridge is awash with pools – keep left to miss the worst of the spongy ground. Traverse to the ridge path and mount northward to the summit, with the occasional stake stump from the old metal estate fence as a guide.

Via Lingy End   634m/2080ft   4.7km/3 miles

4 This special route, ideal for anyone looking for an unusual ascent (possibly using the Greenup Gill path for a circular return), ventures onto the northern rim of the valley bound for Low Saddle. Follow the approach to GREAT CRAG page 108, via Lingy End. After crossing the stile ascend until a wall is seen riding up to the right. Ford the gill, the outflow of Dock Tarn, and climb with the wall to the right over the shoulder of High Crag. Delight in the view beyond – over the meeting of the Greenup Gill and Langstrath valleys, with Eagle and Sergeant's Crags centre-stage, and the long view to Bowfell at the head of Langstrath quite unforgettable. The route traverses rough ground to come alongside the wall that protects the edge. The wall has the scenic impact of some heroic stone frontier, rising and falling in these stirring mountain surroundings. Keep alongside the wall until a gill re-entrant breaks the steady progress, then angle up the rough slopes to the cairn on Low Saddle – a viewpoint that provides the best survey of the northern sector of the Central Fells. Follow the ridge up to High Saddle, join the fence, crossing a stile at the top, and head south to the summit.

ASCENT FROM WATENDLATH (5)

Via Blea Tarn   470m/1540ft   5.2km/3¼ miles

5 One wonders how many visitors to this gorgeous little community have stood on the packhorse bridge, looked across the tarn and known they were looking straight at Ullscarf – even the local farmers call it Coldbarrow Fell! This is an efficient start-point – consult BELL CRAGS page 31, Route 9. Ford the beck precisely at the outflow of Blea Tarn and follow the western shore, nipping up onto the ridge at the first bay – there is nothing to impede, nor anything to encourage, speed! Climb steadily to crest Low Saddle.

Harrop Tarn from Tarn Crag. Thirlmere is the backdrop.

ASCENT FROM DOBGILL (18)

Via Harrop Tarn   550m/1800ft   4km/2½ miles

Eastern approaches are so different – is this the same mountain? When viewed across Thirlmere, through the trees from the main road, the near eastern skyline is so craggy that it suggests great tidings for the explorer. The early stages of all approaches reinforce this perception, but Ullscarf is no alpine peak, and the backing slopes soon falter into mediocre moorland. What am I saying? This is Lakeland! Given sunshine and the right day, even these barren slopes have their beauty. **6** From Dob Gill a made-path climbs directly to the outflow of Harrop Tarn. **7** A further path begins from the road south of Dobgill Bridge, rising via hand-gates to cross the forest fence by a ladder-stile and subsequent duck-boarding to reach the footbridge below the outflow. The main forest track leads west; as it forks on two occasions keep up left (though on the latter occasion it is more straight on, rising as a path to the double kissing-gate exiting the conifers). The bridle path mounts the slope to the broad depression traversed by a fence. Do not go through the hand-gate, but instead turn left, following the fence by a pool to the base of Standing Crag. Bear up left, via an easy gully, clambering to the top to rejoin the fence. Take the opportunity to stand at the brink of the cliff (origin of the crag name) to gaze at the fine view north. Follow the fence up to the acute corner, walking free of the fence on the left, to attain the summit cairn.

Standing Crag

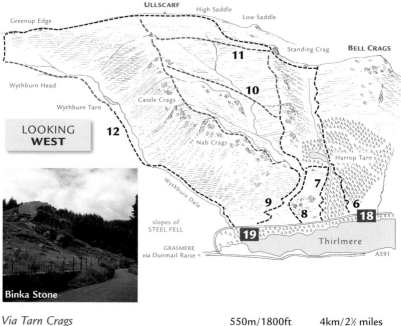

ULLSCARF   High Saddle   Low Saddle

Greenup Edge

Standing Crag   **BELL CRAGS**

11

Wythburn Head

10

Castle Crags

Wythburn Tarn

LOOKING WEST   **12**

Nab Crags

Harrop Tarn

Wythburn Dale

7

9   **6**

8

18

slopes of STEEL FELL

19   Thirlmere

GRASMERE *via* Dunmail Raise <

A591

Binka Stone

Via Tarn Crags	550m/1800ft	4km/2½ miles

8 Start from a roadside gate at GR318138, south of the glacially smoothed outcrop known as the Binka Stone, so called from its likeness to a 'binka' (a dialect term for a doorstep). Angle diagonally left across the slope beneath Birk Crag, and a groove leads through the juniper to a rising wall. At the top either venture to the cairn on top of the crag and a smart descent to Harrop Tarn via a tall hand-gate, or cross the adjacent stile and follow the plantation fence to ford Ullscarf Gill. Bear left on a green path that curves up onto the ridge above a cluster of sheepfolds, then becomes lost as a tangible path. Continue onto the rising ridge to gain the edge of Tarn Crags, a fine viewpoint for Bell Crags (see that fell chapter's title image) and over the plantations surrounding Harrop Tarn. Hold to the edge, stepping down a rock band or two, and crossing marshy ground to reach the ridge fence above Standing Crag.

ASCENT FROM STEEL END (19)

Via Ullscarf Gill	550m/1800ft	4.4km/2¾ miles

9 This route is best begun from the Steel End car park. Follow the road right to go through the yard and gates at Stenkin (barn). Follow the wall to the site of the original West Head Farm – almost all trace of this farmstead has gone. Its economic footing was lost when the reservoir stole its valley pasture, and its name was taken by the one farm that remained, which had previously had the topographically appropriate name of

Steel End. Bear up left by the fence to a hand-gate in the fell-bounding wall. A continuing shepherds' path of ancient purpose winds up the rough fellside, coming close to the rising wall shielding Birk Crag; this path is more obscure in the damp ground. Continue to a wall-gap; the shepherds' path progresses to sheepfolds within Ullscarf Gill. However, as soon as you pass through the wall, bear up left to the prominent wall cairn, known as The Beacon. The short length of wall set up as The Beacon is a replacement for a finer structure thrown down over 50 years ago – vandalism is not new!

The continuing ridge, rising above Nab Crags, gives ample scope for the inventive fell-wanderer. There is no path, which seems strange considering how bold the ridge appears when viewed from the Armboth road-end at the A591. Pass a curious ruin in the shelter of the first step of the ridge, and thereafter make whatever progress appeals in order to culminate upon a modest cairn directly overlooking the foot-

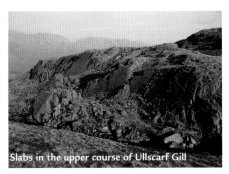
Slabs in the upper course of Ullscarf Gill

bridge far below in the jaws of Wythburn Dale. The ridge now turns west and it is less easy to keep to the scenic edge. (A deep re-entrant gill may tempt the more intrepid fellsman to ascend from the depths of Wythburn Dale, but such a notion comes with a health warning!) The ridge rises progressively to a cluster of pools above Castle Crags.

Old path above the former West Head Farm

10 This point can be reached (less impressively it has to be said) from Route 8 by following Ullscarf Gill, via a slabby ravine, then curving south without the benefit of a path towards the brink. **11** An old shepherds' traverse can be attempted from Standing Crag, formerly marked by a string of cairns bee-lining to Black Knott, though now only one cairn remains across the pretty torrid headstream terrain. Black Knott is a rocky oasis on the ridge west of the clusters of pools. Head west to meet up with the ridge path, then turn north to the summit.

Via Wythburn Dale   565m/1860ft   6.8km /4¼ miles

12 A soft route... underfoot! From the Steel End car park go left to a kissing-gate or continue over the bridge a few further strides to a hand-gate and steps leading down into the meadow. The two paths advance in harmony either side of the fenced Wythburn Beck, via gates, ladder-stiles or stiles, to reunite at a wooden footbridge. Continue on the dale path climbing above the southern bank of Wythburn Beck. There are two fine waterslide cascades, which are all the more exciting when a strong wind surges spray back. Pass the twin portal moraines anciently breached, draining the former Wythburn Dale Tarn. Pass the sinuous vestigal tarn also known, not without cause, as The Bog. The old path dissolves underfoot and from here you progress pathless up the mossy dale to unite with the ancient east–west bridle path fording Mere Beck. Traverse Wythburn Head, climbing by Flour Gill onto the plateau pass of Greenup Edge to join the ridge path that follows the line of fence-stake stumps north to the summit.

Low Saddle looking to High Saddle

North from the acute fence corner on Ullscarf

THE SUMMIT

Ullscarf summit cairn

Walkers cross the summit and think little of the event, heaping greatest praise on Low Saddle as the panoramic highpoint of their visit. There are broad acres of acidic grassland declining into the peaty wastes of Ullscarf Gill to the east, and coarser slopes spill quickly westward to Greenup and Bleatarn Gills. The stumps of the old estate fence may cause some visitors to stumble, but it is far better to have the stumps than to have the fell-top ruined with an actual fence. Sadly, from this point on, up the spine of the range to Bleaberry Fell and a little beyond, a stock-proof fence has been reinstated.

SAFE DESCENTS

Well, the fence has one merit, but only one. In mist the fence, that has its acute corner some 350m north of the summit cairn, is a sure guide. Follow it to the right, to the top of Standing Crag, and the path veers right to work down a gully to its base, then on beside the continuing fence to a hand-gate in the damp depression. From here join the old bridle path linking Watendlath left (through the gate) and Thirlmere (Dob Gill). Anyone caught in mist, with Borrowdale as their destination, should cross the stile at the acute corner and go left, hugging the fence down to the wall that runs along the edge above the Greenup Gill valley. Follow this wall to the right to reach Dock Tarn and the path down through the woods by Lingy End.

RIDGE ROUTES

BELL CRAGS	↓210m/690ft	↑30m/100ft	2.8km/1¾ miles

Head north to the acute corner of the fence and go right, following the fence to the top of Standing Crag. Bear down right to the crag base, where the fence resumes. Follow this beyond the pools and ridge-top hand-gate, skirting marshy ground to bear half-right onto the short summit ridge.

HIGH RAISE	↓120m/390ft	↑155m/510ft	4km/2½ miles

Go south – a definite path with the old metal fence stakes as guides gives confidence – until you dip to an area of large pools that gives cause to watch one's footing, and where a right-hand bias ensures driest boots. Cross the Greenup Edge depression, climbing south-south-west via Low White Stones to the Ordnance Survey pillar and wind-shelter that mark this, the roof of the range.

PANORAMA

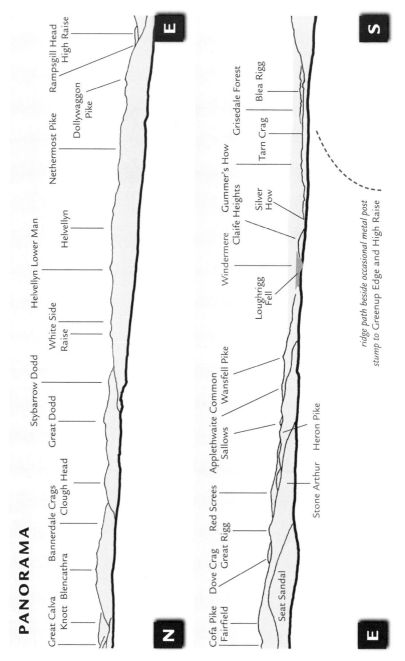

ridge path beside occasional metal post stump to Greenup Edge *and* High Raise

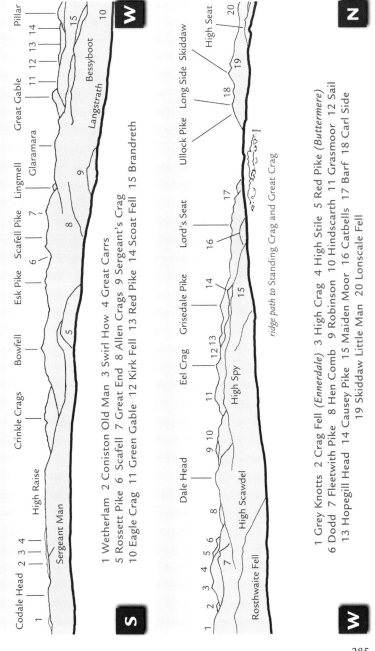

N

Pillar

15

10

Bessyboot

Langstrath

Great Gable

11 12 13 14

Glaramara

9

Lingmell

7

Scafell Pike

6

8

Esk Pike

Bowfell

5

Crinkle Crags

High Raise

Sergeant Man

Codale Head 2 3 4

1

W

S

1 Wetherlam 2 Coniston Old Man 3 Swirl How 4 Great Carrs
5 Rossett Pike 6 Scafell 7 Great End 8 Allen Crags 9 Sergeant's Crag
10 Eagle Crag 11 Green Gable 12 Kirk Fell 13 Red Pike 14 Scoat Fell 15 Brandreth

High Seat

20

19

Skiddaw

Long Side

18

Ullock Pike

17

Lord's Seat

16

Grisedale Pike

14

Eel Crag

12 13

11

High Spy

9 10

Dale Head

8

High Scawdel

7

1 2 3 4 5 6

Rosthwaite Fell

ridge path to Standing Crag and Great Crag

15

W

1 Grey Knotts 2 Crag Fell (*Ennerdale*) 3 High Crag 4 High Stile 5 Red Pike (*Buttermere*)
6 Dodd 7 Fleetwith Pike 8 Hen Comb 9 Robinson 10 Hindscarth 11 Grasmoor 12 Sail
13 Hopegill Head 14 Causey Pike 15 Maiden Moor 16 Catbells 17 Barf 18 Carl Side
19 Skiddaw Little Man 20 Lonscale Fell

28 WALLA CRAG *(379m, 1243ft)*

Travellers venturing south from Keswick along the Borrowdale Road get their first taste of the rocky dramas ahead when they see, rising above the green canopy of Great Wood, the massive 'wall of crag' appropriately called Walla Crag. Strictly the fell is the north-west shoulder of Bleaberry Fell, separated from the higher ground by a wide upland hollow drained by Brockle Beck. To the south the short incursion of Cat Gill separates the fell from Falcon Crag, which has no pretensions to separate fell status, even though it is a major two-tiered sporting venue for rock climbers.

There is no doubting the individualistic qualities of this imposing facade so luxuriantly wreathed in trees. At its

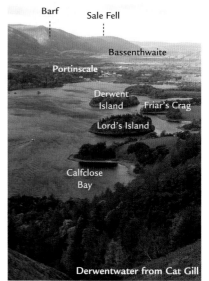

Barf   Sale Fell

Bassenthwaite

Portinscale

Derwent Island   Friar's Crag

Lord's Island

Calfclose Bay

Derwentwater from Cat Gill

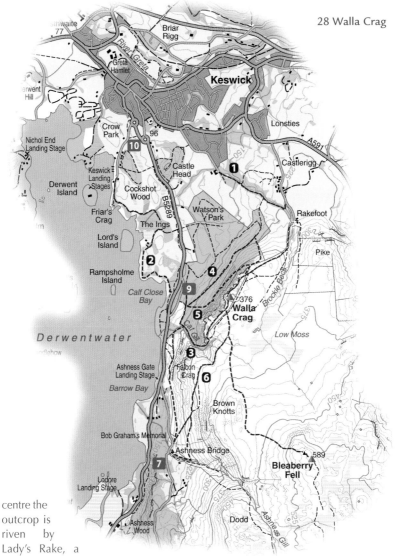

centre the outcrop is riven by Lady's Rake, a damp vegetated gully. Do not be tempted even to try to ascend this rotten cliff – even climbers give it a miss! Down the decades the summit has been a prime objective for evening strolls from Keswick. It is unrivalled for its views across to the Keswick vale, and blessed too with a lovely view over Derwentwater. While the bold escarpment suggests a difficult climb, it can be out-flanked to give the gentlest of climbs. However, steeper lines need not be resisted, and these include a secretive under-cliff trod which can be awkward in damp conditions when tree roots are slick.

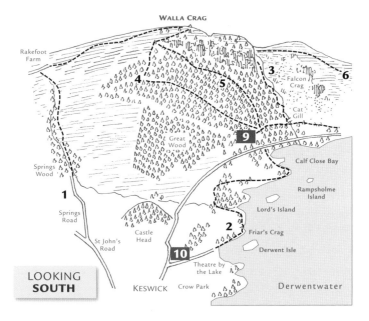

WALLA CRAG

Rakefoot
Farm

4

5

3

Falcon
Crag

6

Cat
Gill

9

Great
Wood

Calf Close Bay

Rampsholme
Island

Springs
Wood

Lord's Island

1

Springs
Road

2

Friar's Crag

St John's
Road

Castle
Head

10

Derwent Isle

LOOKING
SOUTH

Theatre by
the Lake

KESWICK   Crow Park

Derwentwater

Castlehead Wood backed by Keswick

ASCENT FROM KESWICK (10)

Via Springs Wood   300m/990ft   3.2km/2 miles

1 Start from the Moot Hall in Market Square at the centre of Keswick. Head south-east following the pavement of St John's Street, which becomes the Old Ambleside Road after Castlehead Close, to turn right into Springs Road (note there is no scope for car parking in this vicinity). Pass beyond Springs Farm via a gate into Springs Wood and ascend beside the gill on a popular path in close harmony with the beck, then switch right to run alongside pasture fencing. After the Great Wood path merges from the right, pass through a kissing-gate and soon dip into the dell and cross a foot-bridge, then rise to meet the minor road at steps and a hand-gate. Go right and the road forks at Rakefoot Farm, where you go right, signed 'Wallacrag'. Cross the foot-bridge, rising with a wall right to a stile, and ascend with the wall to the right. Either go through the first hand-gate and wind up within the scarp-edge enclosure or continue to the top and cross a stile to the summit cairn.

Via Friar's Crag and Calfclose Bay   3.5km/2¼ miles

2 A lovely lakeside approach from the Lake Road car park, via Friar's Crag, Ings Wood and Calfclose Bay, makes the ideal start to the climb.

ASCENT FROM GREAT WOOD (9)

Via Cat Gill   300m/990ft   0.8km/½ mile

Three contrasting and delightfully sylvan routes (Routes 3–5) lead to the top from the National Trust car park. **3** To go via Cat Gill head south, passing above the former car park area. Ignore the forest track that swings left, and keep forward upon the footpath that leads to the footbridge spanning Cat Gill. Do not cross, but instead ascend the cobbled path that rises steeply beside the cacophony of the ravine via two hand-gates. Pass through a kissing-gate then via a zig-zag stepped section to another kissing-gate. As it follows up the steps by the wall the slope eases. Either continue, with the wall left, or cross the stile to complete the ascent within the tree-fringed scarp enclosure. Take one notable early 'spur opportunity' to wander left for a special view over Derwentwater. Continue to reach and cross a stile in the wall – you are now above the inaccessible gully of Lady's Rake – and advance on a popular path to the open summit.

Via forest tracks or the under-cliff path   1.2km/¾ mile

4 The undoubted beauties of Great Wood fully deserve a more leisurely line along the forest tracks. You have a choice here. The first option is to head north, switching right as the gate to the valley road comes into view. As you gently rise, ignore the track to the left into the Watson's Park section of the wood. The track swings right and merges with the footpath from Springs Wood and promptly bears off up the bank, with a small gill to the right. Alternatively, this point can be reached more directly by

Blencathra from the balcony

advancing south from the car park, and this time swinging left to climb steadily with the forest track. Where the track levels and shapes to descend, cross a small gill. Bear up sharp right. Ford the gill below the enclosure fence corner, and continue now up the right bank. Emerge from the woodland and keep the fence on the right until the slope eases onto heathery ground, with superb views of Skiddaw and Blencathra the rich reward. Either go through the hand-gate in the wall to complete the ascent, principally in the pasture, or keep up the escarpment edge, attractively garnished with heather. A matter of metres beyond the hand-gate notice the small balcony viewpoint. This is not only a fine moment to pause and survey a sumptuous prospect towards Keswick, but it marks the top of the sub-edge or under-cliff path.

5 The under-cliff path, very much the third way, requires a degree of confidence as there is some awkward footing. At the point where the forestry track sweeps left, spot an unwaymarked narrow path rising directly up through the conifers. This climbs and winds assiduously towards the foot of the crag directly beneath Lady's Rake. It duly drifts left, seeking ledges and tight tree passages. The path remains consistent, but is never more than a thin trod. Keep directly below the escarpment outcrop. Towards the end of the traverse, after a gill, one particular ledge at a dry gully may be found troublesome in damp conditions. On emerging at the aforementioned balcony, go right to climb the attractive escarpment edge.

ASCENT FROM ASHNESS BRIDGE (7)

Via Falcon Crag   160m/530ft   1.5km/1 mile

Few visitors miss the opportunity to admire and photograph the famous view from above the bridge. What the majority fail to realise is that this is but one component of a suite of four stunning viewpoints of this prospect of Skiddaw. **6** To draw the composition together one should embark on a circular expedition, best begun from this, the first formal car park up the Watendlath road, GR269196. Advance north recrossing the bridge. One may follow the footpath that contours ahead to a hand-gate in the down-wall subsequently forks half-right up the bracken slope. The path climbs, less than comfortably in places, up to a stile in a modern fence to join the higher path in a wet patch devoid of bracken.

Alternatively, bear up directly from the bridge, cross the fence-stile beside the old fold, and ascend to where a path bears off to the left up the bracken slope. Then continue to a hand-gate in the wall. This point can also be attained from the lower path – after passing through the hand-gate, rise directly with the wall to your right (though bracken does tend to diminish one's enthusiasm) to reach an adjacent hand-gate in the fence. The prominent path climbs steadily to easier ground.

Watch for a side path, half-left, which can be followed down the grassy spur to the cairn on the top of Falcon Crag. This is the second notable viewpoint of the tour (Ashness Bridge being the first), providing a superb prospect over Great Wood framed by Walla Crag and Derwentwater.

Climb back up to the path to traverse above the steep re-entrant of Cat Gill and ford the gill en route to the stile into the Walla Crag escarpment enclosure. The summit of Walla Crag provides the third viewpoint.

To reach the fourth, continue down the northern scarp, through the heather, to the small balcony at the top of the under-cliff path. This provides the most pleasing view of Skiddaw and Blencathra. Head on down the edge-path to reach the forest track and turn left, retracing Route 5 to meet the lower footpath. Bear left to cross the Cat

Lower and upper tiers of Falcon Crag

Gill footbridge and traverse the undulating path below Falcon Crag, at one point slipping through a gorse tunnel. The crag is famed for its climbs and, appropriately, resident peregrines.

THE SUMMIT

Nature has provided the fell with a bald crown of naked rock, and to the west the ground falls precipitously. Heather enlivens the near ground, which is interlaced with native trees that line the edge to north and south. This is a momentous belvedere from which to admire the perennially attractive fell-surround of Derwentwater. The summit cairn is set back from this brink. Beyond the wall the fell merges into sheep pasture. In recent years the fell's height has been reassessed, 3m being added to its height.

All visitors are drawn to the rocky western edge for the best views – as if to confirm this, the panorama is taken from this spot. Standing on the fell witness the stark division between the sleeker lines of the Skiddaw slates, as expressed by the North-Western Fells across the lake, and the igneous rocks of the Borrowdale Volcanic group gathering in force to the south and culminating upon Scafell Pike.

SAFE DESCENTS

For Great Wood car park, Cat Gill and the paths that swing down from the north are fine, but avoid the under-cliff path. The easiest option of all is to head for Rakefoot Farm on the green tracks across the open pasture to the north-east, and to descend the sheltered Spring Wood path.

Walla Crag summit looking east

Walla Crag from the top of Falcon Crag

RIDGE ROUTE

BLEABERRY FELL	↓45m/150ft	↑255m/840ft	2km/1¼ miles

Head south and cross the wall-stile, following the Ashness Bridge path. After some 200m bear half-left (south-south-east) at a cairn and join the path crossing the upper Cat Gill ford. The line becomes clearer after traversing the damp ground. Rise to glance by a sheepfold to the east of a knoll and skirt the peaty hollow before climbing the steep north-west prow on a the smart new path to a viewpoint cairn. Continue via a further large cairn to the summit wind-shelter cairn.

PANORAMA

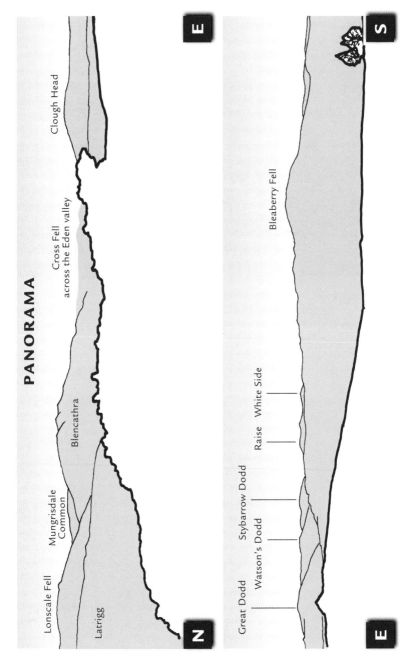

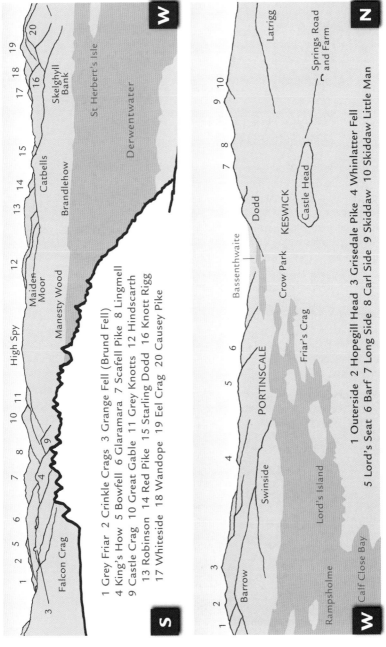

1 Grey Friar 2 Crinkle Crags 3 Grange Fell (Brund Fell)
4 King's How 5 Bowfell 6 Glaramara 7 Scafell Pike 8 Lingmell
9 Castle Crag 10 Great Gable 11 Grey Knotts 12 Hindscarth
13 Robinson 14 Red Pike 15 Starling Dodd 16 Knott Rigg
17 Whiteside 18 Wandope 19 Eel Crag 20 Causey Pike

1 Outerside 2 Hopegill Head 3 Grisedale Pike 4 Whinlatter Fell
5 Lord's Seat 6 Barf 7 Long Side 8 Carl Side 9 Skiddaw 10 Skiddaw Little Man

nurture
lakeland

Helicopter delivering path-
building rock on the steep
slopes of Dollywaggon Pike

FIXING THE FELLS
FOR THE FUTURE

In preparing this guide I am ever more keenly
aware of the work being done to secure the fell
paths, making the whole fell environment visu-
ally a better place. The National Park Authority
in conjunction with the National Trust are play-
ing crucial roles within the structure of the Fix
the Fells Project (visit: www.fixthefells.co.uk).

A huge amount of work has been devoted
to stabilising paths, including intelligent pre-emptive work. Capital projects too,
have seen mechanical diggers carried high onto the fells at key points to heal sorely
worn paths. Huge quantities of path-pitching stone is carried most economically
by helicopter. Sadly worn paths of Wainwright's day have been given a new lease
of life. While some walkers may gripe that the hard pitching is tough on the ankles
and knees, at least it's not so tough on the mountains themselves. All of which has
to be good.

See the difference – 'before and after' on the
path above Comb Crags on the upper slopes
of Nethermost Pike

In common with so many countryside projects Fix the Fells faces a
'strapped for cash' future, and for
its work to continue unabated it
looks to Nurture Lakeland (www.
nurturelakeland.org) for assist-
ance. As an associate member of
the organisation I am committed
to supporting its work. The char-
ity actively encourages businesses,
particularly those that benefit from
tourism, to pay into environmental-
project funding through 'Payback'
schemes that sustain the beautiful landscape so many visitors and
locals adore.

INDEX

Bold indicates Fell Chapters (annotations on panoramas excluded)

297

LISTING OF CICERONE GUIDES

Walking in the Cevennes
Walking in the Dordogne
Walking in the Haute Savoie
   North & South
Walking in the Languedoc
Walking in the Tarentaise and
   Beaufortain Alps
Walking on Corsica

GERMANY
Germany's Romantic Road
Hiking and Biking in the
   Black Forest
Walking in the Bavarian Alps
Walking the River Rhine Trail

HIMALAYA
Annapurna
Bhutan
Everest: A Trekker's Guide
Garhwal and Kumaon:
   A Trekker's and Visitor's Guide
Kangchenjunga:
   A Trekker's Guide
Langtang with Gosainkund
   and Helambu:
   A Trekker's Guide
Manaslu: A Trekker's Guide
The Mount Kailash Trek
Trekking in Ladakh
Trekking in the Himalaya

ICELAND & GREENLAND
Trekking in Greenland
Walking and Trekking in Iceland

IRELAND
Irish Coastal Walks
The Irish Coast to Coast Walk
The Mountains of Ireland

ITALY
Gran Paradiso
Sibillini National Park
Stelvio National Park
Shorter Walks in the Dolomites
Through the Italian Alps
Trekking in the Apennines
Trekking in the Dolomites
Via Ferratas of the Italian
   Dolomites: Vols 1 & 2
Walking in Abruzzo
Walking in Sardinia
Walking in Sicily
Walking in the Central Italian Alps

Walking in the Dolomites
Walking in Tuscany
Walking on the Amalfi Coast
Walking the Italian Lakes

MEDITERRANEAN
Jordan – Walks, Treks, Caves,
   Climbs and Canyons
The Ala Dag
The High Mountains of Crete
The Mountains of Greece
Treks and Climbs in Wadi Rum,
   Jordan
Walking in Malta
Western Crete

NORTH AMERICA
British Columbia
The Grand Canyon
The John Muir Trail
The Pacific Crest Trail

SOUTH AMERICA
Aconcagua and the
   Southern Andes
Hiking and Biking Peru's
   Inca Trails
Torres del Paine

SCANDINAVIA
Walking in Norway

**SLOVENIA, CROATIA AND
MONTENEGRO**
The Julian Alps of Slovenia
The Mountains of Montenegro
Trekking in Slovenia
Walking in Croatia
Walking in Slovenia:
   The Karavanke

SPAIN AND PORTUGAL
Costa Blanca: West
Mountain Walking in
   Southern Catalunya
The Mountains of Central Spain
The Northern Caminos
Trekking through Mallorca
Walking in Madeira
Walking in Mallorca
Walking in Menorca
Walking in the Algarve
Walking in the
   Cordillera Cantabrica
Walking in the Sierra Nevada

Walking on Gran Canaria
Walking on La Gomera and
   El Hierro
Walking on La Palma
Walking on Tenerife
Walking the GR7 in Andalucia
Walks and Climbs in the
   Picos de Europa

SWITZERLAND
Alpine Pass Route
Canyoning in the Alps
Central Switzerland
The Bernese Alps
The Swiss Alps
Tour of the Jungfrau Region
Walking in the Valais
Walking in Ticino
Walks in the Engadine

TECHNIQUES
Geocaching in the UK
Indoor Climbing
Lightweight Camping
Map and Compass
Mountain Weather
Moveable Feasts
Outdoor Photography
Polar Exploration
Rock Climbing
Sport Climbing
The Book of the Bivvy
The Hillwalker's Guide to
   Mountaineering
The Hillwalker's Manual

MINI GUIDES
Alpine Flowers
Avalanche!
Navigating with a GPS
Navigation
Pocket First Aid and
   Wilderness Medicine
Snow

MOUNTAIN LITERATURE
8000m
A Walk in the Clouds
Unjustifiable Risk?

For full information on all our
guides, and to order books and
eBooks, visit our website:
www.cicerone.co.uk.

Walking – Trekking – Mountaineering – Climbing – Cycling

Over 40 years, Cicerone have built up an outstanding collection of 300 guides, inspiring all sorts of amazing adventures.

Every guide comes from extensive exploration and research by our expert authors, all with a passion for their subjects. They are frequently praised, endorsed and used by clubs, instructors and outdoor organisations.

All our titles can now be bought as **e-books** and many as iPad and Kindle files and we will continue to make all our guides available for these and many other devices.

Our website shows any **new information** we've received since a book was published. Please do let us know if you find anything has changed, so that we can pass on the latest details. On our **website** you'll also find some great ideas and lots of information, including sample chapters, contents lists, reviews, articles and a photo gallery.

It's easy to keep in touch with what's going on at Cicerone, by getting our monthly **free e-newsletter**, which is full of offers, competitions, up-to-date information and topical articles. You can subscribe on our home page and also follow us on **Facebook** and **Twitter**, as well as our **blog**.

Cicerone – the very best guides for exploring the world.

CICERONE

2 Police Square Milnthorpe Cumbria LA7 7PY
Tel: 015395 62069 info@cicerone.co.uk
www.cicerone.co.uk